독해가 2배 빨라지는
챗GPT
수능독해

독해가 2배 빨라지는
챗GPT 수능독해

초판 1쇄 인쇄　2024년 2월 1일
초판 1쇄 발행　2024년 2월 5일

지은이 | 김지애, 이제종, 황현목, 반병현
펴낸이 | 김승기
펴낸곳 | ㈜생능출판사 / 주소 경기도 파주시 광인사길 143
브랜드 | 생능북스
출판사 등록일 | 2005년 1월 21일 / 신고번호 제406-2005-000002호
대표전화 | (031) 955-0761 / 팩스 (031) 955-0768
홈페이지 | www.booksr.co.kr

책임편집 | 최동진 / 편집 신성민, 이종무
영업 | 최복락, 김민수, 심수경, 차종필, 송성환, 최태웅, 김민정
마케팅 | 백수정, 명하나

ISBN 979-11-92932-46-0 (53740)
값 19,000원

핵심문장이 곧 독해다!

독해가
2배 빨라지는

챗GPT
수능독해

김지애 이제종 황현목 반병현 공저

ΛL 생능북스

왜 수능독해에
챗GPT를?

핵심 문장 밑줄 긋기 실험 결과

54명의 학생을 대상으로 밑줄 긋기가 정답률에 유의미한 차이를 보이는지 분석하였습니다.
분석 결과, 70% 이상 지문에서 밑줄이 있는 경우 정답률이 유의미하게 증가하는 것이 확인되었습니다.
특히 문장을 해석하더라도 내용을 이해하기 어려운 특정 고난도 문제에서는 정답률이
최대 219%까지도 증가했습니다.

핵심 문장
밑줄 긋기 실험

학교, 학원 등 교육 현장에서 영어를 가르치다 보면 고민 상담을 요청하는 학생들이 많은데요, 특히 영어 독해와 관련하여 재미있는 경향성을 발견할 수 있습니다. 평소에 수업을 열심히 듣고, 기본적인 문법이나 단어를 충분히 숙지하고 있는 우수한 학생들 중에서도 독해 문제를 잘 풀지 못해서 고민을 하는 학생들이 꼭 있다는 점입니다.

특히 가장 안타까운 사례는 분명히 영어 문장의 해석은 완벽하게 했지만 정답을 찾기 어려워하는 경우입니다. 영어 실력 자체는 준수하지만 문해력이 이를 뒷받침해 주지 못해서 생기는 경우입니다.

이에 저자들은 지문의 이해를 극적으로 도와줄 수 있는 보조수단이 없을까 고민했습니다. 제한된 시간 안에 사용할 수 있어야 하고, 시험장에서 시도하더라도 부정행위가 아니어야 한다는 조건까지 고려하면서 말입니다.

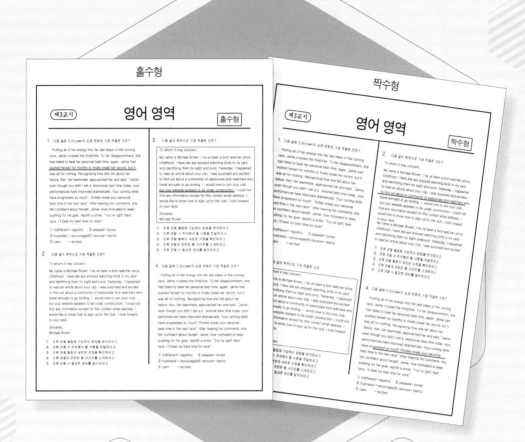

다양한 방법이 있겠습니다만, 저자들은 우선 핵심 문장에 밑줄을 그어 주는 것으로 지문의 이해를 도와줄 수 있을 것인가 실험했습니다.

먼저 동일한 내용의 시험지를 홀수형, 짝수형으로 구분하여 홀수형은 홀수번 문항에만 밑줄을 제공했고, 짝수형은 짝수번 문항에만 밑줄을 제공했습니다. 그리고 시험지를 잘 섞어 무작위로 학생들에게 나눠주고, 정답률이 달라지는지를 확인하였습니다. 과학업계에서는 이와 같은 실험 방식을 대조실험이라고 부릅니다.
실험 결과 재미있는 사실을 알아낼 수 있었습니다. 거의 대부분의 학생들이 밑줄이 제공된 문항에서 보다 정답률이 높았으며, 중위권 학생일수록 밑줄의 도움을 받을 때 정답을 맞힐 확률이 크게 증가하는 것을 확인했습니다.

저자들은 실험 결과에 영감을 받아 이 책을 집필하기로 했습니다.

이 책에서는 수능 및 모의고사 기출문제의 지문을 수집하여, 핵심 문장에는 밑줄을 그어 제공합니다. 여러분께서는 밑줄이 쳐져 있는 문장이 글의 내용을 이해하는 데에 중요한 부분이라는 점을 염두하시며 먼저 문제를 풀어보시기 바랍니다. 문제의 해설에서는 본문의 내용을 직접적으로 해설한 지문을 제공하기보다는, 밑줄을 친 문장이 왜 글의 핵심에 해당하는지를 설명하는 데 노력을 더욱 기울였습니다.

밑줄과 함께 기출문제를 풀고 나면, 기출문제의 지문을 토대로 한 변형문제가 제공됩니다. 수능형 문제와 내신형 문제가 함께 제공되오니, 한 번 이해한 지문을 토대로 여러 문제를 풀어나가는 감각을 느껴보시기 바랍니다.

변형문제 지문에서는 밑줄을 제공하지 않습니다. 앞서 보신 기출문제의 지문과 핵심 문장의 위치가 동일하기 때문입니다. 여러분께서는 변형문제의 지문에서 직접 핵심 문장을 찾아 밑줄을 그어보시고, 앞 페이지의 기출문제 지문에 수록된 밑줄과 동일한지 아닌지를 고민해 보시기 바랍니다.

결과적으로 직접 지문의 핵심 문장을 파악하여 밑줄을 긋는 실력을 조금씩 키워나가실 수 있을 것입니다. 이와 같은 경험이 조금씩 쌓이면 시험장에서도 만족할만한 성과를 만들어낼 수 있을 것입니다.

챗GPT와 함께 밑줄을

지문의 핵심 문장에 밑줄을 긋는 데에는 다양한 방법이 있습니다. 과거에는 단어들을 분석하여 핵심 문장을 찾아주는 〈TextRank〉라는 기술이 인기였습니다. 다만 이 방법은 "왜 이 문장이 핵심 문장인가?"라는 질문에 적절한 대답을 제공하지 못한다는 한계가 있습니다.

하지만 챗GPT는 다릅니다. 세상에서 가장 똑똑한 인공지능인 챗GPT에게 수능 영어 지문을 입력하고 핵심 문장을 찾아달라고 부탁하면, 순식간에 핵심 문장을 찾아줍니다. 그게 왜 핵심 문장에 해당하는지 이유를 물어보면 아주 친절하게 설명해 주기까지 합니다. 예시를 보여드리겠습니다.

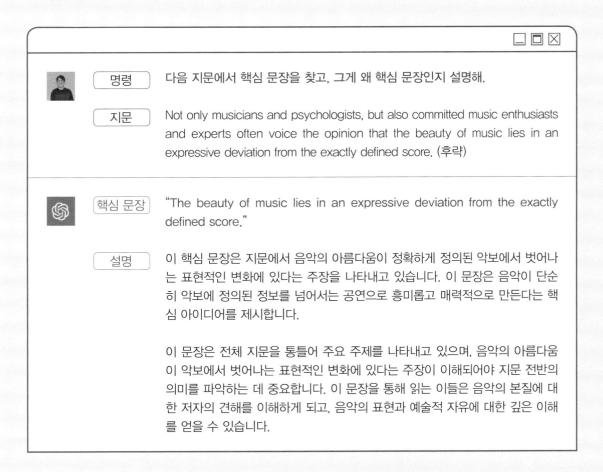

어떤가요? 무척이나 친절한 답변을 제공해주지요?

이처럼 챗GPT를 사용하면 수능 영어 공부에 많은 도움을 받을 수 있습니다. 이 책에서 제공되는 밑줄도 모두 챗GPT를 통해 작성되었답니다.

EBS SW 온라인 강의 무료수강 안내 ☐ ☐ ☒

챗GPT와 함께 핵심 문장을 찾는 과정과 각 유형별 문제 풀이 방법 강의를 무료로 제공합니다.
EBS SW를 통해 강의를 수강하실 수 있습니다. 강의 수강 방법을 안내해드립니다.

1

**EBS SW
회원가입**

https://ebssw.kr 로 접속하여
회원가입 후 로그인합니다.

2

강의찾기

검색창에서 〈Chat GPT를 활용한 수능/모의고사 풀이〉를 검색하여, 위 강의를 찾아 클
릭합니다. 혹은 다음 URL을 주소창에 붙여넣거나 QR 코드를 스캔해도 좋습니다.

https://www.ebssw.kr/lrnng/alctcr/alctcrDetailView.do?alctcrSn=58456

3

수강신청

강의 소개 페이지 상단의 〈수강신청〉 버튼을 클릭합니다.

이 책의 저자들이 직접 제공하는 무료 강의를 마음껏 수강하세요!

학습용 애플리케이션 사용 방법

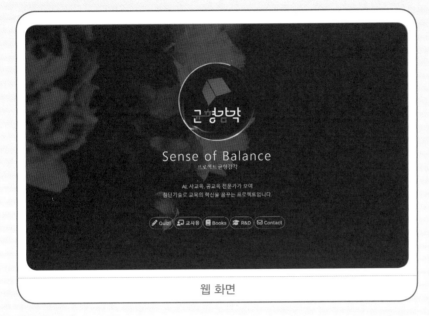

웹 화면

구글 플레이스토어

1 웹으로 사용(모든 스마트폰, 태블릿 가능)

> https://bhban.kr/ai_voca

2 안드로이드
왼쪽의 QR 코드를 찍어주세요.

3 앱 활용하기

- 〈AI 족집게 수능영단어〉 책에 수록된 "AI가 선정한 이번 수능에 많이 나올 단어" 퀴즈를 풀어
볼 수 있습니다.
- 이 책에 수록된 독해 퀴즈를 풀어볼 수 있습니다. (2024년 상반기 중 업데이트 예정)

차 례

PART

01

내용
파악

유형

01 글의 목적 파악하기

CASE 01

기출문제
정복하기

2020년 수능
18번 문제

난이도 ★☆☆☆☆

Dear Mr. Kayne,

I am a resident of Cansinghill Apartments, located right next to the newly opened Vuenna Dog Park. As I live with three dogs, I am very happy to let my dogs run around and safely play with other dogs from the neighborhood. However, the noise of barking and yelling from the park at night is so loud and disturbing that I cannot relax in my apartment. Many of my apartment neighbors also seriously complain about this noise. I want immediate action to solve this urgent problem. **Since you are the manager of Vuenna Dog Park, I ask you to take measures to prevent the noise at night**. I hope to hear from you soon.

Sincerely,
Monty Kim

윗글의 목적으로 가장 적절한 것은?

① 애완견 예방 접종 일정을 확인하려고
② 애완견 공원의 야간 이용 시간을 문의하려고
③ 아파트 내 애완견 출입 금지 구역을 안내하려고
④ 아파트 인근에 개장한 애완견 공원을 홍보하려고
⑤ 애완견 공원의 야간 소음 방지 대책을 촉구하려고

Dear Mr. Kayne,

I am a resident of Cansinghill Apartments, located right next to the newly opened Vuenna Dog Park. As I live with three dogs, I am very happy to let my dogs run around and safely play with other dogs from the neighborhood. However, the noise (of barking and yelling from the park at night)is so loud and disturbing that I cannot relax in my apartment. Many of my apartment neighbors also seriously complain about this noise. I want immediate action to solve this urgent problem. Since you are the manager of Vuenna Dog Park, I ask you to take measures to prevent the noise at night. I hope to hear from you soon.

Sincerely,
Monty Kim

핵심 문장인 이유

해당 문장은 글의 전반에 반복되는 키워드 '야간소음'을 언급하고 있고, 이를 해결해줄 것을 촉구하므로 지문 전체를 아우르는 핵심 문장에 해당한다.

본문 해설

글쓴이를 포함한 많은 아파트 주민들이 공원에서 나는 '야간소음'에 불편함을 겪고 있으니 이 긴급한 문제를 해결하기 위해 조치를 취해달라는 것이 지문 내용이다. 글에서 반복적으로 언급되는 '야간소음'과 '문제 해결'을 포함하고 있고 글의 의도를 정확하게 서술하고 있는 선택지는 ⑤번이다.

문제 풀이 전략

수능 5개년 모두 이메일 형식을 띤 편지글로 출제되었다. 같은 키워드가 반복되며 선택지 답안까지도 연결된다. 이때 키워드가 파생어의 형태로 바뀌거나 유의어로 대체되기도 한다.

글의 분위기가 전환되며 글쓴이의 의도가 드러나기 때문에 역접의 접속사(however, but, on the other hand etc.) 이후를 집중해서 보는 것이 중요하다.

또한, 최근 5개년 중 정답이 "Would you like to~?, I would like to~, I ask you to~" 형식이므로 이 문형을 유의해서 본다면 정답에 한층 가까워질 수 있다.

정답 ⑤

Dear Mr. Kayne,

I am a resident of Cansinghill Apartments, located right next to the newly opened Vuenna Dog Park. As I live with three dogs, I am very happy to let my dogs run around and safely play with other dogs from the neighborhood. However, the noise of barking and yelling from the park at night is so loud and disturbing that I cannot relax in my apartment. Many of my apartment neighbors also seriously complain about this noise. I want immediate action to solve this urgent problem. Since you are the manager of Vuenna Dog Park, I ask you to take measures to prevent the noise at night. I hope to hear from you soon.

Sincerely,
Monty Kim

Monty Kim에 관한 윗글의 내용과 일치하지 <u>않는</u> 것은?

① Vuenna Dog Park 옆에 위치한 Cansinghill Apartments에 살고 있다.

② 세 마리의 강아지와 살고 있다.

③ 공원의 소음이 너무 커서 집에서 휴식을 취할 수 없다.

④ Vuenna Dog Park의 매니저로 일하고 있다.

⑤ Mr. Kayne로부터 빠른 소식을 듣길 원한다.

Dear Mr. Kayne,

I am a resident of Cansinghill Apartments, located right next to the newly opened Vuenna Dog Park. As I live with three dogs, I am very happy to let my dogs run around and safely play with other dogs from the neighborhood. However, the noise of barking and yelling from the park at night is (A) 너무 시끄럽고 불안해서 아파트에서 쉴 수 없습니다. Many of my apartment neighbors also seriously complain about this noise. I want immediate action to solve this urgent problem. Since you are the manager of Vuenna Dog Park, I ask you to take measures to prevent the noise at night. I hope to hear from you soon.

Sincerely,
Monty Kim

밑줄 친 (A)의 우리말에 맞게 아래의 단어를 배열하시오. (필요 시 어형 변화 가능)

(loud / apartment / and / that / relax / so / I / disturb / in / my / can)

④ Since you are the manager of Vuenna Dog Park,~ 이 부분에서 편지를 받는 대상인 Mr. Kayne가 Vuenna Dog Park의 매니저임을 알 수 있다. 따라서 이 선택지는 지문 내용과 일치하지 않는다.

① I am a resident of Cansinghill Apartments, located right next to the newly opened Vuenna Dog Park.
② As I live with three dogs, ~
③ However, the noise of barking and yelling from the park at night is so loud and disturbing that I cannot relax in my apartment.
⑤ I hope to hear from you soon.

정답 ④

실전! 내신대비!

can을 cannot으로 바꾸어 so 형용사/부사 that 주어 can't 구문을 사용하고, disturb(v.방해하다)를 disturbing(adj.불안한) 형태로 바꾸어 단어를 배열하면 된다.

> **아래의 프롬프트를 챗GPT에 입력해 보세요.**
> "so that can't 구문을 활용한 예시 3개 보여줘."
> "so that can't를 대신해서 사용할 수 있는 구문 예시를 3개 보여줘."

정답 so loud and disturbing that I cannot relax in my apartment

글의 목적 파악하기

CASE 02

난이도 ★☆☆☆☆

Dear Friends,

Season's greetings. As some of you already know, we are starting the campus food drive. This is how you participate. **You can bring your items for donation to our booths.** Our donation booths are located in the lobbies of the campus libraries. Just drop off the items there during usual library hours from December 4 to 23. The donated food should be non-perishable like canned meats and canned fruits. Packaged goods such as jam and peanut butter are also good. We will distribute the food to our neighbors on Christmas Eve. We truly appreciate your help.

Many blessings,
Joanna at Campus Food Bank

윗글의 목적으로 가장 적절한 것은?

① 음식 기부에 참여하는 방법을 안내하려고
② 음식 배달 자원봉사 참여에 감사하려고
③ 도서관 이용 시간 변경을 공지하려고
④ 음식물 낭비의 심각성을 알려 주려고
⑤ 크리스마스 행사 일정을 문의하려고

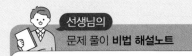

Dear Friends,

   Season's greetings. As some of you already know, we are starting the campus food drive. This is how you participate. You can bring your items for donation to our booths. Our donation booths are located in the lobbies of the campus libraries. Just drop off the items there during usual library hours from December 4 to 23. The donated food should be non-perishable like canned meats and canned fruits. Packaged goods such as jam and peanut butter are also good. We will distribute the food to our neighbors on Christmas Eve. We truly appreciate your help.

Many blessings,
Joanna at Campus Food Bank

핵심 문장인 이유

해당 문장은 글의 전반에 반복되는 키워드 '기부'를 포함하며 '음식 기부'에 참여하는 방법을 안내하므로 지문 전체를 아우르는 핵심 문장에 해당한다.

본문 해설

"Campus Food Bank"에서 "food drive"를 시작함을 알리며 음식 기부에 참여하는 방법과 조건 등 상세한 정보를 안내하는 지문이다. 글에서 반복적으로 언급되는 '기부'를 포함하고 있고 '참여 방법'을 안내하는 내용이므로, 글의 목적으로 가장 적절한 것은 ①번이다.

문제 풀이 전략

글의 도입에서 "This is how you participate." 문장을 통해 참여하는 방법이 뒤따라 나올 것을 명시해주고 있다. 이렇게 전체 내용을 포괄하는 문장만 찾아도 정답을 찾아낼 수 있다. 이어지는 글의 내용은 세부적인 방법을 나타내므로 모든 문장을 해석하기보다는 "how to participate"에서 벗어나는 내용이 없는지만 훑어보고 정답을 찾으면 시간을 절약할 수 있다.

2021년 수능 18번 변형 문제

난이도 ★★☆☆☆

Dear Friends,

Season's greetings. As some of you already know, we are starting the campus food drive. This is how you participate. You can bring your items for donation to our booths. Our donation booths are located in the lobbies of the campus libraries. Just drop off the items there during usual library hours from December 4 to 23. The donated food should be non-perishable like canned meats and canned fruits. Packaged goods such as jam and peanut butter are also good. We will distribute the food to our neighbors on Christmas Eve. We truly appreciate your help.

Many blessings,
Joanna at Campus Food Bank

Food Donation에 관한 윗글의 내용과 일치하지 <u>않는</u> 것은?

① Campus food drive는 Campus Food Bank에서 주관한다.
② 기부할 물품을 부스로 가져오면 참여할 수 있다.
③ 기부 부스는 캠퍼스 도서관 로비에 위치해 있다.
④ 도서관 열람 시간과 상관없이 12월 4일부터 23일까지 참여할 수 있다.
⑤ 기부된 음식은 크리스마스 이브에 이웃들에게 나눠질 것이다.

2021년 수능 18번 서답형 변형 문제

난이도 ★★★☆☆

Dear Friends,

Season's greetings. As some of you already know, we are starting the campus food drive. This is how you participate. You can bring your items for donation to our booths. Our donation booths (A) <u>locate</u> in the lobbies of the campus libraries. Just drop off the items there during usual library hours from December 4 to 23. The (B) <u>donate</u> food should be non-perishable like canned meats and canned fruits. (C) <u>Package</u> goods such as jam and peanut butter are also good. We will distribute the food to our neighbors on Christmas Eve. We truly appreciate your help.

Many blessings,
Joanna at Campus Food Bank

밑줄 친 (A)∼(C)의 동사를 어법에 맞게 변형하시오.

(A) _____
(B) _____
(C) _____

④ Just drop off the items there during usual library hours from December 4 to 23. 문장에서 도서관의 평소 운영시간 동안
  만 물품을 가져와야 함을 알 수 있다. 따라서 이 선택지는 지문 내용과 일치하지 않는다.

① ~ we are starting the campus food drive. 문장과 Joanna at Campus Food Bank 문구를 통해 일치함을 알 수 있다.

② You can bring your items for donation to our booths.

③ Our donation booths are located in the lobbies of the campus libraries.

⑤ We will distribute the food to our neighbors on Christmas Eve.

정답 ④

(A)는 '위치해 있다' 수동태 표현으로 쓰되 복수 주어와 수를 일치시키고 시제를 현재형으로 쓴다.

(B)는 "donate"가 뒤에 나오는 명사 "food"를 수동의 의미로 꾸며주므로 수동형으로 쓴다.

(C)는 "Package"가 뒤에 나오는 명사 "goods"를 수동의 의미로 꾸며주므로 수동형으로 쓴다. 이때 본동사 "are"을 확인하
여 "goods such as~" 명사구를 목적어로 취하는 동명사 주어가 아님을 주의한다.

> ⟳ 아래의 프롬프트를 챗GPT에 입력해 보세요.
> "수동태 표현이 들어간 예문을 3개 보여줘."
> "명사를 수식하는 현재분사와 과거분사가 들어간 예문을 각각 2개씩 보여줘."
> "동명사 주어로 시작하는 예문을 2개 보여줘."

정답 (A) are located (B) donated (C) Packaged

글의 목적 파악하기

난이도 ★☆☆☆☆

Dear Mr. Reese,

A few days ago, I submitted my application and recipe for the 2nd Annual DC Metro Cooking Contest. However, I would like to change my recipe if it is possible. I have checked the website again, but I could only find information about the contest date, time, and prizes. I couldn't see any information about changing recipes. I have just created a great new recipe, and I believe people will love this more than the one I have already submitted. **Please let me know if I can change my submitted recipe.** I look forward to your response.

Best Regards,
Sophia Walker

윗글의 목적으로 가장 적절한 것은?
① 요리 대회 일정을 안내하려고
② 요리 대회 심사 결과를 확인하려고
③ 요리법 변경 가능 여부를 문의하려고
④ 새로운 요리법 개발을 요청하려고
⑤ 요리 대회 불참을 통보하려고

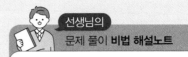
Dear Mr. Reese,

  A few days ago, I submitted my application and recipe for the 2nd Annual DC Metro Cooking Contest. However, I would like to change my recipe if it is possible. I have checked the website again, but I could only find information about the contest date, time, and prizes. I couldn't see any information about changing recipes. I have just created a great new recipe, and I believe people will love this more than the one I have already submitted. Please let me know if I can change my submitted recipe. I look forward to your response.

Best Regards,
Sophia Walker

핵심 문장인 이유

해당 문장은 글의 전반에 반복되는 키워드 '요리법 변경'을 포함하여 '가능 여부'를 알려달라는 요지를 드러내므로 지문 전체를 아우르는 핵심 문장에 해당한다.

본문 해설

이미 요리 대회에서 사용할 요리법을 제출하였으나, 새로운 레시피를 개발하여 요리법을 변경하고 싶으니 가능 여부를 알려달라는 것이 지문 내용이다. 글에서 반복적으로 언급되는 '요리법 변경'을 포함하고 있고 가능 여부를 문의하는 내용의 글이므로, 글의 목적으로 가장 적절한 것은 ③번이다.

문제 풀이 전략

주어진 지문의 하단에서 핵심적인 주제와 목적을 파악한다. 특히, "Please~"로 시작하는 구문에 글쓴이가 전달하려고 하는 메시지가 잘 드러나므로 유의해서 읽는다.

Dear Mr. Reese,

A few days ago, I submitted my application and recipe for the 2nd Annual DC Metro Cooking Contest. However, I would like to change my recipe if it is possible. I have checked the website again, but I could only find information about the contest date, time, and prizes. I couldn't see any information about changing recipes. I have just created a great new recipe, and I believe people will love this more than the one I have already submitted. Please let me know if I can change my submitted recipe. I look forward to your response.

Best Regards,
Sophia Walker

Sophia Walker에 관한 윗글의 내용과 일치하지 <u>않는</u> 것은?

① Annual DC Metro Cooking Contest에 참가한다.
② 요리법 변경과 관련된 내용을 찾기 위해 웹사이트에 방문했다.
③ 이미 제출한 요리법에 약간의 요리법을 추가하기를 원한다.
④ 사람들이 새로운 요리법을 더 좋아할 것이라고 생각한다.
⑤ Mr. Reese로부터 연락을 기다리고 있다.

Dear Mr. Reese,

A few days ago, I submitted my application and recipe for the 2nd Annual DC Metro Cooking Contest. However, (A) 나는 가능하다면 내 요리법을 변경하고 싶다. I have checked the website again, but I could only find information about the contest date, time, and prizes. I couldn't see any information about changing recipes. I have just created a great new recipe, and I believe people will love this more than the one I have already submitted. (B) 제출된 제 요리법을 수정할 수 있는지를 알려주세요. I look forward to your response.

Best Regards,
Sophia Walker

1. 밑줄 친 (A)의 우리말에 맞게 아래의 단어를 배열하시오. (필요 시 어형 변화 가능)

(my / change / will / possible / like / to / it / recipe / if / I / be)

_____

2. 밑줄 친 (B)를 다음 〈조건〉을 충족시켜 영작하시오.

〈조건〉 (1) Please로 시작하는 명령문을 사용하시오.
        (2) 명사절 접속사 if를 사용하시오.

_____

③ However, I would like to change my recipe if it is possible. 문장에서 글쓴이는 요리법 추가가 아닌 변경을 원하고 있음을 알 수 있다. 따라서 이 선택지는 지문 내용과 일치하지 않는다.

① ~ recipe for the 2nd Annual DC Metro Cooking Contest.

② I have checked the website again, ~

④ ~ I believe people will love this more than the one I have already submitted.

⑤ I look forward to your response.

정답 ③

1. '~하고 싶다'라는 의미의 "would like to~" 표현을 사용하고 뒤에 if 조건절을 붙여 '~하다면'의 의미를 완성하도록 단어를 배열하면 된다.

2. '나에게 알려줘'를 명령문 "let me know"로 나타내고 목적격 보어로 나온 동사 "know"의 목적절로서 if 명사절을 사용한다. '~인지 아닌지'의 의미를 가진 명사절 whether도 있으나 명사절 접속사 if를 사용하라는 조건에 유의한다.

> 🐾 아래의 프롬프트를 챗GPT에 입력해 보세요.
>
> "명사절 접속사 if가 사용된 예문을 5개 보여줘."
>
> "명사절 접속사 whether가 사용된 예문을 5개 보여줘."

정답 1. I would like to change my recipe if it is possible.
2. Please let me know if I can change my submitted recipe.

글의 목적 파악하기

난이도 ★☆☆☆☆

Dear Ms. Larson,

 I am writing to you with new information about your current membership. Last year, you signed up for our museum membership that provides special discounts. As stated in the last newsletter, this year we are happy to be celebrating our 50th anniversary. **So we would like to offer you further benefits.** These include free admission for up to ten people and 20% off museum merchandise on your next visit. You will also be invited to all new exhibition openings this year at discounted prices. We hope you enjoy these offers. For any questions, please feel free to contact us.

Best regards,
Stella Harrison

윗글의 목적으로 가장 적절한 것은?

① 박물관 개관 50주년 기념행사 취소를 공지하려고
② 작년에 가입한 박물관 멤버십의 갱신을 요청하려고
③ 박물관 멤버십 회원을 위한 추가 혜택을 알려 주려고
④ 박물관 기념품점에서 새로 판매할 상품을 홍보하려고
⑤ 박물관 전시 프로그램에서 변경된 내용을 안내하려고

Dear Ms. Larson,

I am writing to you with new information about your current membership. Last year, you signed up for our museum membership that provides special discounts. As stated in the last newsletter, this year we are happy to be celebrating our 50th anniversary. So we would like to offer you further benefits. These include free admission for up to ten people and 20% off museum merchandise on your next visit. You will also be invited to all new exhibition openings this year at discounted prices. We hope you enjoy these offers. For any questions, please feel free to contact us.

Best regards,
Stella Harrison

핵심 문장인 이유

해당 문장은 글의 전반에 반복되는 키워드 '멤버십', '할인' 등을 통칭하는 단어 '혜택'을 포함하고 있고 이 '혜택'을 추가 제공하고자 하는 요지를 드러내므로 지문 전체를 아우르는 핵심 문장에 해당한다.

본문 해설

편지를 받는 대상인 Ms. Larson에게 현재 이용하고 있는 멤버십에 대해 추가 혜택을 제공하고자 쓴 글이며 그에 대한 상세한 혜택 내용이 담겨 있는 지문이다. 글 전체에 걸친 키워드 '멤버십', '혜택'을 포함하고 있고 정보를 제공하고자 하는 내용의 글이므로, 글의 목적으로 가장 적절한 것은 ③번이다.

문제 풀이 전략

어휘나 문장 구조에서 특별한 힌트를 찾아내어 읽는다. 일부 단어나 표현은 글쓴이의 의도나 목적을 드러낼 수 있는데 특히, 'So〜'로 시작하는 구문은 글쓴이가 진정으로 하고자 하는 말을 드러내므로 특히 유의해서 읽는다.

정답 ③

Dear Ms. Larson,

I am writing to you with new information about your current membership. Last year, you signed up for our museum membership that provides special discounts. As stated in the last newsletter, this year we are happy to be celebrating our 50th anniversary. So we would like to offer you further benefits. These include free admission for up to ten people and 20% off museum merchandise on your next visit. You will also be invited to all new exhibition openings this year at discounted prices. We hope you enjoy these offers. For any questions, please feel free to contact us.

Best regards,
Stella Harrison

Ms. Larson에 관한 윗글의 내용과 일치하지 않는 것은?

① 현재 박물관 멤버십 회원이다.
② 작년에 특별 할인을 제공하는 박물관 멤버십에 가입했다.
③ 최대 10명에 20% 할인을 해주는 상품은 따로 구매를 해야 한다.
④ 올해 새로운 전시회에 할인된 가격으로 초대될 것이다.
⑤ 질문이 생기면 언제든지 편하게 연락하면 된다.

Dear Ms. Larson,

I am writing to you with new information about your current membership. Last year, you signed up for our museum membership that provides special discounts. As (A) state in the last newsletter, this year we are happy to be celebrating our 50th anniversary. So we would like to offer you further benefits. These include free admission for up to ten people and 20% off museum merchandise on your next visit. You will also be invited to all new exhibition openings this year at (B) discount prices. We hope you enjoy these offers. For any questions, please feel free to contact us.

Best regards,
Stella Harrison

밑줄 친 (A)~(B)의 동사를 어법에 맞게 변형하시오.

(A) _____

(B) _____

③ These include free admission for ~ 문장에서 멤버십 회원에게는 추가 혜택으로 무료 등록이 가능하며 따로 구매하지 않아도 됨을 알 수 있다. 따라서 이 선택지는 지문 내용과 일치하지 않는다.

① I am writing to you with new information about your current membership.
② Last year, you signed up for our museum membership that provides special discounts.
④ You will also be invited to all new exhibition openings this year at discounted prices.
⑤ For any questions, please feel free to contact us.

정답 ③

(A)는 지난 뉴스레터에 '서술된 것처럼'이라는 의미의 수동태 표현이 필요하므로 "stated"로 쓴다.
(B)는 "discount"가 뒤에 나오는 명사 "prices"를 수동의 의미로 꾸며주므로 수동형으로 쓴다.

> 🐾 아래의 프롬프트를 챗GPT에 입력해 보세요.
> "명사를 수식하는 현재분사와 과거분사가 들어간 예문을 각각 2개씩 보여줘."

정답 (A) stated (B) discounted

주제 파악하기

난이도 ★★☆☆☆

An important advantage of disclosure, as opposed to more aggressive forms of regulation, is its flexibility and respect for the operation of free markets. Regulatory mandates are blunt swords; they tend to neglect diversity and may have serious unintended adverse effects. For example, energy efficiency requirements for appliances may produce goods that work less well or that have characteristics that consumers do not want. **Information provision, by contrast, respects freedom of choice.** If automobile manufacturers are required to measure and publicize the safety characteristics of cars, potential car purchasers can trade safety concerns against other attributes, such as price and styling. If restaurant customers are informed of the calories in their meals, those who want to lose weight can make use of the information, leaving those who are unconcerned about calories unaffected. Disclosure does not interfere with, and should even promote, the autonomy (and quality) of individual decision-making.

윗글의 주제로 가장 적절한 것은?

① steps to make public information accessible to customers
② benefits of publicizing information to ensure free choices
③ strategies for companies to increase profits in a free market
④ necessities of identifying and analyzing current industry trends
⑤ effects of diversified markets on reasonable customer choices

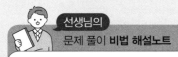
An important advantage of disclosure, ⟨as opposed to more aggressive forms of⟩regulation, is its flexibility and respect for the operation of free markets. Regulatory mandates are blunt swords; they tend to neglect diversity and may have serious unintended adverse effects. For example, energy efficiency requirements for appliances may produce goods that work less well or that have characteristics that consumers do not want. Information provision, ⟨by contrast,⟩respects freedom of choice. If automobile manufacturers are required to measure and publicize the safety characteristics of cars, potential car purchasers can trade safety concerns against other attributes, such as price and styling. If restaurant customers are informed of the calories in their meals, those who want to lose weight can make use of the information, leaving those who are unconcerned about calories unaffected. Disclosure does not ⟨interfere with, and should even promote, the autonomy (and quality) of individual decision-making.

> 기호참고
> D : disclosure
> R : regulatory

핵심 문장인 이유

글의 키워드는 정보, 규제, 공개를 들 수 있다. 이 글은 정보를 공개했을 때와 제한했을 때의 경우를 예시를 들어 보여주고 있다. 그 중, 정보를 공개하는 것에 대한 장점으로 글을 시작하였고, 해당 문장 이후로도 정보공개의 장점으로 '선택의 범위를 늘려줄 수 있는 점'을 반복하여 말하고 있으므로 위의 문장이 핵심 문장이라 할 수 있다.

본문 해설

정보 공개의 장점에 대하여 자동차 구매와 식당에서의 예시를 들어 규제와는 달리 사람들의 선택권을 늘려준다는 내용을 반복적으로 설명하고 있다. 정보공개의 장점과 그 내용을 정확하게 포함한 선택지는 ②번이다.

문제 풀이 전략

반복되는 어휘를 살펴보고 키워드가 무엇인지 정확하게 파악해야 한다. 대조적인 개념이 나올 경우 그 개념에 관련된 내용을 분류하여 표시하여 답을 찾을 때 쉽게 참고할 수 있도록 활용하는 전략이 중요하다.

> 🐾 아래의 프롬프트를 챗GPT에 입력해 보세요.
> '위에 소개한 지문의 키워드를 알려줘.'

정답 ②

An important advantage of disclosure, as opposed to more aggressive forms of regulation, is its flexibility and respect for the operation of free markets. Regulatory mandates are blunt swords; they tend to neglect diversity and may have serious unintended adverse effects.

(A) If restaurant customers are informed of the calories in their meals, those who want to lose weight can make use of the information, leaving those who are unconcerned about calories unaffected. Disclosure does not interfere with, and should even promote, the autonomy (and quality) of individual decision−making.

(B) Information provision, by contrast, respects freedom of choice. If automobile manufacturers are required to measure and publicize the safety characteristics of cars, potential car purchasers can trade safety concerns against other attributes, such as price and styling.

(C) For example, energy efficiency requirements for appliances may produce goods that work less well or that have characteristics that consumers do not want.

다음 중 주어진 글 다음에 올 글의 순서로 가장 적절한 것은?

① (B)−(C)−(A)

② (A)−(B)−(C)

③ (C)−(A)−(B)

④ (C)−(B)−(A)

⑤ (A)−(C)−(B)

An important advantage of disclosure, as opposed to more aggressive forms of regulation, ① is its flexibility and respect for the operation of free markets. Regulatory mandates are blunt swords; they tend to neglect diversity and may have serious unintended adverse effects. For example, energy efficiency requirements for appliances may produce goods that ② working less well or that have characteristics that consumers do not want. Information provision, by contrast, respects freedom of choice. If automobile manufacturers ③ are required to measure and publicize the safety characteristics of cars, potential car purchasers can trade safety concerns against other attributes, such as price and styling. If restaurant customers ④ are informed of the calories in their meals, those who want to lose weight can make use of the information, leaving those who are unconcerned about calories unaffected. Disclosure does not interfere with, and should even ⑤ promote, the autonomy (and quality) of individual decision−making.

윗글의 밑줄 친 부분 중, 어법상 틀린 것은?

① is

② working

③ are required

④ are informed

⑤ promote

제시문에서 정보 공개의 중요성에 대하여 설명하고 있고, 규제의 단점을 제시하며 서술을 이어가고 있다. 규제의 단점에 대한 예시를 들어주는 (C)가 먼저 이어져야 하며, 그 반대 개념인 (B)가 이어지는 것이 적절하다. (A)에서는 (B)에서 설명하고 있는 개념을 부연 설명하고 결론을 제시하고 있으므로 (A)는 (B) 다음에 배치되는 것이 적절하다.

정답 ④

이 문제에서 오답은 B 선택지인 "② working"이다. goods를 선행사로 취하는 관계사절의 동사 역할을 수행할 수 있는 work가 들어가야 한다.

① 'is : An important advantage'는 단수 명사이므로 동사 'is'가 이를 수반하는 것이 문법적으로 옳다.
③ are required : 이 부분은 동사 'are'와 과거분사 'required'로 구성된 수동태이다. 'automobile manufacturers'와 동사가 행위가 요구된다는 수동의 의미를 가지므로 수동태가 쓰여야 한다.
④ are informed : 이것 역시 수동태인 'are informed'의 사용이 적절하다. 주어 'restaurant customers'가 정보를 제공받는 수동적인 위치에 있기 때문이다.
⑤ promote : 여기서 'promote'는 주어 'Disclosure'의 동작을 설명하는 동사이며, should와 함께 사용되었으므로 원형이 적절하다.

정답 ②

주제 파악하기

CASE 02

난이도 ★★★☆☆

There are pressures within the museum that cause it to emphasise what happens in the galleries over the activities that take place in its unseen zones. In an era when museums are forced to increase their earnings, they often focus their energies on modernising their galleries or mounting temporary exhibitions to bring more and more audiences through the door. In other words, as museums struggle to survive in a competitive economy, their budgets often prioritise those parts of themselves that are consumable: infotainment in the galleries, goods and services in the cafes and the shops. The unlit, unglamorous storerooms, if they are ever discussed, are at best presented as service areas that process objects for the exhibition halls. And at worst, as museums pour more and more resources into their publicly visible faces, **the spaces of storage may even suffer, their modernisation being kept on hold or being given less and less space to house the expanding collections and serve their complex conservation needs.**

윗글의 주제로 가장 적절한 것은?

① importance of prioritising museums' exhibition spaces
② benefits of diverse activities in museums for audiences
③ necessity of expanding storerooms for displaying objects
④ consequences of profit-oriented management of museums
⑤ ways to increase museums' commitment to the public good

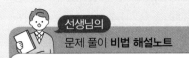
There are pressures *within* the museum that cause it to emphasise what happens in the galleries over the activities that take place in its unseen zones. In an era when museums are forced to increase their earnings, they often focus their energies on modernising their galleries or mounting temporary exhibitions to bring more and more audiences through the door. In other words, as museums struggle to survive in a competitive economy, their budgets often prioritise those parts of themselves that are consumable: infotainment in the galleries, goods and services in the cafes and the shops. The unlit, unglamorous storerooms, if they are ever discussed, are at best presented as service areas[that process objects for the exhibition halls.]And at worst, as museums pour more and more resources into their publicly visible faces, the spaces of storage may even suffer, their modernisation being kept on hold or being given less and less space to house the expanding collections and serve their complex conservation needs.

기호참고

U : unseen zone

핵심 문장인 이유

소장품을 저장하는 공간이 중요함에도 박물관의 수익을 고려하여 점점 그 자리를 잃어가는 내용을 설명하는 글이다. 밑줄 친 문장은 키워드인 박물관의 저장공간과 저장공간이 더 나빠지는 현상을 가장 포괄적으로 담고 있는 문장이므로 이를 핵심 문장이라 할 수 있다.

본문 해설

이 글은 두 가지 소재를 대조적으로 다루고 있다. 미술관의 공공에 개방된 공간(갤러리, 전시관, 카페, 상점 등)과 미술관의 보이지 않는 공간(보관실, 저장소 등)의 불균형에 대하여 대조적으로 보여주고 있다. 미술관은 현재 수익을 증가시킬 수 있는 활동에 집중하고 있으며 이는 현대화, 일시적인 전시회, 소비재 등에 집중한다는 내용과 이에 반해, 저장실 등 보이지 않는 공간은 상대적으로 소홀히 다뤄지고 있는 상황을 부각하고 있다. 이익 위주의 활동에 밀려 점차 자리를 잃어가는 박물관의 저장공간에 대한 처우에 대한 글이므로 모든 키워드와 내용을 담고 있는 ④번이 정답이 된다.

문제 풀이 전략

지문에서 대조적인 개념이 나올 경우 이를 자신만의 기호로 표시하여 내용을 정확하게 구분하는 것이 중요하다.

🎓 아래의 프롬프트를 챗GPT에 입력해 보세요.

'이 글에서 대조되고 있는 내용을 나눠서 정리해줘.'

정답 ④

There are pressures within the museum that cause it to emphasise what happens in the galleries over the activities that take place in its unseen zones. In an era when museums are forced to increase their earnings, they often focus their energies on modernising their galleries or mounting temporary exhibitions to bring more and more audiences through the door. In other words, as museums struggle to survive in a competitive economy, their budgets often prioritise those parts of themselves that are _____ : infotainment in the galleries, goods and services in the cafes and the shops. The unlit, unglamorous storerooms, if they are ever discussed, are at best presented as service areas that process objects for the exhibition halls. And at worst, as museums pour more and more resources into their publicly visible faces, the spaces of storage may even suffer, their modernisation being kept on hold or being given less and less space to house the expanding collections and serve their complex conservation needs.

윗글의 빈칸에 들어갈 말로 가장 적절한 것은?

① available
② capable
③ manageable
④ understandable
⑤ consumable

There are pressures within the museum that cause it to emphasise what happens in the galleries over the activities that take place in its unseen zones. In an era when museums are forced to increase their earnings, they often focus their energies on modernising their galleries or mounting temporary exhibitions to bring more and more audiences through the door. In other words, as museums struggle to survive in a competitive economy, their budgets often prioritise those parts of themselves that are consumable: infotainment in the galleries, goods and services in the cafes and the shops. The unlit, unglamorous storerooms, if they are ever discussed, are at best presented as service areas that process objects for the exhibition halls. And at worst, as museums pour more and more resources into their publicly visible faces, the spaces of storage may even suffer, their modernisation being kept on hold or being given less and less space to house the expanding collections and serve their complex conservation needs.

윗글의 내용을 한 문장으로 요약하고자 한다. 빈칸 (A), (B)에 들어갈 말로 가장 적절한 것은?

Museums, in striving for economic survival, often ____(A)____ the development and maintenance of their storage areas while ____(B)____ the modernization of their publicly visible spaces.

(A)	(B)		(A)	(B)
① neglect	······ prioritizing		② support	······ maintaining
③ provide	······ increasing		④ discuss	······ visualizing
⑤ expand	······ processing			

원문에 따르면, 미술관은 생존을 위해 자신들의 소비 가능한 부분에 초점을 맞춘다. 이어지는 예시들 또한 박물관의 소비 가능한 요소들의 예시이다. 따라서 답은 'consumable'이 되어야 한다.

정답 ⑤

아래의 글은 본문을 요약한 글로, 수익에 대한 압박에 밀려 점차 자리를 잃어가는 저장고와 같은 보이지 않는 공간이 처한 현실을 알려주는 글이다. 글의 내용에 따르면 박물관은 수익 때문에 저장고를 개발하고 유지하는 것을 '등한시(neglect)'하고 있으며 대중들에게 보여지는 공간을 '우선시(prioritizing)'하고 있으므로 ①번이 정답이 된다.

정답 ①

주제 파악하기

난이도 ★★★☆☆

Difficulties arise when we do not think of people and machines as collaborative systems, but assign whatever tasks can be automated to the machines and leave the rest to people. This ends up requiring people to behave in machine-like fashion, in ways that differ from human capabilities. We expect people to monitor machines, which means keeping alert for long periods, something we are bad at. We require people to do repeated operations with the extreme precision and accuracy required by machines, again something we are not good at. **When we divide up the machine and human components of a task in this way, we fail to take advantage of human strengths and capabilities but instead rely upon areas where we are genetically, biologically unsuited.** Yet, when people fail, they are blamed.

윗글의 주제로 가장 적절한 것은?

① difficulties of overcoming human weakness to avoid failure

② benefits of allowing machines and humans to work together

③ issues of allocating unfit tasks to humans in automated systems

④ reasons why humans continue to pursue machine automation

⑤ influences of human actions on a machine's performance

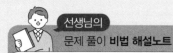
　　Difficulties arise when we do not think of people and machines as collaborative systems, but assign whatever tasks can be automated to the machines and leave the rest to people. This ends up requiring people to behave in machine-like fashion, in ways that differ from human capabilities. We expect people to monitor machines, which means keeping alert for long periods, something we are bad at. We require people to do repeated operations with the extreme precision and accuracy required by machines, again something we are not good at. When we divide up the machine and human components of a task in this way, we fail to take advantage of human strengths and capabilities but instead rely upon areas where we are genetically, biologically unsuited. Yet, when people fail, they are blamed.

핵심 문장인 이유

키워드인 people과 machines의 관계를 고려할 때 모든 자동화 할 수 있는 일을 기계에 맡기고 인간이 잘하지 못하는 일을 하게 된다면, 인간의 강점과 능력을 취하지 못하고 인간에게 맞지 않는 일을 하게 될 것이라는 점을 알 수 있다. 이를 가장 잘 포괄하는 문장이 핵심 문장이 된다.

본문 해설

이 글은 사람과 기계의 협업 시스템에 대한 어려움을 설명하고 있다. 기계가 자동화할 수 있는 모든 작업을 기계에 맡기고 나머지를 사람에게 맡기는 방식으로 작업을 나누면 문제가 발생한다고 주장한다. 이러한 방식으로 문제를 나누게 되면 인간의 장점과 능력을 활용할 수 없게 되고 우리에게 적합하지 않은 영역에 의존하게 된다고 설명하고 있다. 자동화된 시스템에서 인간에게 적절하지 않은 일을 할당하는 것에 대한 문제점을 잘 담고 있는 ③번 선택지가 정답이 된다.

문제 풀이 전략

글 안에서 나타나는 키워드와 반복되는 논리를 잘 파악하여야 한다. 어떤 논리로 글을 전개하고 있는지 내용을 정확하게 파악하여, 앞뒤 문장과 연결을 시켜보자.

> 🔖 아래의 프롬프트를 챗GPT에 입력해 보세요.
> '이 글의 중심 문장을 찾고, 이유를 설명해줘.'

정답 ③

난이도 ★★★★☆

Difficulties arise when we do not think of people and machines as collaborative systems, but assign whatever tasks can be automated to the machines and leave the rest to people. This ends up requiring people to behave in machine−like fashion, in ways that differ from human capabilities. We expect people to monitor machines, which means keeping alert for long periods, something we are bad at. We require people to do repeated operations with the extreme precision and accuracy required by machines, again something we are not good at. When we divide up the machine and human components of a task in this way, we fail to take advantage of _____ but instead rely upon areas where we are genetically, biologically unsuited. Yet, when people fail, they are blamed.

윗글의 빈칸에 들어갈 말로 가장 적절한 것은?

① the emotionless objectivity

② the efficiency and speed

③ human strengths and capabilities

④ unchanging consistency

⑤ capacity to work

난이도 ★★☆☆☆

Difficulties arise when we do not think of people and machines as collaborative systems, but assign whatever tasks can be automated to the machines and leave the rest to people. This ends up requiring people to behave in machine−like fashion, in ways that differ from human capabilities. We expect people to monitor machines, which means keeping alert for long periods, something we are bad at. We require people to do repeated operations with the extreme precision and accuracy required by machines, again something we are not good at. When we divide up the machine and human components of a task in this way, we fail to take advantage of human strengths and capabilities but instead rely upon areas where we are genetically, biologically unsuited. Yet, when people fail, they are blamed.

윗글 중 작가의 주장과 일치하지 <u>않는</u> 것은?

① 사람과 기계는 협력 시스템으로 고려되어야 한다.

② 사람들은 기계의 작업을 수행하는 데 필요한 극도의 정밀성과 정확성을 자연스럽게 가지고 있다.

③ 사람들이 긴 시간 동안 경계를 늦추지 않는 것은 그들이 잘하지 못하는 일이다.

④ 사람들이 기계의 업무를 수행하는 것은 인간의 능력과 다르다.

⑤ 잘못된 업무 분배는 사람들이 자신들의 강점과 능력을 활용하지 못하게 한다.

인간에게 맞지 않는 방식으로 일하게 되면서, '인간의 힘과 능력'의 이점을 취하지 못하게 된다.

감정없는 객관성, 효율성과 속도, 변하지 않는 일관성, 일하는 능력은 주제와 부합하지 않으며, 빈칸에 어울리지 않는다.

정답 ③

사람과 기계가 협력 시스템으로 생각되지 않을 때 어려움이 발생하며, 사람들이 긴 시간 동안 경계를 늦추지 않는 것, 기계의 업무를 수행하는 것은 인간의 능력과 다른 것, 이러한 방식으로 업무를 분배한다면 사람들이 자신의 강점과 능력을 활용하지 못하게 한다는 것은 모두 사실이다.

극도의 정밀성과 정확성은 기계의 영역으로 사람의 능력과는 다른 사실이므로 정답은 ②번이 된다.

정답 ②

주제 파악하기

CASE 04

난이도 ★★★☆☆

Libraries are becoming increasingly interested in the services they are providing for their users. This is an important focus —especially as more and more information becomes available electronically. However, **the traditional strengths of libraries have always been their collections**. This is true still today — especially in research libraries. Also, collection makeup is the hardest thing to change quickly. For example, if a library has a long tradition of heavily collecting materials published in Mexico, then even if that library stops purchasing all Mexican imprints, its Mexican collection will still be large and impressive for several years to come unless they start withdrawing books. Likewise, if a library has not collected much in a subject, and then decides to start collecting heavily in that area it will take several years for the collection to be large enough and rich enough to be considered an important research tool.

윗글의 주제로 가장 적절한 것은?

① lasting significance of library collections even in the digital age
② changing roles of local libraries and their effects on society
③ growing needs for analyzing a large volume of library data
④ online services as a key to the success of research libraries
⑤ rare book collectors' contributions to a library's reputation

Libraries are becoming increasingly interested in the services they are providing for their users. This is an important focus —especially as more and more information becomes available electronically. However, the traditional strengths of libraries have always been their collections. This is true still today —especially in research libraries. Also, collection makeup is the hardest thing to change quickly. For example, if a library has a long tradition of heavily collecting materials published in Mexico, then even if that library stops purchasing all Mexican imprints, its Mexican collection will still be large and impressive for several years to come unless they start withdrawing books. Likewise, if a library has not collected much in a subject, and then decides to start collecting heavily in that area it will take several years for the collection to be large enough and rich enough to be considered an important research tool.

예시

핵심 문장인 이유

전자매체로 변화가 이루어지는 과정에서도 여전히 도서관에 소장된 물리적인 자료가 가지는 존재감에 대해서 말하고 있으므로 그 키워드와 논리를 잘 담고 있는 해당 문장이 핵심 문장이라고 할 수 있다.

본문 해설

전자매체로 이용 가능한 도서관의 자료들이 많아짐에도 불구하고, 도서관이 직접 소장하고 있는 자료가 가진 힘과 신속하게 바꾸기 어려운 특성을 예시를 통해 설명하며, 도서관에서 소장하고 있는 자료의 비중을 독자들에게 소개하는 순서로 글을 전개하고 있다. 이를 가장 잘 담고 있는 선택지는 ①번이다.

문제 풀이 전략

키워드를 찾아내고, 반복되는 논리를 정확하게 파악하는 점이 중요하고, 이를 통해 관련없는 선택지를 정확하게 가려내는 과정이 필수적이다.

> 🗨️ 아래의 프롬프트를 챗GPT에 입력해 보세요.
> '글에서 일관성 있게 제시되는 내용을 정리해줘'

정답 ①

Libraries are becoming increasingly interested in the services they are providing for their users. This is an important focus —especially as more and more information becomes available electronically.

(A) For example, if a library has a long tradition of heavily collecting materials published in Mexico, then even if that library stops purchasing all Mexican imprints, its Mexican collection will still be large and impressive for several years to come unless they start withdrawing books.

(B) However, the traditional strengths of libraries have always been their collections. This is true still today —especially in research libraries. Also, collection makeup is the hardest thing to change quickly.

(C) Likewise, if a library has not collected much in a subject, and then decides to start collecting heavily in that area it will take several years for the collection to be large enough and rich enough to be considered an important research tool.

주어진 글 다음에 이어질 글의 순서로 가장 적절한 것을 고르시오.

① (C) − (A) − (B)
② (B) − (A) − (C)
③ (C) − (B) − (A)
④ (A) − (B) − (C)
⑤ (B) − (C) − (A)

Libraries are becoming increasingly interested in the services they are providing for their users. This is an important focus —especially as more and more information becomes available electronically. However, _____. This is true still today —especially in research libraries. Also, collection makeup is the hardest thing to change quickly. For example, if a library has a long tradition of heavily collecting materials published in Mexico, then even if that library stops purchasing all Mexican imprints, its Mexican collection will still be large and impressive for several years to come unless they start withdrawing books. Likewise, if a library has not collected much in a subject, and then decides to start collecting heavily in that area it will take several years for the collection to be large enough and rich enough to be considered an important research tool.

윗글의 빈칸에 들어갈 말로 가장 적절한 것은?

① physical collections are more popular than digital resources
② the traditional strengths of libraries lie in their collections
③ libraries can only provide research tools through physical collections
④ librarians prefer to work with physical collections
⑤ digital resources require too much storage space

제시문에서 디지털 정보의 증가에 따른 도서관 서비스의 변화에 대한 설명을 시작한다.

(B)에서 전통적인 도서관의 강점에 대해 언급하며 이것을 빠르게 변화시키는 것이 어려움을 설명한다. 이어서 (A)에서는 앞서 말한 소장 자료를 변화시키는 것에 대한 어려움에 대한 예시를 들고 있으므로 그 다음 이어질 문장으로 적절하다. 또한 (C)에서 '이와 같이'로 시작하여 예시에 대한 또 다른 설명을 덧붙이고 있으므로 글의 순서는 (B)-(A)-(C)가 적절하다.

정답 ②

키워드 간의 관계를 살펴보면 도서관의 자료가 전자매체로 바뀌어 가고 있는 과정에서도 여전히 도서관에 실제로 소장된 자료가 가지는 강점에 대한 것을 말하고 있는 글이다. "the traditional strengths of libraries lie in their collections."가 이를 가장 잘 나타내고 있다.

정답 ②

유형 03 제목 파악하기

기출문제 정복하기

2023년 9월 평가원 24번 문제

난이도 ★★★☆☆

Not only musicians and psychologists, but also committed music enthusiasts and experts often voice the opinion that the beauty of music lies in an expressive deviation from the exactly defined score. Concert performances become interesting and gain in attraction from the fact that they go far beyond the information printed in the score. In his early studies on musical performance, Carl Seashore discovered that musicians only rarely play two equal notes in exactly the same way. Within the same metric structure, there is a wide potential of variations in tempo, volume, tonal quality and intonation. **Such variation is based on the composition but diverges from it individually. We generally call this 'expressivity'.** This explains why we do not lose interest when we hear different artists perform the same piece of music. It also explains why it is worthwhile for following generations to repeat the same repertoire. New, inspiring interpretations help us to expand our understanding, which serves to enrich and animate the music scene.

윗글의 제목으로 가장 적절한 것은?

① How to Build a Successful Career in Music Criticism
② Never the Same: The Value of Variation in Music Performance
③ The Importance of Personal Expression in Music Therapy
④ Keep Your Cool: Overcoming Stage Fright When Playing Music
⑤ What's New in the Classical Music Industry?

Not only musicians and psychologists, but also committed music enthusiasts and experts/often voice the opinion (that the beauty of music lies in/an expressive deviation from/the exactly defined score.)//Concert performances become interesting and gain in attraction/from the fact (that they go far beyond the information printed in the score.) In his early studies/on musical performance/ Carl Seashore discovered/[that musicians only rarely play two equal notes in exactly the same way.] Within the same metric structure/ there is a wide potential of variations in tempo, volume, tonal quality and intonation./Such variation is based on the composition but diverges from it individually.// We generally call this 'expressivity'.//This explains/[why we do not lose interest/[when we hear/ different artists perform the same piece of music.]]It also explains/[why it is worthwhile for following generations to repeat the same repertoire.] New, inspiring interpretations/help/us/to expand/our understanding, which serves to enrich and animate/the music scene.//

핵심 문장인 이유

해당 문장은 지문의 핵심 개념인 '표현력'을 소개한다. 음악가들이 개별적으로 곡을 해석하고 연주하는 과정에서 표현되는 다양성과 창의성을 '표현력'이라고 하는데, 이는 지문 전체의 중심 주제이다.

가장 핵심이 되는 키워드를 소개하고 그에 대한 중요한 이해를 제공하면서 지문 전체에 대한 요약을 제공하므로 핵심 문장에 해당한다.

본문 해설

음악의 아름다움은 악보의 정확한 지시에서 벗어난 표현에서 나온다. 우리는 이러한 '표현성'으로 인해 다양한 연주자들의 동일한 곡 연주에 대한 흥미를 유지하고, 결과적으로 음악계는 풍부해지고 활기를 갖게 된다는 내용의 글이다.

따라서 글의 제목으로 가장 적절한 것은 ② '절대 같지 않음: 음악 연주에서 변화의 가치'가 가장 적절하다.

문제 풀이 전략

글에 들어가기 전에 선택지의 제목을 먼저 읽고 대략적으로 무엇에 관한 글인지 일반적인 아이디어를 캐치한 후에 문제를 푸는 것이 좋다. 제목을 읽은 상태로 글을 읽다 보면 내용과 제목이 일치하는 것을 훨씬 빠르게 확인할 수 있다.

① 음악 비평에서 성공적인 경력을 쌓는 방법
③ 음악 치료에서 개인적 표현의 중요성
④ 냉정을 유지하세요: 음악 연주 시 무대 공포 극복하기
⑤ 클래식 음악 산업의 최신 동향은 무엇인가요?

정답 ②

Not only musicians and psychologists, but also committed music enthusiasts and experts often voice the opinion ① that the beauty of music lies in an expressive deviation from the exactly defined score. Concert performances become interesting and gain in attraction from the fact that they go far beyond the information ② printed in the score. In his early studies on musical performance, Carl Seashore discovered that musicians only rarely play two equal notes in exactly the same way. Within the same metric structure, there is a wide potential of variations in tempo, volume, tonal quality and intonation. Such variation is based on the composition but ③ diverging from it individually. We generally call this 'expressivity'. This explains why we do not lose interest when we hear different artists perform the same piece of music. It also explains why ④ it is worthwhile for following generations to repeat the same repertoire. New, inspiring interpretations help us ⑤ to expand our understanding, which serves to enrich and animate the music scene.

윗글의 밑줄 친 부분 중, 어법상 틀린 것은?

Not only musicians and psychologists, but also committed music enthusiasts and experts often voice the opinion that the beauty of music lies in an expressive deviation from the exactly defined score. Concert performances become interesting and gain in attraction from the fact that they go far beyond the information printed in the score. In his early studies on musical performance, Carl Seashore discovered that musicians only rarely play two equal notes in exactly the same way. Within the same metric structure, there is a wide potential of variations in tempo, volume, tonal quality and intonation. Such variation is based on the composition but diverges from it individually. We generally call this 'expressivity'. This explains why we do not lose interest when we hear different artists perform the same piece of music. It also explains why it is worthwhile for following generations to repeat the same repertoire. New, inspiring interpretations help us to expand our understanding, which serves to enrich and animate the music scene.

윗글의 내용을 한 문장으로 요약하고자 한다. 빈칸 (A), (B)에 들어갈 말로 가장 적절한 것은?

The beauty of music stems from its ___(A)___, where individual interpretations of scores ___(B)___ performances and maintain audience interest.

	(A)	(B)		(A)	(B)
①	monotony	⋯⋯ limit	②	monotony	⋯⋯ alter
③	expressivity	⋯⋯ reverse	④	expressivity	⋯⋯ vary
⑤	individuality	⋯⋯ control			

③ Such variation이 주어이고 is가 동사이며, 등위접속사 but에 의해 동사가 하나 더 나온 병렬구조이다. 앞에 연결된 동사와 시제를 일치시켜 diverges가 오는 것이 적절하다.

① 앞에 나오는 명사 opinion을 수식하는 동격의 that으로 적절하다.

② 선행하는 명사를 꾸미는 분사표현으로 어떻게 수식하느냐에 따라서 형태가 달라진다. '악보에 인쇄된 정보'로 해석이 되는 수동의 의미를 가지므로 과거분사 형태가 적절하다.

④ 의미상의 주어 for 구문과 진주어 to~를 가지므로 가주어 it이 오는 것이 적절하다.

⑤ 준사역동사 help는 목적격보어로 동사원형과 to부정사 형태를 모두 취할 수 있으므로 to expand는 적절하다.

아래의 프롬프트를 챗GPT에 입력해 보세요.

"that의 종류와 쓰임 알려줘."

"명사를 수식하는 현재분사와 과거분사의 쓰임과 예시 알려줘."

"가주어, 의미상의 주어, 진주어 (it, for, to)가 포함된 예시 3개 보여줘."

"준사역동사 help가 포함된 예시 3개 보여줘."

정답 ③

음악의 진정한 아름다움은 그것을 어떻게 표현하느냐로부터 나오며, 연주자 개개인의 악보 해석이 음악을 더욱 풍성하게 만들어 청자들로 하여금 흥미를 잃지 않도록 한다는 내용이다.

따라서 빈칸 (A), (B)에 들어갈 말로 가장 적절한 것은 ④ '표현력' – '다양하게 하다'이다.

	(A)	(B)
①	단조로움	– 제한하다
②	단조로움	– 바꾸다
③	표현성	– 뒤집다
⑤	개성	– 변화시키다

아래의 프롬프트를 챗GPT에 입력해 보세요.

"위에 소개한 지문의 핵심 단어들을 모두 고르고 뜻도 알려줘."

정답 ④

제목 파악하기

난이도 ★★★☆☆

Mending and restoring objects often require even more creativity than original production. The preindustrial blacksmith made things to order for people in his immediate community; customizing the product, modifying or transforming it according to the user, was routine. Customers would bring things back if something went wrong; repair was thus an extension of fabrication. With industrialization and eventually with mass production, making things became the province of machine tenders with limited knowledge. **But repair continued to require a larger grasp of design and materials, an understanding of the whole and a comprehension of the designer's intentions.** "Manufacturers all work by machinery or by vast subdivision of labour and not, so to speak, by hand," an 1896 Manual of Mending and Repairing explained. "But all repairing must be done by hand. We can make every detail of a watch or of a gun by machinery, but the machine cannot mend it when broken, much less a clock or a pistol!"

윗글의 제목으로 가장 적절한 것은?

① Still Left to the Modern Blacksmith: The Art of Repair
② A Historical Survey of How Repairing Skills Evolved
③ How to Be a Creative Repairperson: Tips and Ideas
④ A Process of Repair: Create, Modify, Transform!
⑤ Can Industrialization Mend Our Broken Past?

Mending and restoring objects often require even more creativity than original production. The preindustrial blacksmith made things to order for people in his immediate community; customizing the product, modifying or transforming it according to the user, was routine. Customers would bring things back if something went wrong; repair was thus an extension of fabrication. With industrialization and eventually with mass production, making things became the province of machine tenders with limited knowledge. But repair continued to require a larger grasp of design and materials, an understanding of the whole and a comprehension of the designer's intentions. "Manufacturers all work by machinery or by vast subdivision of labour and not, so to speak, by hand," an 1896 Manual of Mending and Repairing explained. "But all repairing must be done by hand. We can make/every detail of a watch or of a gun/by machinery, but the machine cannot mend it when broken, much less a clock or a pistol!"
(it is)

핵심 문장인 이유

해당 문장은 지문 전체의 중심 주제인 '수리가 제작보다 더 큰 창의성과 이해를 요구한다'는 개념을 가장 직접적이고 요약적으로 드러내고 있으므로 핵심 문장에 해당한다.

본문 해설

수리와 복원은 종종 원래의 제작보다 더 많은 창의력을 필요로 한다. 산업화 이전과 대량 생산의 시대에도 제품을 수리하는 것은 설계와 재료에 대한 깊은 이해와 디자이너의 의도를 파악하는 능력을 필요로 했다.

따라서 수리가 단순한 기능적 작업이 아니라 창의성과 기술, 전체를 이해하는 능력 등을 요구하는 예술적인 작업이라는 것을 강조하는 ① '현대 대장장이에게 여전히 남겨진 것: 수리의 기술'이 제목으로 가장 적절하다.

② 수리 기술의 역사적 조망
③ 창의적인 수리인이 되는 방법: 팁과 아이디어
④ 수리의 과정: 창조, 수정, 변형!
⑤ 산업화가 우리 과거를 치유할 수 있을까요?

문제 풀이 전략

글의 첫 번째와 마지막 단락에는 일반적으로 주제에 대한 중요한 정보가 들어 있다. 도입부에는 주제를 소개하며 결론 부분은 주요 포인트를 요약하거나 해결책을 제공하기 때문이다. 이 부분을 특히 유의하여 읽으면 지문의 핵심 내용을 효과적으로 이해하여 문제 푸는 데 도움이 된다.

정답 ①

With industrialization and eventually with mass production, making things became the province of machine tenders with limited knowledge.

Mending and restoring objects often require even more creativity than original production. (①) The preindustrial blacksmith made things to order for people in his immediate community; customizing the product, modifying or transforming it according to the user, was routine. (②) Customers would bring things back if something went wrong; repair was thus an extension of fabrication. (③) But repair continued to require a larger grasp of design and materials, an understanding of the whole and a comprehension of the designer's intentions. (④) "Manufacturers all work by machinery or by vast subdivision of labour and not, so to speak, by hand," an 1896 Manual of Mending and Repairing explained. (⑤) "But all repairing must be done by hand. We can make every detail of a watch or of a gun by machinery, but the machine cannot mend it when broken, much less a clock or a pistol!"

글의 흐름으로 보아, 주어진 문장이 들어가기에 가장 적절한 곳을 고르시오.

Mending and restoring objects often require even more creativity than original production. The preindustrial blacksmith made things to order for people in his immediate community; customizing the product, modifying or transforming it according to the user, ① were routine. Customers would bring things back ② if something went wrong; repair was thus an extension of fabrication. With industrialization and eventually with mass production, making things became the province of machine tenders with ③ limited knowledge. But repair continued ④ to require a larger grasp of design and materials, an understanding of the whole and a comprehension of the designer's intentions. "Manufacturers all work by machinery or by vast subdivision of labour and not, so to speak, by hand," an 1896 Manual of Mending and Repairing explained. "But all repairing must be done by hand. We can make every detail of a watch or of a gun by machinery, but the machine cannot mend it when ⑤ broken, much less a clock or a pistol!"

윗글의 밑줄 친 부분 중, 어법상 틀린 것은?

With industrialization and eventually with mass production, making things became the province of machine tenders with limited knowledge. 문장은 산업화와 대량 생산과 함께 물건을 만드는 것이 '제한된 지식을 가진' 기계 관리자의 영역이 되었다는 내용이다.

(③) 뒷문장은 수리에 설계와 재료에 대한 더 큰 이해, 전체에 대한 이해와 설계자의 의도에 대한 이해가 '계속 요구되었다'는 내용으로 역접의 접속사 "But"을 기준으로 상반되는 내용이 나온다.

따라서, ③에 오는 것이 적절하다.

🔁 아래의 프롬프트를 챗GPT에 입력해 보세요.
"분사구문을 활용한 문장 5개 보여줘."

정답 ③

① 동명사 주어 customizing ~, modifying~, transforming~이 등위접속사 or에 의해 병렬구조로 이루어져 있기 때문에 단수로 취급해야 한다. 따라서 were이 아닌 was가 적절하다.

② 조건 접속사 if는 어떤 상황이나 조건을 나타낼 때 사용한다. 고객들이 '제품에 문제가 생기면' 가지고 돌아온다는 내용으로 조건을 나타내는 if가 적절하다.

③ 뒤에 나오는 명사 knowledge를 수식하면서 수동의 의미를 가지므로 과거분사 형태인 limited가 적절하다.

④ continue뒤에 나오는 동사의 형태로 to 부정사와 동명사 형태 모두 가능하므로 to require는 적절하다.

⑤ 문맥에서 주어와 be동사가 명확하게 이해될 때, when절에서 그것들을 생략할 수 있다. 앞 문장에서 주어는 "a watch or a gun"으로 명확하게 이해되므로 주어와 be동사는 it과 be동사 is가 생략된 형태는 적절하다.

🔁 아래의 프롬프트를 챗GPT에 입력해 보세요.
"조건절과 명사절을 나타내는 if가 쓰인 예시 3개씩 보여줘."
"when절에서 주어와 be동사가 생략되는 예시 3개 보여줘."

정답 ①

제목 파악하기

난이도 ★★★☆☆

Hyper-mobility — the notion that more travel at faster speeds covering longer distances generates greater economic success — seems to be a distinguishing feature of urban areas, where more than half of the world's population currently reside. By 2005, approximately 7.5 billion trips were made each day in cities worldwide. In 2050, there may be three to four times as many passenger-kilometres travelled as in the year 2000, infrastructure and energy prices permitting. Freight movement could also rise more than threefold during the same period. **Mobility flows have become a key dynamic of urbanization, with the associated infrastructure invariably constituting the backbone of urban form.** Yet, despite the increasing level of urban mobility worldwide, access to places, activities and services has become increasingly difficult. Not only is it less convenient — in terms of time, cost and comfort — to access locations in cities, but the very process of moving around in cities generates a number of negative externalities. Accordingly, many of the world's cities face an unprecedented accessibility crisis, and are characterized by unsustainable mobility systems.

윗글의 제목으로 가장 적절한 것은?

① Is Hyper-mobility Always Good for Cities?
② Accessibility: A Guide to a Web of Urban Areas
③ A Long and Winding Road to Economic Success
④ Inevitable Regional Conflicts from Hyper-mobility
⑤ Infrastructure: An Essential Element of Hyper-mobility

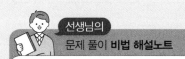
Hyper-mobility — the notion (that more travel at faster speeds/covering longer distances/generates/ greater economic success) — seems to be a distinguishing feature/of urban areas, where more than half (of the world's population) currently reside./By 2005,/approximately 7.5 billion trips were made each day/in cities/worldwide.//In 2050, there may be three to four times as many passenger-kilometres travelled as in the year 2000, infrastructure and energy prices permitting.] Freight movement could also rise/more than threefold/during the same period./Mobility flows have become/ a key dynamic of urbanization,/with the associated infrastructure (invariably constituting the backbone of urban form.)/Yet, despite the increasing level of urban mobility worldwide,/access (to) places, activities (and) services/has become increasingly difficult./Not only is (it) less convenient/— in terms of time, cost and comfort — (to) access locations in cities,/but the very process (of moving around in cities)/generates a number of negative externalities./Accordingly,/many (of the world's cities) face an unprecedented accessibility crisis,/and are characterized by unsustainable mobility systems.//

핵심 문장인 이유

해당 문장은 "Mobility flows", "urbanization", "associated infrastructure" 등 여러 가지 핵심 키워드를 포함하고 있다. 도시화와 이동성 사이의 관계를 명확히 하며, 인프라가 어떻게 도시 형태와 기능에 중요한 영향을 미치는지를 설명하는 등 지문의 전반적인 주제와 밀접한 연관이 있으며, 이후 문단에서 다루어지는 접근성과 부정적 외부성과 같은 문제들을 이해하는 데 필수적인 기반을 제공한다.

따라서 이 지문의 핵심 메시지를 가장 명확하게 전달하는 핵심 문장에 해당한다.

본문 해설

하이퍼 모빌리티는 세계 도시 지역의 이동성을 더 빠른 속도로 증가시킬 수 있지만, 장소와 활동 및 서비스에 대한 접근은 점점 더 어려워지고 도시의 장소에 접근하는 것이 덜 편리할 뿐만 아니라 부정적인 외부 효과를 발생시킨다는 내용의 글이다.
따라서 제목으로 가장 적절한 것은 ① '하이퍼 모빌리티는 도시에 항상 이로운가?'이다.

② 접근성: 도시 지역들의 네트워크 안내서
③ 경제적 성공으로 이어지는 긴 노력의 길
④ 초고이동성으로 인한 불가피한 지역 갈등
⑤ 인프라: 초고이동성의 필수 요소

문제 풀이 전략

때로는 지문에 중요하지 않은 세부 사항이 포함되어 있을 수 있으므로 주제와 관련이 없는 정보를 식별하고 제거하는 연습을 통해 핵심 메시지에 집중한다. 핵심 주제나 목적에 기여하지 않는 세부 사항을 무시하여 옵션을 소거하면서 정답을 찾는다.

정답 ①

Yet, despite the increasing level of urban mobility worldwide, access to places, activities and services has become increasingly difficult.

Hyper—mobility — the notion that more travel at faster speeds covering longer distances generates greater economic success — seems to be a distinguishing feature of urban areas, where more than half of the world's population currently reside. By 2005, approximately 7.5 billion trips were made each day in cities worldwide. In 2050, there may be three to four times as many passenger—kilometres travelled as in the year 2000, infrastructure and energy prices permitting. (①) Freight movement could also rise more than threefold during the same period. (②) Mobility flows have become a key dynamic of urbanization, with the associated infrastructure invariably constituting the backbone of urban form. (③) Not only is it less convenient — in terms of time, cost and comfort — to access locations in cities, but the very process of moving around in cities generates a number of negative externalities. (④) Accordingly, many of the world's cities face an unprecedented accessibility crisis, and are characterized by unsustainable mobility systems. (⑤)

글의 흐름으로 보아, 주어진 문장이 들어가기에 가장 적절한 곳을 고르시오.

Hyper—mobility — the notion that more travel at faster speeds covering longer distances generates greater economic success — seems to be a distinguishing feature of urban areas, where more than half of the world's population currently reside. By 2005, approximately 7.5 billion trips were made each day in cities worldwide. In 2050, there may be three to four times as many passenger—kilometres travelled as in the year 2000, infrastructure and energy prices permitting. Freight movement could also rise more than threefold during the same period. Mobility flows have become a key dynamic of urbanization, with the associated infrastructure invariably constituting the backbone of urban form. Yet, despite the increasing level of urban mobility worldwide, access to places, activities and services has become increasingly difficult. Not only is it less convenient — in terms of time, cost and comfort — to access locations in cities, but the very process of moving around in cities generates a number of negative externalities. Accordingly, many of the world's cities face an unprecedented accessibility crisis, and are characterized by unsustainable mobility systems.

윗글의 주제로 가장 적절한 것은?

① Strategies to improve accessibility in cities
② The benefits of hyper—mobility in urban areas
③ The economic implications of increasing urban mobility
④ Urban mobility's impact on city accessibility and sustainability
⑤ The relationship between urbanization and transportation infrastructure

주어진 문장은 접속사 "Yet"으로 시작하며 전 세계적으로 증가하는 도시 이동성 수준에도 불구하고, 장소, 활동 및 서비스에 대한 접근은 점점 더 어려워졌다는 내용이다.

(③)을 기준으로 앞 문장은 이동성 흐름이 관련 사회 기반 시설의 변화 없이 도시 형태의 중추를 구성하면서 도시화의 핵심 동력이 되었다는 내용이 나온다. (③) 뒷 문장은 시간, 비용 및 편안함 측면에서 보면, 도시에서 장소에 접근하는 것이 덜 편리할 뿐만 아니라, 도시에서 돌아다니는 바로 그 과정이 많은 부정적인 외부 효과를 발생시킨다는 내용이다.

이동성 흐름이 도시화를 가능하게 했으나 서비스에 대한 접근이 더 어려워져 오히려 부정적인 외부 효과를 발생시킨다는 내용이 자연스러우므로 주어진 문장이 들어가기에 가장 적절한 곳은 ③번이다.

> 🔁 아래의 프롬프트를 챗GPT에 입력해 보세요.
> "위에 소개한 지문의 핵심 단어들을 모두 고르고 뜻도 알려줘."
> "위에 소개한 지문을 핵심적인 내용이 모두 포함되도록 영어 한 문장으로 요약해줘."

정답 ③

하이퍼 모빌리티는 도시의 특징적인 요소이며, 도시의 형태와 발전에 핵심적인 역할을 하는 인프라의 중추를 형성한다.

그러나 동시에, 도시 내 이동성 증가는 접근성의 문제와 지속가능성에 영향을 미치며 도시의 이동성 시스템이 지속 불가능할 수 있다는 내용의 글이므로, 글의 주제로 가장 적절한 것은 ④ '도시 이동성이 도시의 접근성과 지속가능성에 미치는 영향'이다.

① 도시에서 접근성을 개선하는 전략들
② 도시 지역에서 하이퍼 모빌리티의 혜택들
③ 도시 내 이동성 증가의 경제적 영향
⑤ 도시화와 교통 인프라 사이의 관계

정답 ④

제목 파악하기

난이도 ★★★☆☆

A defining element of catastrophes is the magnitude of their harmful consequences. To help societies prevent or reduce damage from catastrophes, a huge amount of effort and technological sophistication are often employed to assess and communicate the size and scope of potential or actual losses. This effort assumes that people can understand the resulting numbers and act on them appropriately. However, recent behavioral research casts doubt on this fundamental assumption. Many people do not understand large numbers. **Indeed, large numbers have been found to lack meaning and to be underestimated in decisions unless they convey affect (feeling).** This creates a paradox that rational models of decision making fail to represent. On the one hand, we respond strongly to aid a single individual in need. On the other hand, we often fail to prevent mass tragedies or take appropriate measures to reduce potential losses from natural disasters.

윗글의 제목으로 가장 적절한 것은?

① Be Careful, Numbers Magnify Feelings!
② Preventing Potential Losses Through Technology
③ How to Reach Out a Hand to People in Desperate Need
④ Power of Numbers: A Way of Classifying Natural Disasters
⑤ Insensitivity to Mass Tragedy: We Are Lost in Large Numbers

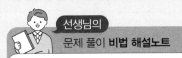
[large numbers에만 focus → affect(feeling) 전달 X → insensitivity to tragedy]

A defining element (of catastrophes) is the magnitude of their harmful consequences. To help societies prevent or reduce damage from catastrophes,/a huge amount (of effort and technological sophistication) are often employed/to assess and communicate/the size and scope (of potential or actual losses.)//This effort assumes that people can understand/the resulting numbers and act on them appropriately.//However, recent behavioral research casts doubt/on this fundamental assumption.//Many people do not understand large numbers. Indeed, large numbers have been found/to lack meaning and to be underestimated in decisions unless they convey affect (feeling). This creates a paradox (that rational models of decision making fail to represent.)//On the one hand, we respond strongly to aid a single individual (in need.)//On the other hand, we often fail to prevent mass tragedies or take appropriate measures to reduce potential losses from natural disasters.//

핵심 문장인 이유

해당 문장은 앞서 언급된 내용을 강조하면서 핵심 키워드인 '큰 숫자'의 부재한 의미와 그로 인해 발생하는 '문제'를 강조하며 전체적인 주장을 더 강화하는 역할을 한다. 따라서 이 지문의 핵심 메시지를 가장 명확하게 전달하는 핵심 문장에 해당한다.

본문 해설

큰 재해가 생기면 그 규모와 피해액을 표현하는 거대한 수에 매몰되어 그 실상을 파악하지 못하는 경향이 있음을 설명하는 글이다. 그리하여 사람들이 개인의 고통에는 강하게 반응하는 반면, 대규모 재난이나 피해를 예방하거나 감소시키는 적절한 조치를 취하기 힘들어지는 역설이 생긴다는 것이다.

따라서 제목으로 가장 적절한 것은 ⑤ '대규모 비극에 대한 무감각: 우리는 큰 수에 매몰되어 있다'이다.

① 조심해, 숫자는 감정을 불어넣는다!
② 기술을 통한 잠재적 손실 예방
③ 극심한 필요를 가진 사람들에게 손 내밀기
④ 숫자의 힘: 자연 재해를 분류하는 방법

문제 풀이 전략

지문을 빠르게 훑어가며 제목과 관련된 키워드나 핵심 구문을 캐치하여 키워드들을 잘 녹여내고 있는 제목을 찾는다. 이때 주의해야 할 점은 단순히 키워드가 포함된 것이 아닌 키워드를 제시하는 뉘앙스를 잘 구분해야 한다. (긍정적인지, 부정적인지, 혹은 개선될 필요가 있는지, 방법을 얘기하고자 하는지 등).

A defining element of catastrophes is the magnitude of their harmful consequences.

(A) However, recent behavioral research casts doubt on this fundamental assumption. Many people do not understand large numbers. Indeed, large numbers have been found to lack meaning and to be underestimated in decisions unless they convey affect (feeling).

(B) This creates a paradox that rational models of decision making fail to represent. On the one hand, we respond strongly to aid a single individual in need. On the other hand, we often fail to prevent mass tragedies or take appropriate measures to reduce potential losses from natural disasters.

(C) To help societies prevent or reduce damage from catastrophes, a huge amount of effort and technological sophistication are often employed to assess and communicate the size and scope of potential or actual losses. This effort assumes that people can understand the resulting numbers and act on them appropriately.

주어진 글 다음에 이어질 글의 순서로 가장 적절한 것을 고르시오.

① (A) − (C) − (B) ② (B) − (A) − (C) ③ (B) − (C) − (A)
④ (C) − (A) − (B) ⑤ (C) − (B) − (A)

A defining element of catastrophes is the magnitude of their harmful consequences. To help societies prevent or reduce ① damage from catastrophes, a huge amount of effort and technological sophistication are often employed to assess and communicate the size and scope of potential or actual losses. This effort assumes that people can understand the resulting numbers and act on them ② appropriately. However, recent behavioral research casts doubt on this fundamental assumption. Many people do not understand large numbers. Indeed, large numbers have been found to lack meaning and to be ③ overestimated in decisions unless they convey affect (feeling). This creates a paradox that rational models of decision making fail to represent. On the one hand, we respond strongly to ④ aid a single individual in need. On the other hand, we often fail to ⑤ prevent mass tragedies or take appropriate measures to reduce potential losses from natural disasters.

윗글의 밑줄 친 부분 중 문맥상 적절하지 않은 것은?

(C) 단락이 먼저 오는 것이 적절하다. 이 단락은 재앙의 심각성과 대응을 위한 노력에 대한 이유와 방법을 설명하고 있기 때문에 주어진 문장의 재앙의 특징 뒤에 오는 것이 자연스럽다.

(A) 단락은 역접의 접속사 However을 사용하여, 앞선 문장에서 언급된 사람들이 "resulting numbers"를 이해하고 적절하게 행동할 수 있다는 가정에 대한 의문을 제기한다.

마지막으로 (B) 단락은 (A) 단락 마지막 문장에서 언급된 큰 수에 대한 이해 부족과 관련하여 의사결정 모델의 역할에 대한 역설을 제기한다.

> 🔖 아래의 프롬프트를 챗GPT에 입력해 보세요.
> "위에 소개한 지문의 핵심 단어들을 모두 고르고 뜻도 알려줘."
> "위에 소개한 지문을 핵심적인 내용이 모두 포함되도록 영어 한 문장으로 요약해줘."

정답 ④

지문은 사람들이 큰 수를 진정으로 이해하지 못하고, 이 큰 수들이 의사결정에서 감정적인 영향을 전달하지 않는 한 과소평가되는 경향이 있다는 내용의 글이다.

따라서 ③의 overestimated를 underestimated와 같은 낱말로 바꾸는 것이 적절하다.

정답 ③

요지 파악하기

CASE 01

난이도 ★★☆☆☆

Historically, drafters of tax legislation are attentive to questions of economics and history, and less attentive to moral questions. Questions of morality are often pushed to the side in legislative debate, labeled too controversial, too difficult to answer, or, worst of all, irrelevant to the project. But, in fact, the moral questions of taxation are at the very heart of the creation of tax laws. Rather than irrelevant, moral questions are fundamental to the imposition of tax. Tax is the application of a society's theories of distributive justice. Economics can go a long way towards helping a legislature determine whether or not a particular tax law will help achieve a particular goal, but economics cannot, in a vacuum, identify the goal. **Creating tax policy requires identifying a moral goal, which is a task that must involve ethics and moral analysis.**

윗글의 요지로 가장 적절한 것은?

① 분배 정의를 실현하려면 시민 단체의 역할이 필요하다.
② 사회적 합의는 민주적인 정책 수립의 선행 조건이다.
③ 성실한 납세는 안정적인 정부 예산 확보의 기반이 된다.
④ 경제학은 세법을 개정할 때 이론적 근거를 제공한다.
⑤ 세법을 만들 때 도덕적 목표를 설정하는 것이 중요하다.

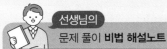
기존의 사실
기존 Historically, drafters of tax legislation are attentive to questions of economics and history, and less attentive to moral questions. Questions of morality are often pushed to the side in legislative debate, labeled too controversial, too difficult to answer, or, worst of all, irrelevant to the project. But, in fact, the moral questions of taxation are at the very heart of the creation of tax laws. Rather than irrelevant, moral questions are fundamental to the imposition of tax. Tax is the application of a society's theories of distributive justice. Economics can go a long way towards helping a legislature determine whether or not a particular tax law will help achieve a particular goal, but economics cannot, in a vacuum, identify the goal. Creating tax policy requires identifying a moral goal, which is a task that must involve ethics and moral analysis.

핵심 문장인 이유

지문의 저자는 세금과 관련된 '도덕적인 질문'이 실제로는 세법 제정의 핵심이라고 주장한다. 역사적으로는 조세 정책을 만들 때 moral question에 주의를 덜 기울이는 경향이 있으나, 세금 정책 제정에 있어서 도덕적인 목표를 밝히는 것이 필요하다는 요지를 글의 전반에서 찾아볼 수 있다.

본문 해설

글에서 반복적으로 등장하는 키워드를 살펴보면 tax legislation, moral question과 의미를 함께하는 단어들이 등장한다. 세금 관련 법률 제정자들이 종종 경제학과 역사에 주의를 기울이지만 도덕적인 문제에는 덜 주의를 기울인다는 사실에 초점을 맞추고 있으며, 세금 정책의 제정은 단지 경제적인 측면만을 고려하는 것이 아니라, 도덕적인 측면도 반드시 고려해야 한다는 것이 이 지문의 핵심 메시지이다. 이를 가장 잘 포괄하고 있는 선택지는 ⑤번이다.

문제 풀이 전략

키워드를 찾아낸 후 키워드 간의 관계에 주의를 기울이며 주제를 찾아내는 것이 중요하다.

> 🔖 아래의 프롬프트를 챗GPT에 입력해 보세요.
> "본문에서 중점적으로 다루고 있는 주제나 문제는 무엇인가?"

정답 ⑤

Historically, drafters of tax legislation are attentive to questions of economics and history, and less attentive to moral questions. Questions of morality are often pushed to the side in legislative debate, labeled too ① controversial, too difficult to answer, or, worst of all, irrelevant to the project. But, in fact, the moral questions of taxation are at the ② periphery of the creation of tax laws. Rather than ③ irrelevant, moral questions are fundamental to the imposition of tax. Tax is the application of a society's theories of distributive justice. Economics can go a long way towards helping a legislature determine whether or not a particular tax law will help achieve a particular goal, but economics cannot, in a vacuum, ④ identify the goal. Creating tax policy requires identifying a ⑤ moral goal, which is a task that must involve ethics and moral analysis.

윗글의 밑줄 친 부분 중, 문맥상 어휘의 쓰임이 올바르지 <u>않은</u> 것은?

Historically, drafters of tax legislation are attentive to questions of economics and history, and less attentive to moral questions. Questions of morality are often pushed to the side in legislative debate, labeled too controversial, too difficult to answer, or, worst of all, irrelevant to the project. But, in fact, the moral questions of taxation are at the very heart of the creation of tax laws. Rather than irrelevant, moral questions are fundamental to the imposition of tax. Tax is the application of a society's theories of distributive justice. Economics can go a long way towards helping a legislature determine whether or not a particular tax law will help achieve a particular goal, but economics cannot, in a vacuum, identify the goal. Creating tax policy requires identifying a moral goal, which is a task that must involve ethics and moral analysis.

다음 중 윗글의 내용과 일치하지 <u>않는</u> 것은?

① Drafters of tax legislation have historically paid attention to economic and historical factors.

② Moral issues are often regarded as irrelevant to tax law creation.

③ The imposition of tax is related to a society's concepts of distributive justice.

④ Economic considerations alone can determine the goals of tax legislation.

⑤ The process of creating tax policy requires ethical and moral analysis.

이 글은 세금 제정에 있어서 도덕적 목표 설정이 중요함을 주장하고 있다. 도입부에서는 도덕적 목표 설정이 여러 가지 이유로 차순위로 밀리고 있음을 서술하였지만, 글의 중반부부터는 도덕적 목표 설정의 중요함을 설명하고 있다.

주어가 세금 제정에서의 도덕적 질문이며, "periphery"는 "중심"이 아닌 "주변"을 의미하기 때문에 글의 논리에서 벗어나므로 ②번이 정답이다.

정답 ②

---

④ Economic considerations alone can determine the goals of tax legislation.
　　(경제적 고려만이 세법 제정의 목표를 결정할 수 있다.)

목표를 식별하는 데 있어서 경제적 고려만으로는 부족하며, 도덕적 목표의 확인이 필요하다고 명시적으로 언급하고 있다.

① Drafters of tax legislation have historically paid attention to economic and historical factors.
　　(과세법을 만드는 사람들은 역사적, 경제적 요인에 주목해왔다.)
② Moral issues are often regarded as irrelevant to tax law creation.
　　(도덕적 문제들은 종종 세법 제정과 관련하여 무관하다고 여겨진다.)
③ The imposition of tax is related to a society's concepts of distributive justice.
　　(세금 부과는 사회의 분배적 정의 개념과 관련이 있다.)
⑤ The process of creating tax policy requires ethical and moral analysis.
　　(세제 정책을 만드는 과정은 윤리적, 도덕적 분석을 필요로 한다.)

정답 ④

유형
04 **요지 파악하기**

CASE 02

기출문제
정복하기

2023년 수능
22번 문제

난이도 ★★★☆☆

Urban delivery vehicles can be adapted to better suit the density of urban distribution, which often involves smaller vehicles such as vans, including bicycles. **The latter have the potential to become a preferred 'last-mile' vehicle, particularly in high-density and congested areas.** In locations where bicycle use is high, such as the Netherlands, delivery bicycles are also used to carry personal cargo (e.g. groceries). Due to their low acquisition and maintenance costs, cargo bicycles convey much potential in developed and developing countries alike, such as the becak (a three-wheeled bicycle) in Indonesia. Services using electrically assisted delivery tricycles have been successfully implemented in France and are gradually being adopted across Europe for services as varied as parcel and catering deliveries. Using bicycles as cargo vehicles is particularly encouraged when combined with policies that restrict motor vehicle access to specific areas of a city, such as downtown or commercial districts, or with the extension of dedicated bike lanes.

윗글의 요지로 가장 적절한 것은?

① 도시에서 자전거는 효율적인 배송 수단으로 사용될 수 있다.

② 자전거는 출퇴근 시간을 줄이기 위한 대안으로 선호되고 있다.

③ 자전거는 배송 수단으로의 경제적 장단점을 모두 가질 수 있다.

④ 수요자의 요구에 부합하는 다양한 용도의 자전거가 개발되고 있다.

⑤ 세계 각국에서는 전기 자전거 사용을 장려하는 정책을 추진하고 있다.

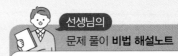
Urban delivery vehicles can be adapted to better suit the density of urban distribution, which often involves smaller vehicles such as vans, including bicycles. The latter have the potential to become a preferred 'last-mile' vehicle, particularly in high-density and congested areas. In locations where bicycle use is high, such as the Netherlands, delivery bicycles are also used to (예시) carry personal cargo (e.g. groceries). Due to their low acquisition and maintenance costs, cargo bicycles convey much potential in developed and developing countries alike, such as the becak (a three-wheeled bicycle) in Indonesia. Services using electrically assisted delivery tricycles have been successfully implemented in France and are gradually being adopted across Europe for services as varied as parcel and catering deliveries. Using bicycles as cargo vehicles is particularly encouraged when combined with policies that restrict motor vehicle access to specific areas of a city, such as downtown or commercial districts, or with the extension of dedicated bike lanes.

핵심 문장인 이유

해당 문장은 키워드인 자전거를 포함하며 특히 밀집도가 높은 공간에서 자전거가 최적의 배달 수단이 될 수 있음을 예시와 뒷받침 문장을 활용하여 반복적으로 설명하고 있다.

본문 해설

글 전체에서 반복되는 키워드를 살펴보면 도시에 적합한 배달 수단 중 특히 자전거에 대하여 서술하고 있다는 것을 확인할 수 있다. 복잡한 도시의 특성상 자전거가 유용하게 활용될 수 있다는 사실을 서술하고 예시(네덜란드, cargo bicycle 등)로 이를 뒷받침하고 있다. 이를 가장 잘 포괄하고 있는 선택지는 ①번이다.

문제 풀이 전략

반복되어 설명하고 있는 개념을 글을 읽어가며 빠르게 파악하는 것이 중요하다. 도시에서 배달 수단으로서의 자전거가 글에서 어떻게 설명되고 있는지, 개념이 일관되게 서술되고 있는지 확인하고 선택지와 비교해 보는 것이 바람직하다.

🐌 **아래의 프롬프트를 챗GPT에 입력해 보세요.**
'이 글의 중심 문장은 무엇이고, 이를 뒷받침하는 근거는 무엇인가?'

정답 ①

Urban delivery vehicles can be adapted to better suit the density of urban distribution, which often involves smaller vehicles such as vans, including bicycles. The latter have the potential to become a preferred 'last−mile' vehicle, particularly in ① high−density and congested areas. In locations where bicycle use is ② high, such as the Netherlands, delivery bicycles are also used to carry personal cargo (e.g. groceries). Due to their ③ low acquisition and maintenance costs, cargo bicycles convey much potential in developed and developing countries alike, such as the becak (a three−wheeled bicycle) in Indonesia. Services using electrically assisted delivery tricycles have been ④ successfully implemented in France and are gradually being adopted across Europe for services as varied as parcel and catering deliveries. Using bicycles as cargo vehicles is particularly encouraged when combined with policies that ⑤ motivate motor vehicle access to specific areas of a city, such as downtown or commercial districts, or with the extension of dedicated bike lanes.

윗글의 밑줄 친 부분 중, 문맥상 낱말의 쓰임이 적절하지 <u>않은</u> 것은?

The latter have the potential to become a preferred 'last−mile' vehicle, particularly in high−density and congested areas.

Urban delivery vehicles can be adapted to better suit the density of urban distribution, which often involves smaller vehicles such as vans, including bicycles. (①) In locations where bicycle use is high, such as the Netherlands, delivery bicycles are also used to carry personal cargo (e.g. groceries). (②) Due to their low acquisition and maintenance costs, cargo bicycles convey much potential in developed and developing countries alike, such as the becak (a three−wheeled bicycle) in Indonesia. (③) Services using electrically assisted delivery tricycles have been successfully implemented in France and are gradually being adopted across Europe for services as varied as parcel and catering deliveries. (④) Using bicycles as cargo vehicles is particularly encouraged when combined with policies that restrict motor vehicle access to specific areas of a city, such as downtown or commercial districts, or with the extension of dedicated bike lanes. (⑤)

주어진 문장이 들어갈 곳으로 가장 적절한 곳은?

본문의 전반부는 도시 배송에 적합한 다양한 교통수단에 대한 언급과 특히 자전거의 효용성에 중점을 둔다. 그러나 "motivate motor vehicle access"라는 표현은 자동차 접근을 독려한다는 뜻으로, 이 문장의 맥락과 일치하지 않는다. 본문의 주제와 관련하여 자전거나 다른 친환경 교통수단의 사용을 촉진하려는 의도가 담겨 있기 때문에 "motivate" 대신 "restrict"와 같이 자동차 접근을 제한하는 의미의 단어가 더 적절하다.

정답 ⑤

주어진 문장에서 "The latter"는 앞서 언급된 'bicycles'를 가리킨다. 이 문장은 자전거가 특히 고밀도 및 혼잡한 지역에서 유용한 수송 수단으로서 선호될 가능성이 있다는 내용을 설명하고 있으며, 이어지는 문장에서 자전거의 유용함을 부연하고 있다. 그러므로 자전거에 대한 설명이 처음으로 등장하는 문장 바로 다음에 들어가는 것이 가장 자연스럽다.

정답 ①

요지 파악하기

CASE 03

난이도 ★★★☆☆

Music is a human art form, an inseparable part of the human experience everywhere in the world. Music is social, and tightly woven into the tapestry of life, and young children are very much a part of this multifaceted fabric. The musical experiences they have provide opportunities for them to know language, behaviors, customs, traditions, beliefs, values, stories, and other cultural nuances. As they become musically skilled through experiences in song and instrumental music, young children can also grow cultural knowledge and sensitivity. Music is an extremely important aspect of culture, shaping and transmitting the above-mentioned aspects that characterize groups of people. **Exposing young children to the world's musical cultures brings them into the cultural conversation, allowing them to learn about self and others in an artistically meaningful and engaging way.** Prior to the development of social biases and cultural preferences that all too easily turn into prejudices, the opportunity to know people through song, dance, and instrument play is a gift to all who work for the well-balanced development of young children into the responsible citizens they will one day become.

윗글의 요지로 가장 적절한 것은?

① 아이들의 균형 잡힌 성장을 위해서는 다양한 경험이 중요하다.
② 사회적 편견과 문화적 선호도는 서로 밀접하게 관련되어 있다.
③ 어린 나이에 다양한 음악에 노출되면 예술적 감각이 향상된다.
④ 음악을 포함한 예술은 특정 문화에 대한 당대의 사회적 시각을 반영한다.
⑤ 음악은 아이들을 사회 · 문화적으로 균형 잡힌 시민으로 성장하게 해 준다.

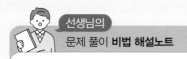

Music is a human art form, an inseparable part of the human experience everywhere in the world. Music is social, and tightly woven into the tapestry of life, and young children are very much a part of this multifaceted fabric. The musical experiences they have provide opportunities for them to know language, behaviors, customs, traditions, beliefs, values, stories, and other cultural nuances. As they become musically skilled through experiences in song and instrumental music, young children can also grow cultural knowledge and sensitivity. Music is an extremely important aspect of culture, shaping and transmitting the above-mentioned aspects that characterize groups of people. Exposing young children to the world's musical cultures brings them into the cultural conversation, allowing them to learn about self and others in an artistically meaningful and engaging way. Prior to the development of social biases and cultural preferences that all too easily turn into prejudices, the opportunity to know people through song, dance, and instrument play is a gift to all who work for the well-balanced development of young children into the responsible citizens they will one day become.

핵심 문장인 이유

글의 전반부에서는 음악이 인간 경험에 미치는 장점, 후반부에서는 음악이 아이들의 발달에 미치는 영향을 서술하고 있다. 해당 문장은 앞서 말한 글의 전체적인 흐름을 가장 잘 요약하고 있는 중심 문장이라고 할 수 있다.

본문 해설

전체적으로 반복되는 어휘를 바탕으로 키워드를 찾아보면 '음악적 경험'이 인간, 특히 '아이들에게 미치는 영향'임을 알 수 있다. 글의 후반부에서 사회적, 문화적인 관점에서 아이들에게 균형 잡힌 성장에 영향을 줄 수 있다는 점을 서술한다. 이를 가장 잘 반영한 선택지는 ⑤번이다.

문제 풀이 전략

글에서 반복되어 나오는 어휘들의 공통점을 확인하여 음악이 인간에게 미치는 영향에 대하여 파악하는 것이 중요하다. 즉, 글을 읽으면서 키워드 간의 관계를 파악하고 공통적으로 등장하는 논리에 주의를 기울여야 한다.

> 🔊 **아래의 프롬프트를 챗GPT에 입력해 보세요.**
> "다음 글의 키워드를 찾고 키워드 간의 관계를 나열하시오."

정답 ⑤

Music is a human art form, an inseparable part of the human experience everywhere in the world. Music is social, and tightly woven into the tapestry of life, and young children are very much a part of this multifaceted fabric. The musical experiences they have provide opportunities for them to know language, behaviors, customs, traditions, beliefs, values, stories, and other cultural nuances. As they become musically skilled through experiences in song and instrumental music, young children can also grow cultural knowledge and sensitivity. Music is an extremely important aspect of culture, shaping and transmitting the above-mentioned aspects that characterize groups of people. Exposing young children to the world's musical cultures brings them into the cultural conversation, allowing them to learn about self and others in an artistically meaningful and engaging way. Prior to the development of social biases and cultural preferences that all too easily turn into prejudices, the opportunity to know people through song, dance, and instrument play is a gift to all who work for the well-balanced development of young children into the responsible citizens they will one day become.

윗글의 내용을 한 문장으로 요약하고자 한다. 빈칸 (A), (B)에 들어갈 말로 가장 적절한 것은?

| Music enhances kids' understanding of diverse ___(A)___ , ___(B)___ early biases. |

(A)   (B)
① theories   ······ fostering
③ culture   ······ preventing
⑤ instrument ······ consuming

(A)   (B)
② creativity ······ contemplating
④ principles ······ obtain

Music is a human art form, an inseparable part of the human experience everywhere in the world. Music is social, and tightly woven into the tapestry of life, and young children are very much a part of this multifaceted fabric. The musical experiences they have provide opportunities for them to know language, behaviors, customs, traditions, beliefs, values, stories, and other cultural nuances. As they become musically skilled through experiences in song and instrumental music, young children can also grow cultural knowledge and sensitivity. Music is an extremely important aspect of culture, shaping and transmitting the above-mentioned aspects that characterize groups of people. Exposing young children to the world's musical cultures brings them into the cultural conversation, allowing them to learn about self and others in an artistically meaningful and engaging way. Prior to the development of social biases and cultural preferences that all too easily turn into prejudices, the opportunity to know people through song, dance, and instrument play is a gift to all who work for the well-balanced development of young children into the responsible citizens they will one day become.

윗글을 읽고 알 수 없는 정보는?
① 음악이 인간의 경험에 얼마나 중요한 역할을 하는가
② 음악이 어린 아이들에게 언어, 행동, 관습, 전통 등을 배우는 데 어떤 도움을 주는가
③ 음악이 문화를 어떻게 형성하고 전달하는가
④ 음악을 통해 아이들이 자신과 다른 사람들에 대해 어떻게 배울 수 있는가
⑤ 저자가 특정 음악 스타일이나 장르에 대해 어떻게 생각하는가

글의 핵심은 음악이 아이들을 사회적, 문화적인 관점을 길러주어 아이들의 성장에 긍정적 영향을 줄 수 있다는 것이다. 음악은 아이들이 다양한 문화(diverse culture)를 경험하고 이해할 수 있도록 돕고, 편견과 편향된 사고(bias)를 막아(preventing) 균형 잡힌 발달을 이루게 하므로 정답은 ③번이 된다.

정답 ③

이 글에서는 저자의 특정 음악 스타일이나 장르에 대한 선호나 생각에 대해서는 언급하지 않았으므로 정답은 ⑤번이다.

정답 ⑤

요지 파악하기

CASE 04

난이도 ★★★☆☆

Environmental hazards include biological, physical, and chemical ones, along with the human behaviors that promote or allow exposure. Some environmental contaminants are difficult to avoid (the breathing of polluted air, the drinking of chemically contaminated public drinking water, noise in open public spaces); in these circumstances, exposure is largely involuntary. **Reduction or elimination of these factors may require societal action, such as public awareness and public health measures.** In many countries, the fact that some environmental hazards are difficult to avoid at the individual level is felt to be more morally egregious than those hazards that can be avoided. Having no choice but to drink water contaminated with very high levels of arsenic, or being forced to passively breathe in tobacco smoke in restaurants, outrages people more than the personal choice of whether an individual smokes tobacco. These factors are important when one considers how change (risk reduction) happens.

윗글의 요지로 가장 적절한 것은?

① 개인이 피하기 어려운 유해 환경 요인에 대해서는 사회적 대응이 필요하다.
② 환경오염으로 인한 피해자들에게 적절한 보상을 하는 것이 바람직하다.
③ 다수의 건강을 해치는 행위에 대해 도덕적 비난 이상의 조치가 요구된다.
④ 환경오염 문제를 해결하기 위해서는 사후 대응보다 예방이 중요하다.
⑤ 대기오염 문제는 인접 국가들과의 긴밀한 협력을 통해 해결할 수 있다.

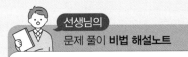
Environmental hazards include biological, physical, and chemical ones, along with the human behaviors that promote or allow exposure. Some environmental contaminants are difficult to avoid (the breathing of polluted air, the drinking of chemically contaminated public drinking water, noise in open public spaces); in these circumstances, exposure is largely involuntary. Reduction or elimination of these factors may require societal action, such as public awareness and public health measures. In many countries, the fact that some environmental hazards are difficult to avoid at the individual level is felt to be more morally egregious than those hazards that can be avoided. Having no choice but to drink water contaminated with very high levels of arsenic, or being forced to passively breathe in tobacco smoke in restaurants, outrages people more than the personal choice of whether an individual smokes tobacco. These factors are important when one considers how change (risk reduction) happens.

예시)

핵심 문장인 이유

'인간 활동'에 의해 만들어진 환경적 위험이 있으며 이는 사람들이 피하기 힘들다는 점을 글 전반에서 언급하고 있다. 이를 해결하기 위해 사회적 대응이 필요함을 서술하며 글쓴이의 의견을 전달하는 위의 문장이 핵심이라 할 수 있다.

본문 해설

사람들은 환경 위험에 노출되는 것을 피할 수 없고, 이에 대한 사회적 행동이 필요할 수 있다는 주장을 펼치고 있는 글이다. 글의 후반부에서 피할 수 없는 환경 위험에 대하여 사람들이 더 큰 분노를 느끼고 있다는 말로 이를 보충 설명하고 있다.

문제 풀이 전략

글에 등장하는 예시와 보충 설명 문장이 공통적으로 무엇을 설명하고 있는지 정확하게 파악하여야 한다.

> **아래의 프롬프트를 챗GPT에 입력해 보세요.**
> '글의 주제를 찾고, 해당 문장이 주제가 되는 근거를 제시하시오.'

Environmental hazards include biological, physical, and chemical ones, along with the human behaviors that promote or allow exposure. Some environmental contaminants are difficult to avoid (the breathing of polluted air, the drinking of chemically contaminated public drinking water, noise in open public spaces); in these circumstances, exposure is largely involuntary. Reduction or elimination of these factors may require societal action, such as public awareness and public health measures. In many countries, the fact that some environmental hazards _____ at the individual level is felt to be more morally egregious than those hazards that can be avoided. Having no choice but to drink water contaminated with very high levels of arsenic, or being forced to passively breathe in tobacco smoke in restaurants, outrages people more than the personal choice of whether an individual smokes tobacco. These factors are important when one considers how change (risk reduction) happens.

윗글의 빈칸에 들어갈 말로 가장 적절한 것은?

① are difficult to avoid
② can be avoided
③ are not easily favored
④ are largely voluntary
⑤ are easy to prevent

Having no choice but to drink water contaminated with very high levels of arsenic, or being forced to passively breathe in tobacco smoke in restaurants, outrages people more than the personal choice of whether an individual smokes tobacco.

Environmental hazards include biological, physical, and chemical ones, along with the human behaviors that promote or allow exposure. (①) Some environmental contaminants are difficult to avoid (the breathing of polluted air, the drinking of chemically contaminated public drinking water, noise in open public spaces); in these circumstances, exposure is largely involuntary. (②) Reduction or elimination of these factors may require societal action, such as public awareness and public health measures. (③) In many countries, the fact that some environmental hazards are difficult to avoid at the individual level is felt to be more morally egregious than those hazards that can be avoided. (④) These factors are important when one considers how change (risk reduction) happens. (⑤)

윗글 중 제시문이 들어갈 위치로 가장 적절한 곳은?

문장의 주요 포인트는 일부 환경적 위험요소가 개인 수준에서 피하기 어렵다는 것이다.
후반부에 서술되는 내용 또한 피할 수 없는 환경적 위험요소들을 설명하고 있다.

② can be avoided : 글에서는 일부 환경 위험요소가 피하기 어렵다는 점을 강조하고 있으므로 글의 내용과 상반된다.

③ are not easily favored : 글의 주제는 "피하기 어려움"이지 "쉽게 선호되지 않음"이 아니다.

④ are largely voluntary : "voluntary"는 자발적으로 선택할 수 있다는 의미로, 주어진 문맥과 상반되는 내용이다.

⑤ are easy to prevent : 이 선택지는 문맥과 상반된다. 글은 환경 위험요소가 "피하기 어렵다"는 것을 강조하고 있다.

정답 ①

본문에서는 환경적 위험요인들, 그리고 이런 요인들을 피하거나 줄이는 것이 어렵다는 것에 대해 언급하고 있다. 그리고 이런 요인들은 대부분 사회적 행동으로 해결해야 할 문제들이라는 주장을 하고 있다.
이 문장은 앞서 등장한 개념인 불가피한 환경 요인에 대하여 더 세부적으로 설명하고 있으며, 불가피한 환경 요인들이 어떻게 사람들을 더 크게 분노시키는지를 명확히 하므로 해당 위치가 적절하다.

정답 ④

PART
02

의미
이해

주장 파악하기

난이도 ★★★☆☆

At every step in our journey through life we encounter junctions with many different pathways leading into the distance. Each choice involves uncertainty about which path will get you to your destination. Trusting our intuition to make the choice often ends up with us making a suboptimal choice. Turning the uncertainty into numbers has proved a potent way of analyzing the paths and finding the shortcut to your destination. **The mathematical theory of probability hasn't eliminated risk, but it allows us to manage that risk more effectively.** The strategy is to analyze all the possible scenarios that the future holds and then to see what proportion of them lead to success or failure. This gives you a much better map of the future on which to base your decisions about which path to choose.

윗글에서 필자가 주장하는 바로 가장 적절한 것은?

① 성공적인 삶을 위해 미래에 대한 구체적인 계획을 세워야 한다.
② 중요한 결정을 내릴 때에는 자신의 직관에 따라 판단해야 한다.
③ 더 나은 선택을 위해 성공 가능성을 확률적으로 분석해야 한다.
④ 빠른 목표 달성을 위해 지름길로 가고자 할 때 신중해야 한다.
⑤ 인생의 여정에서 선택에 따른 결과를 스스로 책임져야 한다.

At every step in our journey through life we encounter junctions with many different pathways leading into the distance. Each choice involves uncertainty about which path will get you to your destination. Trusting our intuition to make the choice often ends up with us making a suboptimal choice. Turning the uncertainty into numbers has proved a potent way of analyzing the paths and finding the shortcut to your destination. The mathematical theory of probability hasn't eliminated risk, but it allows us to manage that risk more effectively. The strategy is to analyze all the possible scenarios that the future holds and then to see what proportion of them lead to success or failure. This gives you a much better map of the future on which to base your decisions about which path to choose.

핵심 문장인 이유

이 글은 인생에서의 선택, 직관에 의존하는 것의 한계, 그리고 불확실성을 숫자로 바꾸어 선택의 최적화를 도모하는 방법에 대한 내용을 다루고 있다. 해당 핵심 문장은 확률의 수학적 이론이 위험을 제거하지는 못하더라도 위험과 불확실성을 효과적으로 관리할 수 있음을 주장하는 문장으로, 전체 글의 메시지를 요약하는 중요한 부분이다.

본문 해설

우리가 선택을 할 때, 직관을 믿기보다 불확실성을 숫자(확률)로 바꾸어 효과적으로 이를 관리해줄 수 있다는 장점을 여러 문장에 걸쳐 설명하고 있으므로 정답은 ③번이 된다.

문제 풀이 전략

반복적으로 등장하는 논리를 파악하는 것이 중요하다. 여러 문장에 걸쳐 반복되는 내용을 캐치하고, 문장과 문장 간의 관련성을 찾아보는 전략이 필요하다.

> 🌐 아래의 프롬프트를 챗GPT에 입력해 보세요.
> "글에서 제시된 주장과 그 근거를 분석하고, 그 관계를 설명하세요."

정답 ③

2023년 수능 20번 변형 문제 난이도 ★★★☆☆

At every step in our journey through life we encounter junctions with many different pathways leading into the distance. Each choice involves uncertainty about which path will get you to your destination. Trusting our intuition to make the choice often ends up with us making a suboptimal choice. Turning the uncertainty into numbers has proved a potent way of analyzing the paths and finding the shortcut to your destination. The mathematical theory of _____ hasn't eliminated risk, but it allows us to manage that risk more effectively. The strategy is to analyze all the possible scenarios that the future holds and then to see what proportion of them lead to success or failure. This gives you a much better map of the future on which to base your decisions about which path to choose.

윗글의 빈칸에 들어갈 말로 가장 적절한 것은?

① chance

② certainty

③ probability

④ logic

⑤ prediction

2023년 수능 20번 변형 문제 난이도 ★★★★☆

At every step in our journey through life we encounter junctions with many different pathways leading into the distance.

(A) Turning the uncertainty into numbers has proved a potent way of analyzing the paths and finding the shortcut to your destination. The mathematical theory of probability hasn't eliminated risk, but it allows us to manage that risk more effectively.

(B) Each choice involves uncertainty about which path will get you to your destination. Trusting our intuition to make the choice often ends up with us making a suboptimal choice.

(C) The strategy is to analyze all the possible scenarios that the future holds and then to see what proportion of them lead to success or failure. This gives you a much better map of the future on which to base your decisions about which path to choose.

주어진 글 다음에 이어질 글의 순서로 가장 적절한 것은?

① (C) − (A) − (B)

② (B) − (A) − (C)

③ (A) − (C) − (B)

④ (B) − (C) − (A)

⑤ (C) − (B) − (A)

이 문장의 전후 문맥을 살펴보면, 선택에 대한 불확실성을 숫자로 전환하는 방법이 강력한 해석 도구가 될 수 있다는 주장이 이어진다. 본문의 논리 흐름을 따르면, 이 빈칸에는 '불확실성을 숫자로 변환하는 수학적 이론'이 들어가야 한다. 그리고 그 이론이 바로 '확률 (probability)'이므로 정답은 ③번이다.

① chance는 확률과 유사한 의미를 가지지만, 수학적 이론을 지칭하는 것은 아니므로 본문과 부합하지 않는다.
② certainty는 불확실성의 반대 의미이며, 본문의 맥락과는 맞지 않다.
④ logic은 일반적인 사고 과정이나 논증을 설명하는데 사용되지만, 본문에서 언급하는 불확실성을 관리하는 이론을 의미하는 것은 아니다.
⑤ prediction은 미래의 상황을 예측하는 행위를 의미하지만, 수학적 이론을 지칭하는 것은 아니므로 본문과 부합하지 않는다.

정답 ③

(B)에서는 인생의 여정에서 다양한 선택의 기회가 있고, 그 선택에는 불확실성이 따르며, 종종 직관에만 의존하여 최적이 아닌 선택을 하는 경우가 있음을 나타낸다. (A)는 (B)에서 언급된 불확실성을 확률의 수학적 이론을 사용하여 위험을 관리하는 방법을 소개한다. (C)는 (A)에서 소개된 확률의 수학적 이론을 바탕으로 더 구체적인 전략을 제시한다. 미래의 가능한 시나리오를 분석하고, 어떤 경로가 성공으로 이끌 것인지를 판단하는 기준을 제공한다.

정답 ②

주장 파악하기

난이도 ★★★☆☆

Occasionally individuals do not merely come out as well as clearly state what is troubling them and instead select more indirect means of expressing their annoyance. One companion might talk to the various other in a way that is condescending and also indicates underlying hostility. Numerous other times, partners may mope and even frown without genuinely dealing with an issue. Companions may likewise merely prevent discussing an issue by swiftly switching over topics when the subject turns up or by being incredibly vague. **Such indirect ways of expressing temper are not useful since they don't provide the individual that is the target of the behaviors, an idea of exactly how to react.** They understand their companion is irritated, but the absence of directness leaves them without advice regarding what they can do to solve the issue.

윗글에서 필자가 주장하는 바로 가장 적절한 것은?

① 이성보다 감정에 호소하여 상대방을 설득해야 한다.

② 상대방의 기분을 상하게 하는 행동을 자제해야 한다.

③ 문제 해결을 위해서는 문제를 직접적으로 언급해야 한다.

④ 타인의 입장을 이해하려면 경청하는 자세를 가져야 한다.

⑤ 목표 달성을 방해하는 문제점을 지속적으로 파악해야 한다.

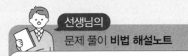
Occasionally individuals do not merely come out as well as clearly state what is troubling them and instead select more indirect means of expressing their annoyance. One companion might talk to the various other in a way that is condescending and also indicates underlying hostility. Numerous other times, partners may mope and even frown without genuinely dealing with an issue. Companions may likewise merely prevent discussing an issue by swiftly switching over topics when the subject turns up or by being incredibly vague. Such indirect ways of expressing temper are not useful since they don't provide the individual that is the target of the behaviors, an idea of exactly how to react. They understand their companion is irritated, but the absence of directness leaves them without advice regarding what they can do to solve the issue.

핵심 문장인 이유

'간접적인 방법으로 자신의 의견을 표현하는 것'에 대한 단점을 설명하는 글로, 이러한 방법은 문제 해결에 도움이 되지 않을 것임을 말하고 있다. 이를 가장 잘 표현하는 문장은 해당 핵심 문장이다.

본문 해설

글 초반부에는 간접적으로 자신의 감정을 표현하는 방법에 대하여 여러 문장에 걸쳐 설명하고 있다. 중반부부터는 간접적인 방법이 유용하지 않으며 그 이유에 대하여 설명하고 있다. 이 내용을 가장 잘 담고 있는 선택지는 ③번이다.

문제 풀이 전략

주요 개념인 '간접성'에 대한 글쓴이의 입장을 정확하게 파악하고 선택지를 고르는 것이 중요하다.

> 📝 아래의 프롬프트를 챗GPT에 입력해 보세요.
> '이 글에서 설명하는 주요개념을 파악하고, 이를 설명하는 방식을 제시하시오.'

Occasionally individuals do not merely come out as well as clearly state what is troubling them and instead select more indirect means of expressing their annoyance. One companion might talk to the various other in a way that is condescending and also indicates underlying hostility. Numerous other times, partners may mope and even frown without genuinely dealing with an issue. Companions may likewise merely prevent discussing an issue by swiftly switching over topics when the subject turns up or by being incredibly vague. Such indirect ways of expressing temper are not useful since they don't provide the individual that is the target of the behaviors, an idea of exactly how to react. They understand their companion is irritated, but _____ leaves them without advice regarding what they can do to solve the issue.

윗글의 빈칸에 들어갈 말로 가장 적절한 것은?

① the absence of assurance

② the failure of hiding anger

③ the habit of getting annoyed

④ the challenge of finding a solution

⑤ the absence of directness

Occasionally individuals do not merely come out as well as clearly state what is troubling them and instead select more indirect means of expressing their annoyance. One companion might talk to the various other in a way that is condescending and also indicates underlying hostility. ① Numerous other times, partners may mope and even frown without genuinely dealing with an issue. ② Companions may likewise merely prevent discussing an issue by swiftly switching over topics when the subject turns up or by being incredibly vague. ③ Consequently, when someone communicates casually, they can more readily acknowledge their emotions and seek resolutions. ④ Such indirect ways of expressing temper are not useful since they don't provide the individual that is the target of the behaviors, an idea of exactly how to react. ⑤ They understand their companion is irritated, but the absence of directness leaves them without advice regarding what they can do to solve the issue.

윗글에서 전체 흐름과 관계 <u>없는</u> 문장은?

글 전체의 내용은 간접적인 방법으로 불만을 표현하는 것과 그 문제점에 관한 것이다. 상대방이 명확하게 자신의 불만이나 화를 표현하지 않기 때문에 문제를 해결하기 위해 어떻게 반응해야 할지 모르는 상황을 설명하고 있다. 이러한 문맥에서 "the absence of directness"는 상대방의 직접적인 표현의 부재를 가리키며, 이 부재 때문에 대상이 어떻게 반응해야 할지 모른다는 사실을 강조한다. ① 확신의 부재, ② 분노 숨기기의 실패, ③ 짜증 내는 습관, ④ 해결책을 찾는 도전 등은 빈칸에 들어갈 말로 적절하지 않다.

정답 ⑤

전체 글의 맥락은 사람들이 간접적인 방법으로 자신의 불만이나 분노를 표현할 때 발생하는 문제점과 어려움에 관한 것이다.
③번 문장은 비공식적이거나 캐주얼한 대화의 긍정적인 측면, 즉 감정을 쉽게 인정하고 해결책을 찾을 수 있다는 내용을 언급하고 있다. 그러나 그 앞뒤 문장들은 간접적인 표현과 소통의 부정적인 측면에 중점을 둔다. 따라서 ③번 문장은 전체 맥락과 일관성이 없다.

정답 ③

유형

05

주장 파악하기

CASE 03

기출문제
정복하기

2021년 9월
평가원
20번 문제

난이도 ★★★☆☆

Given the right conditions, entrepreneurship can be fully woven into the fabric of campus life, greatly expanding its educational reach. One study showed that, within the workplace, peers influence each other to spot opportunities and act on them: the more entrepreneurs you have working together in an office, the more likely their colleagues will catch the bug. A study of Stanford University alumni found that those "who have varied work and educational backgrounds are much more likely to start their own businesses than those who have focused on one role at work or concentrated in one subject at school." **To cultivate an entrepreneurial culture, colleges and universities need to offer students a broad choice of experiences and wide exposure to different ideas.** They are uniquely positioned to do this by combining the resources of academic programming, residential life, student groups, and alumni networks.

윗글에서 필자가 주장하는 바로 가장 적절한 것은?

① 훌륭한 기업가가 되기 위해서 관심 있는 한 분야에 집중해야 한다.

② 대학은 학생들이 기업가 정신을 함양하도록 환경을 조성해야 한다.

③ 좋은 직장을 얻기 위해서 학업과 대외 활동에 충실해야 한다.

④ 기업은 대학생들의 다양한 소모임 활동을 적극 지원해야 한다.

⑤ 대학생은 학업 성취를 위하여 경험과 생각의 폭을 넓혀야 한다.

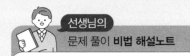
　　Given the right conditions, entrepreneurship can be fully woven into the fabric of campus life, greatly expanding its educational reach. One study showed that, within the workplace, peers influence each other to spot opportunities and act on them: the more entrepreneurs you have working together in an office, the more likely their colleagues will catch the bug. A study of Stanford University alumni found that those "who have varied work and educational backgrounds are much more likely to start their own businesses than those who have focused on one role at work or concentrated in one subject at school." To cultivate an entrepreneurial culture, colleges and universities need to offer students a broad choice of experiences and wide exposure to different ideas. They are uniquely positioned to do this by combining the resources of academic programming, residential life, student groups, and alumni networks.

핵심 문장인 이유

기업가 정신이 교육적으로 사람들에게 미치는 영향과 그 현상을 서술한 글로 기업가 문화를 육성하기 위해 대학에서 할 역할을 알려주고 있다. 이를 가장 잘 담고 있는 위의 문장이 핵심 문장이다.

본문 해설

첫 문장에서 교육에서 기업가 정신과 대학생활과의 연관성이 언급된다. 이어서 기업가 문화를 배양해야 하는 이유를 알려주고, 대학에서 기업가적 문화를 알려줄 것을 주장한다. 이를 가장 잘 표현하고 있는 ②번 선택지가 정답이 된다.

문제 풀이 전략

주제문과 이를 설명하는 문장을 구분하는 능력이 필요하다. 주제 문장과 이를 설명하는 문장을 구분하는 과정을 통해 어떤 것이 중요한 문장인지, 많은 문장에 걸쳐서 설명하려는 개념이 결국에는 무엇인지 문장을 읽어 내려가며 찾아내어야 한다.

　🔅 아래의 프롬프트를 챗GPT에 입력해 보세요.
　'글의 각 문장들이 주제문을 어떻게 서술하는지 그 역할을 구분하여 설명하시오.'

정답 ②

Given the right conditions, entrepreneurship can be fully woven into the fabric of campus life, greatly expanding its educational reach.

(A) They are uniquely positioned to do this by combining the resources of academic programming, residential life, student groups, and alumni networks.

(B) One study showed that, within the workplace, peers influence each other to spot opportunities and act on them: the more entrepreneurs you have working together in an office, the more likely their colleagues will catch the bug.

(C) A study of Stanford University alumni found that those "who have varied work and educational backgrounds are much more likely to start their own businesses than those who have focused on one role at work or concentrated in one subject at school." To cultivate an entrepreneurial culture, colleges and universities need to offer students a broad choice of experiences and wide exposure to different ideas.

주어진 글 다음에 이어질 글의 순서로 가장 적절한 것은?

① (C)−(B)−(A)
② (B)−(A)−(C)
③ (C)−(A)−(B)
④ (B)−(C)−(A)
⑤ (A)−(B)−(C)

① Given the right conditions, entrepreneurship can be fully woven into the fabric of campus life, greatly ② expanding its educational reach. One study showed that, within the workplace, peers influence each other to spot opportunities and act on them: the more entrepreneurs you have ③ working together in an office, the more likely their colleagues will catch the bug. A study of Stanford University alumni found that those "who have varied work and educational backgrounds are much more likely to start their own businesses than those who have focused on one role at work or concentrated in one subject at school." ④ Cultivate an entrepreneurial culture, colleges and universities need to offer students a broad choice of experiences and wide exposure to different ideas. They are uniquely positioned to do this by ⑤ combining the resources of academic programming, residential life, student groups, and alumni networks.

윗글의 밑줄 친 부분 중, 어법상 틀린 것은?

(B)는 사무실 환경에서의 기업가 문화와 그 영향에 대해 이야기한다. 이 문장은 기업가 문화의 전파 방식에 대한 일반적인 개념을 제공한다.

그 다음, (C)는 스탠퍼드 대학교의 졸업생 연구를 통해 대학에서의 교육과 경험이 기업가 문화에 어떻게 영향을 미치는지를 구체적으로 보여준다. 이는 일반적인 기업가 문화의 전파 방식에서 좀 더 구체적인 대학의 맥락으로 이동하는 것이다.

(A)는 대학들이 어떻게 기업가 문화를 촉진할 수 있는지를 구체적으로 제안한다. 이 문장은 대학이 기업가 문화를 통합하고 확장하는 방법에 대한 직접적인 해결책을 제시한다.

정답 ④

Cultivate는 동사의 형태로 활용되어 주어 없이 문장을 형성할 수 없다.

① Given은 조건을 나타내는 데 사용되며, "어떤 조건을 가정할 때"라는 의미로 해석된다. 여기서는 "올바른 조건이 주어진다면"이라는 의미로 사용되었다.
② expanding은 분사구문 형태로 사용되어 주어 'entrepreneurship'이 'its educational reach'를 '확장'한다는 행위를 설명하고 있다.
③ working은 분사로 사용되어 'entrepreneurs'가 'an office'에서 '함께 일하고 있다'는 상황을 표현한다.
⑤ combining은 전치사 뒤에 위치하며 'colleges and universities'가 여러 가지 자원을 '결합'한다는 행위를 설명하고 있다.

정답 ④

주장 파악하기

CASE 04

난이도 ★★★☆☆

At the 2015 *Fortune* Most Powerful Women Summit, Ginni Rometty offered this advice: "When did you ever learn the most in your life? What experience? I guarantee you'll tell me it was a time you felt at risk." To become a better leader, you have to step out of your comfort zone. You have to challenge the conventional ways of doing things and search for opportunities to innovate. Exercising leadership not only requires you to challenge the organizational status quo but also requires you to challenge your internal status quo. You have to challenge yourself. You have to venture beyond the boundaries of your current experience and explore new territory. Those are the places where there are opportunities to improve, innovate, experiment, and grow. **Growth is always at the edges, just outside the boundaries of where you are right now.**

윗글에서 필자가 주장하는 바로 가장 적절한 것은?

① 지도자는 실현 가능한 목표를 설정해야 한다.
② 지도자는 새로운 제도를 적극적으로 도입해야 한다.
③ 지도자는 조직의 현재 상태를 철저히 분석해야 한다.
④ 지도자는 현재의 자신을 넘어서는 도전을 해야 한다.
⑤ 지도자는 기존의 방식과 새로운 방식을 조화시켜야 한다.

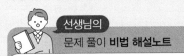
At the 2015 *Fortune* Most Powerful Women Summit, Ginni Rometty offered this advice: "When did you ever learn the most in your life? What experience? I guarantee you'll tell me it was a time you felt at risk." To become a better leader, you <u>have to</u> step out of <u>your comfort zone</u>. You have to <u>challenge the conventional ways</u> of doing things and search for opportunities to innovate. Exercising leadership not only requires you to challenge the organizational status quo but also <u>requires you to challenge your internal status quo</u>. You have to challenge yourself. You have to venture beyond the boundaries of your current experience and explore new territory. Those are the places where there are opportunities to improve, innovate, experiment, and grow. Growth is always at the edges, just outside the boundaries of where you are right now.

핵심 문장인 이유

기존의 방식에서 벗어나 현재의 상태에 도전할 것을 글 전체에서 요구하고 있다. 이를 가장 잘 종합하고 있는 문장이 핵심 문장이다.

본문 해설

자신이 안주하고 있는 영역을 넘어, 도전할 것을 여러 문장에 걸쳐서 나타내고 있다. 이를 가장 잘 반영하는 주장은 ④번이다.

문제 풀이 전략

문장에서 공통요소를 찾아 연결하면서, 반복적으로 등장하는 키워드와 논리를 찾는 과정이 필요하다.

> 🔊 **아래의 프롬프트를 챗GPT에 입력해 보세요.**
> '글의 핵심 키워드를 선정하고, 그 이유를 글에 사용된 문장을 예로 들어 설명하시오.'

정답 ④

At the 2015 *Fortune* Most Powerful Women Summit, Ginni Rometty offered this advice: "When did you ever learn the most in your life? What experience? I guarantee you'll tell me it was a time you felt at risk." To become a better leader, you have to step out of your _____. You have to challenge the conventional ways of doing things and search for opportunities to innovate. Exercising leadership not only requires you to challenge the organizational status quo but also requires you to challenge your internal status quo. You have to challenge yourself. You have to venture beyond the boundaries of your current experience and explore new territory. Those are the places where there are opportunities to improve, innovate, experiment, and grow. Growth is always at the edges, just outside the boundaries of where you are right now.

윗글의 빈칸에 들어갈 말로 가장 적절한 것은?

① boundary

② opportunity

③ growth

④ comfort zone

⑤ challenge

At the 2015 *Fortune* Most Powerful Women Summit, Ginni Rometty offered this advice: "When did you ever learn the most in your life? What experience? I guarantee you'll tell me it was a time you felt at risk." To become a better leader, you have to step out of your comfort zone. You have to challenge the conventional ways of doing things and search for opportunities to innovate. Exercising leadership not only requires you to challenge the organizational status quo but also requires you to challenge your internal status quo. You have to challenge yourself. You have to venture beyond the boundaries of your current experience and explore new territory. Those are the places where there are opportunities to improve, innovate, experiment, and grow. Growth is always at the edges, just outside the boundaries of where you are right now.

윗글의 내용과 일치하는 것은?

① 더 나은 리더가 되려면, 본인의 안락함에서 벗어나고 자신에게 도전해야 한다.

② 더 나은 리더가 되려면, 일하는 방식에 대한 관습을 따르는 것이 좋다.

③ 조직의 현재 상태는 안정성을 유지하기 위해 도전하지 않아야 한다.

④ 현재의 경험의 경계를 넘어서는 것은 성장의 기회를 제한한다.

⑤ 개인의 안전과 보장을 위해 안락한 상태를 유지해야 한다.

이 지문에서 "comfort zone"은 리더가 더 나은 리더가 되기 위해 벗어나야 하는 것이다. 아래 이어지는 글에서 자신에게 주어진 상황과 자기 자신에 도전하는 등 현재의 상태에서 벗어나 새로운 영역으로 향해 나아갈 것을 요구하고 있으므로, 해당 위치에 가장 적합한 단어는 'comfort zone'이다.

① boundary : 이 단어는 지문에서 맥락에 따라 사용되지만, 필요한 개념을 정확하게 대체할 수 없다.
② opportunity : 이 단어는 "comfort zone"을 벗어난 후 발견되는 것이다.
③ growth : 이 단어는 "comfort zone"을 벗어난 후의 결과이다.
⑤ challenge : 이 단어는 "comfort zone"을 벗어나는 방법을 설명하는데 사용되지만, "comfort zone"을 대체할 수 없다.

정답 ④

이 문장은 지문의 주제와 가장 일치하며, "안락한 상태에서 벗어나야 하며, 자신에게 도전해야 한다"라는 내용이 지문에서 강조된 주요 아이디어이다.

• ②는 지문의 "일하는 방식에 대한 관습에 도전해야 한다"라는 내용과 상충한다.
• ③은 지문의 "리더십을 행사하는 것은 단지 조직의 현재 상태에 도전하는 것뿐만 아니라 자신의 내부 상태에도 도전하는 것을 요구한다"라는 내용과 상충한다.
• ④는 지문의 "현재 경험의 경계를 넘어서 새로운 영역을 탐색해야 한다"라는 내용과 상충한다.
• ⑤는 지문의 "더 나은 리더가 되려면, 당신은 안락한 상태에서 벗어나야 한다"라는 내용과 상충한다.

정답 ①

심경, 분위기 파악하기

CASE 01

난이도 ★★☆☆☆

Once again, I had lost the piano contest to my friend. When I learned that Linda had won, I was deeply troubled and unhappy. My body was shaking with uneasiness. My heart beat quickly and my face became reddish. I had to run out of the concert hall to settle down. Sitting on the stairs alone, I recalled what my teacher had said. **"Life is about winning, not necessarily about winning against others but winning at being you.** And the way to win is to figure out who you are and do your best." He was absolutely right. I had no reason to oppose my friend. Instead, I should focus on myself and my own improvement. I breathed out slowly. My hands were steady now. At last, my mind was at peace.

윗글에 드러난 'I'의 심경 변화로 가장 적절한 것은?

① grateful → sorrowful

② upset → calm

③ envious → doubtful

④ surprised → disappointed

⑤ bored → relieved

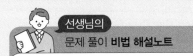
Once again, I had lost the piano contest to my friend. When I learned that Linda had won, I was deeply troubled and unhappy. My body was shaking with uneasiness. My heart beat quickly and my face became reddish. I had to run out of the concert hall to settle down. [Sitting on the stairs alone] I recalled [what my teacher had said.] "Life is about winning, not necessarily about winning against others but winning at being you. And the way to win is to figure out [who you are] and do your best." He was absolutely right. I had no reason to oppose my friend. Instead, I should focus on [myself and my own improvement.] I breathed out slowly. My hands were steady now. At last, my mind was at peace.

핵심 문장인 이유

해당 문장은 글의 주제를 담고 있으며, 글쓴이의 인식이 변하게 되는 전환점으로서 글쓴이 자신과 자기 계발에 집중함을 강조하므로 지문 전체를 아우르는 핵심 문장에 해당한다.

본문 해설

글쓴이가 친구에게 피아노 경연대회에서 져서 감정이 좋지 않았으나 선생님의 자신이 되는 데에서 승리하는 것이라는 조언을 듣고 자신에게 더 집중하고 스스로를 발전시키겠다는 내용이다.

글쓴이는 처음에는 화가 나고 속상했으나 (troubled, unhappy, uneasiness, reddish) 선생님의 조언 이후 마음이 차분해졌음을 (steady, at peace) 알 수 있다. 따라서 'I'의 심경 변화로 가장 적절한 것은 ② '속상한 – 차분한'이다.

① 감사한 – 슬픈
③ 부러워하는 – 의심하는
④ 놀라는 – 실망한
⑤ 지루한 – 안도한

문제 풀이 전략

"심경, 분위기 파악" 유형은 최근 5개년 모두 심경 변화 문제로 출제되었고 앞으로도 심경 변화 문제 유형으로 나올 가능성이 매우 높다. 이 유형은 지문 중간을 제외한 앞, 뒤를 살펴서 문제를 푸는 것이 중요하다.

감정을 나타내는 형용사와 부사를 체크하며 푸는 것이 중요한데, 모든 문장을 꼼꼼히 해석하기보다는 글의 흐름대로 답안을 체크하면 시간을 절약할 수 있다.

정답 ②

Once again, I had lost the piano contest to my friend. When I learned that Linda had won, I was deeply troubled and unhappy. My body was shaking with uneasiness. My heart beat quickly and my face became reddish. I had to run out of the concert hall to settle down. Sitting on the stairs alone, I recalled what my teacher had said. "Life is about winning, not necessarily about winning against others but winning at being you. And the way to win is to figure out who you are and do your best." He was absolutely right. I had no reason to oppose my friend. Instead, I should focus on ＿＿＿＿＿＿＿＿＿＿.
I breathed out slowly. My hands were steady now. At last, my mind was at peace.

윗글의 빈칸에 들어갈 말로 가장 적절한 것을 고르시오.

① prioritizing things to do
② what other people accomplish
③ thinking logically and creatively
④ religious power and believing in it
⑤ myself and my own improvement

Once again, I had lost the piano contest to my friend. When I learned that Linda had won, I was deeply troubled and unhappy. My body was shaking with uneasiness. My heart beat quickly and my face became reddish. I had to run out of the concert hall to settle down. (A) While I sat on the stairs alone, I recalled (B) 나의 선생님께서 말씀하셨던 것. "Life is about winning, not necessarily about winning against others but winning at being you. And the way to win is (C) 네가 누구인지 알아내고 최선을 다하는 것이다." He was absolutely right. I had no reason to oppose my friend. Instead, I should focus on myself and my own improvement. I breathed out slowly. My hands were steady now. At last, my mind was at peace.

1. 밑줄 친 (A)를 분사구문으로 변형하시오.

_____

2. 밑줄 친 (B)를 우리말과 일치하도록 영작하시오.

_____

3. 밑줄 친 (C)의 우리말과 일치하도록 아래의 단어를 배열하시오.

(to / your / out / you / figure / who / are / and / do / best)

_____

접속사 instead를 기준으로 앞, 뒤 내용이 상반되는 것을 알 수 있다. 앞 문장에서 친구에 대적할 것이 아니라 빈칸에 집중해야 한다고 얘기하는 내용의 글이다. 따라서 빈칸에 들어갈 말로 가장 적절한 것은 지문 내에서 '친구'라는 개념과 반대되는 ⑤ '나 자신과 자기발전'이다.

① 해야 할 일들의 우선순위를 정하는 것
② 다른 사람들이 성취하는 것들
③ 논리적이고 창의적으로 생각하는 것
④ 종교적인 힘과 그것을 믿는 것

정답 ⑤

1. 접속사 'While'이 생략되고, 부사절의 주어와 주절의 주어가 같으므로 생략한다. 동사의 시제도 같으므로 'Sitting'으로 시작하는 단순분사구문을 만들면 된다.

2. 선행사를 포함한 관계대명사 'what'은 문장 내에서 주어, 목적어, 보어 역할을 할 수 있는데 여기에서는 'recalled' 동사의 목적어 역할을 한다. 이때 본동사의 시제와 일치시켜야 함을 주의한다.

3. 주격보어로 to 부정사가 필요하고 동사 'figure out'의 목적어로 간접의문문(의문사, 주어, 동사)이 나온다. 등위접속사 and 뒤에 (to)가 생략된 동사원형을 배열하면 된다.

> 아래의 프롬프트를 챗GPT에 입력해 보세요.
>
> "부사절을 분사구문으로 바꾸는 과정을 5개의 예문으로 보여줘."
> "선행사를 포함한 관계대명사 what이 포함된 5개의 예문을 보여줘"
> "간접의문문이 문장 내에서 하는 역할을 5개의 예문으로 보여줘."

정답 1. Sitting on the stairs alone,
　　　 2. what my teacher had said
　　　 3. to figure out who you are and do your best

심경, 분위기 파악하기

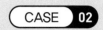
난이도 ★★☆☆☆

It was Evelyn's first time to explore the Badlands of Alberta, famous across Canada for its numerous dinosaur fossils. As a young amateur bone-hunter, she was overflowing with anticipation. She had not travelled this far for the bones of common dinosaur species. Her life-long dream to find rare fossils of dinosaurs was about to come true. She began eagerly searching for them. **After many hours of wandering throughout the deserted lands, however, she was unsuccessful.** Now, the sun was beginning to set, and her goal was still far beyond her reach. Looking at the slowly darkening ground before her, she sighed to herself, "I can't believe I came all this way for nothing. What a waste of time!"

윗글에 나타난 Evelyn의 심경 변화로 가장 적절한 것은?

① confused   → scared

② discouraged → confident

③ relaxed   → annoyed

④ indifferent → depressed

⑤ hopeful   → disappointed

It was Evelyn's first time to explore the Badlands of Alberta, famous across Canada for its numerous dinosaur fossils. As a young amateur bone-hunter, she was overflowing with anticipation. She had not travelled this far for the bones of common dinosaur species. Her life-long dream to find rare fossils of dinosaurs was about to come true. She began eagerly searching for them. After many hours of wandering throughout the deserted lands, however, she was unsuccessful. Now, the sun was beginning to set, and her goal was still far beyond her reach. Looking at the slowly darkening ground before her, she sighed to herself, "I can't believe I came all this way for nothing. What a waste of time!"

핵심 문장인 이유

해당 문장은 글의 주요 전환점을 나타낸다. Evelyn의 기대와 목표가 아직 이루어지지 않았음을 보여주며 이후 이야기에 대한 긴장감과 동기 부여를 제공하기 때문에 핵심 문장에 해당한다.

본문 해설

Evelyn의 오랜 꿈인 희귀한 공룡화석을 찾는 것이 이루어질 생각에 매우 큰 기대를 안고 있었으나 이는 성공적이지 못했다. 해가 지기 시작하며 Evelyn은 자신의 노력과 시간이 헛되었다며 실망한다.

Evelyn은 처음에 기대하고 신났으나 (overflowing with anticipation, life-long dream, eagerly) 황무지에서 발굴작업이 실패하자 매우 실망하고 좌절함을 (unsuccessful, sighed to herself, nothing, a waste of time) 알 수 있으므로 Evelyn의 심경 변화로 가장 적절한 것은 ⑤ '희망적인 – 실망한' 이다.

① 혼란스러운 – 두려운
② 낙담한 – 자신감 있는
③ 편안한 – 짜증난
④ 무관심한 – 우울한

문제 풀이 전략

주어진 지문의 전체적인 문맥을 이해한다. 문장이나 지문의 특정 부분만이 아니라 전반적인 맥락을 파악함으로써 글쓴이의 태도 변화를 더 정확하게 이해할 수 있다.

정답 ⑤

It was Evelyn's first time to explore the Badlands of Alberta, famous across Canada for its numerous dinosaur fossils. As a young amateur bone−hunter, she was overflowing with anticipation.

(A) After many hours of wandering throughout the deserted lands, however, she was unsuccessful. Now, the sun was beginning to set, and her goal was still far beyond her reach.

(B) She had not travelled this far for the bones of common dinosaur species. Her life−long dream to find rare fossils of dinosaurs was about to come true. She began eagerly searching for them.

(C) Looking at the slowly darkening ground before her, she sighed to herself, "I can't believe I came all this way for nothing. What a waste of time!"

주어진 글 다음에 이어질 글의 순서로 가장 적절한 것을 고르시오.

① (A)−(C)−(B)   ② (B)−(A)−(C)
③ (B)−(C)−(A)   ④ (C)−(A)−(B)
⑤ (C)−(B)−(A)

After many hours of wandering throughout the deserted lands, however, she was unsuccessful.

It was Evelyn's first time to explore the Badlands of Alberta, famous across Canada for its numerous dinosaur fossils. (①) As a young amateur bone−hunter, she was overflowing with anticipation. (②) She had not travelled this far for the bones of common dinosaur species. (③) Her life−long dream to find rare fossils of dinosaurs was about to come true. (④) She began eagerly searching for them. (⑤) Now, the sun was beginning to set, and her goal was still far beyond her reach. Looking at the slowly darkening ground before her, she sighed to herself, "I can't believe I came all this way for nothing. What a waste of time!"

글의 흐름으로 보아, 주어진 문장이 들어가기에 가장 적절한 곳을 고르시오.

(B) 단락이 먼저 오는 것이 적절하다. 이 단락은 주어진 문장 마지막 부분에 나오는 Evelyn이 많은 기대감을 가지고 있는 것에 대한 이유를 제공한다.

(A) 단락은 (B) 단락에 나온 부푼 기대와 생각과는 달리 실패로 끝이 났고 그녀의 꿈이 멀어졌음을 나타낸다.

마지막으로 (C) 단락은 (A) 단락에 이어서 기대했던 것이 실패로 끝난 것에 대한 실망과 좌절을 나타낸다.

정답 ②

"After many hours of wandering throughout the deserted lands, however, she was unsuccessful." 문장은 황무지를 많은 시간 배회했으나 화석을 하나도 찾지 못했다는 내용으로 역접의 접속사 however를 포함하여 앞뒤 내용이 반전될 것임을 알 수 있다.

(④)을 기준으로 앞 문장은 그녀가 열성적으로 공룡화석을 찾기 시작한다는 내용이고, 뒷 문장은 그녀의 목표는 여전히 이루기 힘들다는 내용이므로 주어진 문장을 삽입함으로써 글을 반전시키면 된다.

따라서 (④)에 오는 것이 적절하다.

> 아래의 프롬프트를 챗GPT에 입력해 보세요.
> "분사구문을 활용한 문장 5개 보여줘."

정답 ④

심경, 분위기 파악하기

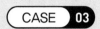

유형 06

기출문제 정복하기

2020년 수능 19번 문제

난이도 ★★☆☆☆

Looking out the bus window, Jonas could not stay calm. He had been looking forward to this field trip. It was the first field trip for his history course. His history professor had recommended it to the class, and Jonas had signed up enthusiastically. He was the first to board the bus in the morning. The landscape looked fascinating as the bus headed to Alsace. Finally arriving in Alsace after three hours on the road, however, Jonas saw nothing but endless agricultural fields. The fields were vast, but hardly appealed to him. **He had expected to see some old castles and historical monuments, but now he saw nothing like that awaiting him.** "What can I learn from these boring fields?" Jonas said to himself with a sigh.

윗글에 드러난 Jonas의 심경 변화로 가장 적절한 것은?

① excited → disappointed
② indifferent → thrilled
③ amazed → horrified
④ surprised → relieved
⑤ worried → confident

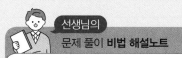

분사구문(= As, While he looked out ~)
[Looking out the bus window,] Jonas could not stay calm. He had been looking forward to this field trip. It was the first field trip for his history course. His history professor had recommended it to the class, and Jonas had signed up enthusiastically. He was the first to board the bus in the morning. The landscape looked fascinating as the bus headed to Alsace. Finally [arriving in Alsace
                                                                              분사구문
after three hours on the road,] however, Jonas saw nothing but endless agricultural fields. The fields
                                                                    (= when he arrived in Alsace
were vast, but hardly appealed to him. He had expected to see some old castles and historical monuments, but now he saw nothing like that awaiting him. "What can I learn from these boring fields?" Jonas said to himself with a sigh.

핵심 문장인 이유

해당 문장은 역사 현장 학습에 대한 Jonas의 기대와 현실 사이의 차이를 나타낸다. 기대와 실망이라는 대조는 글의 주요 주제를 형성하며, Jonas의 감정과 경험을 이해하는데 중요하므로 핵심 문장에 해당한다.

본문 해설

Jonas는 오랫동안 고대하던 역사 현장 학습에 가는 것에 매우 큰 기대를 안고 있었으나 기대와는 달리 오래된 성이나 역사 유적지가 아닌 그를 기다리고 있는 것은 지루한 들판뿐임에 실망한다.

Jonas는 처음에 기대하고 신났으나 (not stay calm, enthusiastically, fascinating) 기대하던 역사 유적지가 아닌 끝없이 펼쳐진 농사용 들판을 보고 매우 실망함 (hardly appealed, boring, with a sigh) 알 수 있으므로, Jonas의 심경 변화로 가장 적절한 것은 ① '기대한 – 실망한'이다.

② 무관심한 – 감격한
③ 놀라운 – 두려워 하는
④ 놀란 – 안도한
⑤ 걱정스러운 – 자신감 있는

문제 풀이 전략

지문에서 사용된 언어적 단서를 활용한다. 특정 단어나 표현은 종종 감정이나 태도를 나타내는 힌트를 제공할 수 있다. 문맥을 고려하여 이러한 단서를 잘 활용하는 것이 좋다.

정답 ①

Finally arriving in Alsace after three hours on the road, however, Jonas saw nothing but endless agricultural fields.

Looking out the bus window, Jonas could not stay calm. He had been looking forward to this field trip. It was the first field trip for his history course. (①) His history professor had recommended it to the class, and Jonas had signed up enthusiastically. (②) He was the first to board the bus in the morning. (③) The landscape looked fascinating as the bus headed to Alsace. (④) The fields were vast, but hardly appealed to him. (⑤) He had expected to see some old castles and historical monuments, but now he saw nothing like that awaiting him. "What can I learn from these boring fields?" Jonas said to himself with a sigh.

글의 흐름으로 보아, 주어진 문장이 들어가기에 가장 적절한 곳을 고르시오.

Looking out the bus window, Jonas could not stay calm. He had been looking forward to this field trip. It was the first field trip for his history course. His history professor had recommended it to the class, and Jonas had signed up enthusiastically. He was the first to board the bus in the morning. The landscape looked (A) <u>fascinate</u> as the bus headed to Alsace. Finally (B) <u>arrive</u> in Alsace after three hours on the road, however, Jonas saw nothing but endless agricultural fields. The fields were vast, but hardly appealed to him. He had expected to see some old castles and historical monuments, but now he saw nothing like that (C) <u>await</u> him. "What can I learn from these boring fields?" Jonas said to himself with a sigh.

밑줄 친 (A)~(C)의 동사를 어법에 맞게 한 단어로 변형하시오.

(A) _____

(B) _____

(C) _____

Finally arriving in Alsace after three hours on the road, however, Jonas saw nothing but endless agricultural fields. 문장은 3시간 이상 걸려 Alsace에 도착했으나 끝없는 농업용 들판만이 있었다는 내용으로 역접의 접속사 however를 포함하여 기대했던 것과는 달랐음을 알 수 있다.

(④)을 기준으로 앞 문장은 Jonas가 Alsace로 가는 길에 매우 기대하는 내용이고, 뒷 문장은 들판이 광활했으나 그의 기대와는 달랐다는 내용이므로 주어진 문장을 삽입함으로써 글을 반전시키면 된다.

따라서 (④)에 오는 것이 적절하다.

정답 ④

(A)는 주어인 'landscape'가 매혹적인 감정을 불러일으키는 것이므로 현재분사 형태인 'fascinating'으로 쓴다.
(B)는 분사구문임을 확인하고 'arriving'으로 쓴다.
(C)는 뒤에 나오는 목적어 'him'를 취하므로 능동의 의미를 가지는 현재분사로 쓴다.

아래의 프롬프트를 챗GPT에 입력해 보세요.
"감정을 나타내는 현재분사와 과거분사가 쓰인 예시 5개씩 보여줘."
"분사구문을 활용한 문장 5개 보여줘."

정답 (A) facinating (B) arriving (C) awaiting

심경, 분위기 파악하기

CASE 04

난이도 ★★☆☆☆

The waves were perfect for surfing. Dave, however, just could not stay on his board. He had tried more than ten times to stand up but never managed it. He felt that he would never succeed. He was about to give up when he looked at the sea one last time. The swelling waves seemed to say, "Come on, Dave. One more try!" Taking a deep breath, he picked up his board and ran into the water. He waited for the right wave. Finally, it came. He jumped up onto the board just like he had practiced. **And this time, standing upright, he battled the wave all the way back to shore.** Walking out of the water joyfully, he cheered, "Wow, I did it!"

윗글에 드러난 Dave의 심경 변화로 가장 적절한 것은?

① frustrated → delighted

② bored → comforted

③ calm → annoyed

④ relieved → frightened

⑤ pleased → upset

　　The waves were perfect for surfing. Dave, however, just could not stay on his board. He had tried more than ten times to stand up but never managed it. He felt that he would never succeed. He was about to give up when he looked at the sea one last time. The swelling waves seemed to say, "Come on, Dave. One more try!" [Taking a deep breath,] he picked up his board and ran into the water. He waited for the right wave. Finally, it came. He jumped up onto the board just like he had practiced. And this time, standing upright, he battled the wave all the way back to shore. [Walking out of the water joyfully,] he cheered, "Wow, I did it!"

(주석: however 위 밑줄 / it =his board / but / 분사구문 (=After he took ~) / V① / V② / it (= the right wave) / 분사구문 (= As he walked out ~))

핵심 문장인 이유

해당 문장은 Dave의 전환점을 나타낸다. 그가 결국 자신의 목표를 달성했음을 보여주며 그의 변화와 성공을 의미한다. 노력과 극복, 마침내 성공까지 이어지는 이야기의 중요한 포인트를 담고 있기 때문에 핵심 문장에 해당한다.

본문 해설

Dave는 계속 도전했으나 도저히 보드를 통제할 수 없음을 느끼고 서핑에 절대 성공하지 못할 것 같다는 생각을 한다. 그러나 마음을 가다듬고 다시 시도하여 마침내 성공해낸 뒤 행복하게 물 밖으로 나온다.

Dave는 처음에 좌절하고 포기하려고 했으나 (never managed, never succeed, give up) 바다를 바라보며 한 번 더 해보자고 마음을 먹고 결국에는 성공해내고 즐거워함을 (joyfully, cheered, I did it!) 알 수 있으므로 Dave의 심경 변화로 가장 적절한 것은 ① '좌절한 – 기쁜'이다.

② 지루한 – 안심한
③ 차분한 – 짜증난
④ 안도한 – 두려워 하는
⑤ 기쁜 – 속상한

문제 풀이 전략

지문이 어떤 상황에서 일어나고 있는지 이해한다. 상황을 이해하면 주어진 감정이나 태도의 원인을 더욱 명확하게 구분할 수 있다.

정답 ①

And this time, standing upright, he battled the wave all the way back to shore.

The waves were perfect for surfing. Dave, however, just could not stay on his board. He had tried more than ten times to stand up but never managed it. (①) He felt that he would never succeed. (②) He was about to give up when he looked at the sea one last time. The swelling waves seemed to say, "Come on, Dave. One more try!" (③) Taking a deep breath, he picked up his board and ran into the water. (④) He waited for the right wave. Finally, it came. He jumped up onto the board just like he had practiced. (⑤) Walking out of the water joyfully, he cheered, "Wow, I did it!"

글의 흐름으로 보아, 주어진 문장이 들어가기에 가장 적절한 곳을 고르시오.

The waves were perfect for surfing. Dave, however, just could not stay on his board. He had tried more than ten times to stand up but never managed it. He felt that he would never succeed. He was about to give up when he looked at the sea one last time. The swelling waves seemed to say, "Come on, Dave. One more try!" (A) 깊은 숨을 들이마신 후, 그는 서핑 보드를 집어들고 물속으로 달려갔다. He waited for the right wave. Finally, (B) it came. He jumped up onto the board just like he had practiced. And this time, standing upright, he battled the wave all the way back to shore. Walking out of the water joyfully, he cheered, "Wow, I did it!"

1. 밑줄 친 (A)의 우리말에 맞게 아래의 단어를 배열하시오.

(breath / into / his / up / taking / a / and / water / deep / he / picked / board / ran / the)

2. 밑줄 친 (B)가 지칭하는 것을 본문 내에서 연속하는 세 단어로 찾아 쓰시오.

And this time, standing upright, he battled the wave all the way back to shore. 문장은 이번에는 똑바로 서서 파도와 맞서 해안까지 싸웠다는 내용으로 앞선 시도와는 다르게 서핑에 성공한 모습을 보여준다.

(⑤)을 기준으로 바로 앞 문장에서 Dave가 연습한 대로 보드에 올라탔다는 내용이 나오고, 뒤에 기분 좋게 해냈다고 외치며 물 밖으로 나오는 내용이 뒤따른다.

따라서 (⑤)에 오는 것이 적절하다.

정답 ⑤

1. 'Taking'으로 시작하는 분사구문을 먼저 적고, 주어는 'he', 시제는 과거로 'picked up'과 'ran into'를 병렬구조로 단어를 배열하면 된다.

2. 앞문장 "He waited for the right wave."에서 적당한 파도를 기다렸는데 마침내 그것이 왔다고 했으므로 'the right wave'를 지칭한다.

> 🐾 아래의 프롬프트를 챗GPT에 입력해 보세요.
> "분사구문을 활용한 예시 5개 보여줘."

정답 1. Taking a deep breath, he picked up his board and ran into the water
2. the right wave

함축적 의미 파악하기

CASE 01

난이도 ★★★★☆

Lawyers sometimes describe ownership as a bundle of sticks. This metaphor was introduced about a century ago, and it has dramatically transformed the teaching and practice of law. **The metaphor is useful because it helps us see ownership as a grouping of interpersonal rights that can be separated and put back together.** When you say *It's mine* in reference to a resource, often that means you own a lot of the sticks that make up the full bundle: the sell stick, the rent stick, the right to mortgage, license, give away, even destroy the thing. Often, though, we split the sticks up, as for a piece of land: there may be a landowner, a bank with a mortgage, a tenant with a lease, a plumber with a license to enter the land, an oil company with mineral rights. Each of these parties owns <u>a stick in the bundle</u>.

밑줄 친 a stick in the bundle이 윗글에서 의미하는 바로 가장 적절한 것은?

① a legal obligation to develop the resource

② a priority to legally claim the real estate

③ a right to use one aspect of the property

④ a building to be shared equally by tenants

⑤ a piece of land nobody can claim as their own

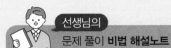
Lawyers sometimes describe/ownership/as a *bundle of sticks*. This metaphor was introduced/about a century ago,/ and it has dramatically transformed/the teaching and practice of law./The metaphor is useful/because it helps us see ownership as a grouping of interpersonal rights (that can be separated and put back together.) When you say *It's mine*/in reference to a resource,/often that means/you own a lot of the sticks (that make up the full bundle: the sell stick, the rent stick, the right to mortgage, license, give away, even destroy the thing.) Often, though, we split the sticks up,/as for a piece of land,/ there may be a landowner, a bank with a mortgage, a tenant with a lease, a plumber with a license to enter the land, an oil company with mineral rights.]//Each of these parties owns a stick in the bundle.

핵심 문장인 이유

해당 문장은 지문의 핵심 키워드인 "ownership"을 "interpersonal rights"의 묶음으로 보는 방식으로 소유권의 복잡성과 다양성을 이해하는 새로운 관점을 제시한다.

또한, that can be seperated and put back together을 통해서 소유권이 얼마나 유연하고 변화 가능한지를 보여준다.

소유권에 대한 전통적인 생각을 넘어서서, 그것을 더 복잡하고 다양한 방식으로 이해하는 방법을 제시하므로 전체 지문의 핵심 주제를 집약적으로 반영하는 핵심 문장에 해당한다.

본문 해설

변호사들은 때때로 소유권을 나무가지 묶음으로 설명한다. 이 비유는 소유권을 개별적인 권리들의 집합으로 보고, 이를 분리하거나 재결합할 수 있다는 것을 보여준다. 따라서 밑줄 친 부분이 의미하는 바로 가장 적절한 것은 ③ '그 재산의 한 측면을 사용할 수 있는 권리'이다.

① 그 자원을 개발할 법적 의무
② 법적으로 그 부동산을 차지할 우선권
④ 임차인들에 의해 동등하게 공유될 건물
⑤ 아무도 자신의 것으로 주장할 수 없는 토지의 한 면

문제 풀이 전략

지문 전체에서 사용된 비유나 은유를 먼저 파악한다. 이러한 비유와 은유는 직접적인 의미가 아닌 간접적인 의미를 나타낼 수 있으므로 비유적 표현에 주의를 기울여 의미하는 바를 찾아야 한다.

정답 ③

Lawyers sometimes describe ownership as a bundle of sticks. This metaphor was introduced about a century ago, and it has dramatically transformed the teaching and practice of law. The metaphor is useful because it helps us see ownership as a grouping of interpersonal rights that can be separated and put back together. When you say *It's mine* in reference to a resource, often that means you own a lot of the sticks that make up the full bundle: the sell stick, the rent stick, the right to mortgage, license, give away, even destroy the thing. Often, though, we split the sticks up, as for a piece of land: there may be a landowner, a bank with a mortgage, a tenant with a lease, a plumber with a license to enter the land, an oil company with mineral rights. Each of these parties owns a stick in the bundle.

윗글의 제목으로 가장 적절한 것은?

① Legal Definitions of Ownership

② The Role of Banks in Property Ownership

③ Ownership: Dissecting the Bundle of Rights

④ The Evolution of Ownership Over the Centuries

⑤ Differentiating Lease, Mortgage, and Licensing

Lawyers sometimes describe ownership as a bundle of sticks. This metaphor was introduced about a century ago, and it has dramatically transformed the teaching and practice of law. The metaphor is useful because it helps us see ownership as a grouping of interpersonal rights that can be separated and put back together. When you say *It's mine* in reference to a resource, often that means you own a lot of the sticks that make up the full bundle: the sell stick, the rent stick, the right to mortgage, license, give away, even destroy the thing. Often, though, we split the sticks up, as for a piece of land: there may be a landowner, a bank with a mortgage, a tenant with a lease, a plumber with a license to enter the land, an oil company with mineral rights. Each of these parties _____.

윗글의 빈칸에 들어갈 말로 가장 적절한 것은?

① disputes a claim on the assets

② owns a stick in the bundle

③ perceives a slice of the pie

④ controls a share in the property

⑤ rejects a portion in the rights

이 지문은 소유권에 대한 개념과 "bundle of sticks"라는 개념에 대해 설명하고 있으며 소유권이 개별 권리들의 번들로 구성되는 것을 강조하고, 이러한 권리들이 분리되고 다시 합쳐질 수 있다는 내용의 글이다. 따라서 글의 제목으로 적절한 것은 ③ '소유권: 권리의 번들 분석'이다.

① 소유권의 법적 정의
② 부동산 소유에 은행의 역할
④ 세기를 거쳐 발전하는 소유권
⑤ 임대, 모기지, 라이센싱의 차이

아래의 프롬프트를 챗GPT에 입력해 보세요.
"위에 소개한 지문의 핵심 단어들을 모두 고르고 뜻도 알려줘."

정답 ③

이 지문은 소유권에 대한 개념을 "bundle of sticks"라는 비유를 통해 설명하고 있다. 소유권이 개별 권리들의 번들로 구성되는 것을 강조하고, 이러한 권리들이 분리되고 다시 합쳐질 수 있다는 점을 설명하고 있다.

Each of these parties owns a stick in the bundle. 이라는 문장은 결국 각각의 당사자들이 소유권의 번들 중 하나의 권리를 소유하고 있다는 의미를 내포하고 있다.

따라서 지문의 내용과 결론을 고려하여 빈칸에 가장 적절한 말은 '② 번들 속의 한 권리를 소유하고 있다.'이다. 이는 소유권의 개념을 잘 나타내며, 이전에 제시한 조건에 부합하는 정답이다.

① 자산에 대한 권리를 반박한다.
③ 일정 부분을 인지한다.
④ 부동산의 지분을 관리한다.
⑤ 권리들 중 일부를 거부한다.

정답 ②

함축적 의미 파악하기

CASE 02

난이도 ★★★★☆

Coming of age in the 18th and 19th centuries, the personal diary became a centerpiece in the construction of a modern subjectivity, at the heart of which is the application of reason and critique to the understanding of world and self, which allowed the creation of a new kind of knowledge. **Diaries were central media through which enlightened and free subjects could be constructed.** They provided a space where one could write daily about her whereabouts, feelings, and thoughts. Over time and with rereading, disparate entries, events, and happenstances could be rendered into insights and narratives about the self, and allowed for the formation of subjectivity. It is in that context that the idea of "the self [as] both made and explored with words" emerges. Diaries were personal and private; one would write for oneself, or, in Habermas's formulation, one would make oneself public to oneself. By making the self public in a private sphere, the self also became an object for self-inspection and self-critique.

밑줄 친 make oneself public to oneself가 윗글에서 의미하는 바로 가장 적절한 것은?

① use writing as a means of reflecting on oneself
② build one's identity by reading others' diaries
③ exchange feedback in the process of writing
④ create an alternate ego to present to others
⑤ develop topics for writing about selfhood

Coming of age in the 18th and 19th centuries, the personal diary became a centerpiece/in the construction of a modern subjectivity, at the heart of which/is the application of reason and critique to the understanding of world and self, which allowed/the creation of a new kind of knowledge.// Diaries were central media/through which enlightened and free subjects/could be constructed./They provided a space/where one could write daily about her whereabouts, feelings, and thoughts./Over time and with rereading, [disparate entries, events, and happenstances] could be rendered/into insights and narratives about the self, and allowed/for the formation of subjectivity.//It is in that context that the idea of "the self [as] both made and explored with words" emerges./Diaries were personal and private;/one would write for oneself, or, in Habermas's formulation,/one would make oneself public to oneself/ By making the self/public/in a private sphere, the self also became an object/for self-inspection and self-critique.//

핵심 문장인 이유

해당 문장은 핵심 키워드인 "diaries"가 어떻게 현대 주체성의 구축에 중심적인 역할을 했는지 명확하게 표현한다.

일기의 중요성과 그것이 개인의 자아 인식과 주체성 형성에 어떻게 영향을 미쳤는지에 대한 전체 지문의 핵심 주제를 집약적으로 반영하는 핵심 문장에 해당한다.

본문 해설

18-19세기에 성장한 일기는 개인의 생활, 감정, 생각을 기록하는 공간으로, 계몽된 자유로운 주체를 구성할 수 있는 중심 매체로서 자신의 행방, 감정, 생각에 대해 매일 쓸 수 있도록 하여 자기 점검과 자기 비판의 대상이 되었다고 했으므로, 밑줄 친 부분이 글에서 의미하는 바로 가장 적절한 것은 ① '글을 자신을 되돌아보는 수단으로 사용하곤'이다.

② 타인의 일기를 읽음으로써 자신의 정체성을 확립하곤
③ 글 쓰는 과정에서 의견을 교환하곤
④ 다른 사람에게 제시하기 위한 대체 자아를 창조하곤
⑤ 자아에 관한 글을 쓰기 위한 주제를 개발하곤

문제 풀이 전략

주어진 단어나 표현 주변의 문맥을 주의 깊게 살펴본다. 종종 부연 설명이 함축적인 의미를 더 잘 이해하도록 도와주기 때문이다.

정답 ①

Coming of age in the 18th and 19th centuries, the personal diary became a centerpiece in the construction of a modern subjectivity, at the heart of ① <u>which</u> is the application of reason and critique to the understanding of world and self, which allowed the creation of a new kind of knowledge. Diaries were central media through which enlightened and free subjects could be constructed. They provided a space ② <u>where</u> one could write daily about her whereabouts, feelings, and thoughts. Over time and with rereading, disparate entries, events, and happenstances could be rendered into insights and narratives about the self, and ③ <u>allowed</u> for the formation of subjectivity. It is in that context that the idea of "the self [as] both made and explored with words" ④ <u>emerge</u>. Diaries were personal and private; one would write for oneself, or, in Habermas's formulation, one would make oneself public to oneself. By making the self ⑤ <u>public</u> in a private sphere, the self also became an object for self-inspection and self-critique.

윗글의 밑줄 친 부분 중, 어법상 틀린 것은?

Coming of age in the 18th and 19th centuries, the personal diary became a centerpiece in the construction of a modern subjectivity, at the heart of which is the application of reason and critique to the understanding of world and self, which allowed the creation of a new kind of knowledge. ① Diaries were central media through which enlightened and free subjects could be constructed. ② They provided a space where one could write daily about her whereabouts, feelings, and thoughts. ③ Over time and with rereading, disparate entries, events, and happenstances could be rendered into insights and narratives about the self, and allowed for the formation of subjectivity. ④ In the meantime, memories, lectures and diaries of the time multiply, and often give controversial but incomplete assessments. ⑤ It is in that context that the idea of "the self [as] both made and explored with words" emerges. Diaries were personal and private; one would write for oneself, or, in Habermas's formulation, one would make oneself public to oneself. By making the self public in a private sphere, the self also became an object for self-inspection and self-critique.

윗글에서 전체 흐름과 관계 <u>없는</u> 문장은?

④ it ~ that 강조구문이고, 주어는 두 번째 that 뒤에 나오는 the idea이므로 emerges가 적절하다. 강조구문이 아니었을 경우 문장은 다음과 같다. "The idea of the self [as] both made and explored with words emerges in that context."

① 바로 앞에 선행하는 a modern subjectivity에 대해 설명하는 관계대명사로 which는 적절하다.
② 뒤따라 나오는 one could write ~ and thoughts라는 완전한 절을 이끌며 공간을 나타내는 a space라는 선행사를 꾸며주기에 관계부사 where은 적절하다.
③ 과거분사 allowed는 그 앞에 생략된 could be와 더불어 수동태의 술어를 이루므로 적절하다.
⑤ 형용사 public은 동사 make의 목적격 보어로 적절하다. (make+목적어+목적격 보어)

> ⟐ 아래의 프롬프트를 챗GPT에 입력해 보세요.
> "부사구를 강조하는 it ~ that 강조 구문 예시 3개 보여줘."
> "관계부사의 종류와 쓰임 알려줘."

정답 ④

이 지문은 18세기와 19세기에 개인 다이어리가 현대적인 자아성 형성과 지식의 창출에 중요한 역할을 한다는 내용의 글이므로, 스트레스를 받는 기간 동안 많은 사람이 일기를 쓰며 위안을 얻곤 한다는 ④는 글의 전체 흐름과 관계가 없다.

> ⟐ 아래의 프롬프트를 챗GPT에 입력해 보세요.
> "위에 소개한 지문의 핵심 단어들을 모두 고르고 뜻도 알려줘."
> "위에 제시된 지문을 핵심으로만 구성된 한 문장으로 요약해줘."

정답 ④

유형
07 함축적 의미 파악하기

CASE 03

기출문제
정복하기

2023년 9월
평가원
21번 문제

난이도 ★★★☆☆

　You may feel there is something scary about an algorithm deciding what you might like. Could it mean that, if computers conclude you won't like something, you will never get the chance to see it? Personally, I really enjoy being directed toward new music that I might not have found by myself. I can quickly get stuck in a rut where I put on the same songs over and over. That's why I've always enjoyed the radio. **But the algorithms that are now pushing and pulling me through the music library are perfectly suited to finding gems that I'll like.** My worry originally about such algorithms was that they might drive everyone into certain parts of the library, leaving others lacking listeners. Would they cause a convergence of tastes? But thanks to the nonlinear and chaotic mathematics usually behind them, this doesn't happen. A small divergence in my likes compared to yours can send us off into different far corners of the library.

밑줄 친 send us off into different far corners of the library가 윗글에서 의미하는 바로 가장 적절한 것은?

① lead us to music selected to suit our respective tastes

② enable us to build connections with other listeners

③ encourage us to request frequent updates for algorithms

④ motivate us to search for talented but unknown musicians

⑤ make us ignore our preferences for particular music genres

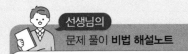

선생님의
문제 풀이 **비법 해설노트**

You may feel/there is something scary about an algorithm deciding(what you might like.)//Could it mean that/ if computers conclude/you won't like something/ you will never get the chance to see it?//Personally,/I really enjoy being directed/toward new music (that I might not have found by myself.)I can quickly get stuck/in a rut/where I put on the same songs over and over.//That's why I've always enjoyed the radio.//But the algorithms(that are now pushing and pulling me through the music library) are perfectly suited to finding gems (that I'll like.)//My worry originally/about such algorithms was/that they might drive/everyone/into certain parts of the library/ leaving others/ lacking listeners.//Would they cause a convergence of tastes? But thanks to the nonlinear and chaotic mathematics usually behind them/ this doesn't happen.//A small divergence (in my likes compared to yours)can send us off into different far corners of the library.

집합, 집중

핵심 문장인 이유

해당 문장은 핵심 키워드인 "algorithm"의 음악 추천의 가치와 효과에 대한 전체적인 주제를 요약하고 강조한다.

또한, 알고리즘이 음악 선택에 어떻게 개인화된 추천을 제공하는지에 대한 긍정적인 견해를 중점적으로 보여주면서 언급된 우려와 걱정에 대한 반론이나 대안적인 시각을 제시하므로 핵심 문장에 해당한다.

본문 해설

알고리즘이 당신이 좋아할 것을 결정하는 것은 무서워 보일 수 있으나 이러한 알고리즘은 개인의 음악 취향을 정확하게 찾아내며, 비선형적이고 혼돈의 수학 덕분에 모든 사람의 취향이 하나로 수렴하지 않게 한다는 내용의 글이다.

따라서 각자의 작은 선호의 차이가 주어라는 점을 고려하면, 밑줄 친 부분이 의미하는 바로 가장 적절한 것은 ① '우리를 각각 자신의 취향에 맞도록 선택된 음악으로 이끌다'이다.

② 우리가 다른 청취자들과 관계를 맺을 수 있게 하다.
③ 우리가 알고리즘을 위한 업데이트를 자주 요구하라고 권하다.
④ 재능이 있지만 알려지지 않은 음악가들을 찾도록 우리에게 동기를 주다.
⑤ 특별한 음악 장르에 대한 우리의 선호를 무시하도록 만들다.

문제 풀이 전략

문장 내에서 사용된 특정 단어나 표현이 함축된 의미를 나타내는 경우가 많으므로 이러한 언어적 힌트를 잘 활용하여 주어진 문장의 실제 의미를 파악한다.

정답 ①

You may feel there is something scary about an algorithm deciding what you might like. Could it mean that, if computers conclude you won't like something, you will never get the chance to see it? Personally, I really enjoy ① being directed toward new music that I might not have found by myself. I can quickly get stuck in a rut ② which I put on the same songs over and over. That's why I've always enjoyed the radio. But the algorithms ③ that are now pushing and pulling me through the music library are perfectly suited to finding gems that I'll like. My worry originally about such algorithms ④ was that they might drive everyone into certain parts of the library, leaving others lacking listeners. Would they cause a convergence of tastes? But thanks to the nonlinear and chaotic mathematics usually behind them, this doesn't happen. A small divergence in my likes ⑤ compared to yours can send us off into different far corners of the library.

윗글의 밑줄 친 부분 중, 어법상 틀린 것은?

You may feel there is something scary about an algorithm deciding what you might like. Could it mean that, if computers conclude you won't like something, you will never get the chance to see it? Personally, I really enjoy being directed toward new music that I might not have found by myself. I can quickly get stuck in a rut where I put on the same songs over and over. That's why I've always enjoyed the radio. But the algorithms that are now pushing and pulling me through the music library are perfectly suited to finding gems that I'll like. My worry originally about such algorithms was that they might drive everyone into certain parts of the library, leaving others lacking listeners. Would they cause a convergence of tastes? But thanks to the nonlinear and chaotic mathematics usually behind them, this doesn't happen. A small divergence in my likes compared to yours can send us off into different far corners of the library.

윗글의 제목으로 가장 적절한 것은?

① The Lost Art of Manual Music Discovery
② The Mathematical Underpinnings of Modern Music
③ Personal Reflections on the Evolution of Music Tastes
④ The Impact of Algorithms on Personalized Music Exploration
⑤ Conventional Radio versus Modern Algorithms in Music Curation

② 뒤따라 나오는 I put on the same songs over and over라는 완전한 절을 이끌며 '틀에 박힌'이라는 의미의 in a rut라는 선행사를 꾸며주려면 관계부사 where이 적절하다. 여기에서 "rut"은 특정 상태가 발생하는 '장소'를 의미한다.

① 동사 enjoy의 목적어로서 동명사구는 적절하다. 주어 "I"가 "being directed toward new music"이라는 행동을 즐긴다는 의미를 전달하며 "new music"을 찾아주는 것에 직접적으로 이끌리거나 안내받는 경험에 대한 감정을 강조한다.
③ 앞에 선행하는 the algorithms을 수식하며 바로 뒤에 동사 are이 뒤따라 나오는 주격 관계대명사로서 that은 적절하다.
④ 주어가 My worry이므로 단수 동사 was는 적절하다.
⑤ 주어를 수식하는 전치사구 내에서 yours(=your likes)와 my likes를 비교하는 과거분사 compared는 적절하다.

아래의 프롬프트를 챗GPT에 입력해 보세요.
"동명사를 목적어로 취하는 동사의 종류와 예시 보여줘."
"장소구를 수식하는 관계부사 where이 사용된 예시 3개 보여줘."
"과거분사의 쓰임 알려줘."

정답 ②

지문은 음악 탐색에 사용되는 알고리즘의 영향과 개인적인 음악 취향에 대한 내용을 다루고 있다. 알고리즘이 음악 추천 및 탐색에 어떻게 영향을 미치는지, 그리고 개인적인 음악 취향과의 관계를 소개하는 내용의 글이다. 따라서 글의 제목으로 가장 적절한 것은 ④ '알고리즘의 개인 맞춤 음악 탐색에 대한 영향'이다.

① 수작업 음악 발견의 잃어버린 예술
② 현대 음악의 수학적 기반
③ 음악 취향 진화에 대한 개인적인 반성
⑤ 전통적 라디오 대 현대 알고리즘 음악 선정

아래의 프롬프트를 챗GPT에 입력해 보세요.
"위에 소개한 지문의 핵심 단어들을 모두 고르고 뜻도 알려줘."
"위에 제시된 지문을 핵심으로만 구성된 한 문장으로 요약해줘."

정답 ④

함축적 의미 파악하기

CASE **04**

난이도 ★★★★☆

Scientists have no special purchase on moral or ethical decisions; a climate scientist is no more qualified to comment on health care reform than a physicist is to judge the causes of bee colony collapse. The very features that create expertise in a specialized domain lead to ignorance in many others. In some cases lay people — farmers, fishermen, patients, native peoples — may have relevant experiences that scientists can learn from. Indeed, in recent years, scientists have begun to recognize this: the Arctic Climate Impact Assessment includes observations gathered from local native groups. So our trust needs to be limited, and focused. It needs to be very particular. Blind trust will get us into at least as much trouble as no trust at all. **But without some degree of trust in our designated experts — the men and women who have devoted their lives to sorting out tough questions about the natural world we live in — we are paralyzed, in effect not knowing whether to make ready for the morning commute or not.**

밑줄 친 whether to make ready for the morning commute or not이 윗글에서 의미하는 바로 가장 적절한 것은?

① questionable facts that have been popularized by non-experts

② readily applicable information offered by specialized experts

③ common knowledge that hardly influences crucial decisions

④ practical information produced by both specialists and lay people

⑤ biased knowledge that is widespread in the local community

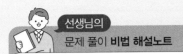

Scientists have no special purchase on moral or ethical decisions/ a climate scientist is no more qualified to comment on health care reform/than a physicist is to judge the causes of bee colony collapse.//The very features (that create expertise in a specialized domain) lead to ignorance/in many others.//In some cases/lay people — farmers, fishermen, patients, native peoples — may have relevant experiences (that scientists can learn from) Indeed/ in recent years/ scientists have begun to recognize this/ the Arctic Climate Impact Assessment includes/observations (gathered from local native groups.)//So our trust needs to be limited, and focused.//It needs to be very *particular*.//Blind trust will get us into/at least/as much trouble as no trust/at all.//But without some degree of trust/in our designated experts/— the men and women (who have devoted their lives to sorting out tough questions/about the natural world (we live in) — we are paralyzed,/in effect not knowing/[whether to make ready for the morning commute or not.]//

핵심 문장인 이유

해당 문장은 지문 전체의 주제인 전문가들에 대한 신뢰가 왜 필요한지를 직접적으로 언급하고 있다. 또한, 전문가들의 중요성과 그들의 역할에 대한 균형 잡힌 관점을 제시하며, 전문가에 대한 맹목적인 신뢰와 전혀 신뢰하지 않는 것 사이의 중요한 균형점을 부각시킨다.

따라서 지문의 중심 주제와 관련된 핵심 메시지를 전달하는 핵심 문장이라고 할 수 있다.

본문 해설

과학자들은 특정 분야에서의 전문가 지식 때문에 다른 분야에서는 지식이 부족할 수 있다. 전문가에 대한 무작정의 신뢰는 위험하며, 때로는 일반인들의 경험이 과학자들에게 중요한 통찰을 제공할 수 있다.

전문 지식에 대한 신뢰는 한정되고 초점이 맞추어져야 하지만, 자연 세계에 관한 어려운 문제들을 해결하기 위해 평생을 바친 사람들의 전문성에 대한 어느 정도의 신뢰가 없다면 아침에 통근 준비를 해야 할지에 대해서도 알 수 없을 것이라고 했으므로, 밑줄 친 부분이 글에서 의미하는 바로 가장 적절한 것은 ② '전문화된 전문가들에 의해 제공된 쉽게 적용할 수 있는 정보'이다.

① 비전문가에 의해 보급된 의심스러운 사실
③ 중대한 결정에 거의 영향을 주지 않는 일반 지식
④ 전문가와 전문가가 아닌 사람들 모두에 의해 생산된 실용적인 지식
⑤ 지역 공동체에 널리 퍼져 있는 편향된 지식

문제 풀이 전략

주어진 문장의 핵심 아이디어에 집중한다. 함축적인 의미는 종종 주요한 핵심 아이디어와 연결되어 있다. 해당 문장이나 구문의 핵심 아이디어를 이해하면 함축된 의미를 더 쉽게 파악할 수 있다.

정답 ②

Scientists have no special purchase on moral or ethical decisions; a climate scientist is no more qualified to comment on health care reform than a physicist is to judge the causes of bee colony collapse. The very features that create expertise in a specialized domain lead to ignorance in many others. In some cases lay people — farmers, fishermen, patients, native peoples — may have relevant experiences that scientists can learn from. Indeed, in recent years, scientists have begun to recognize this: the Arctic Climate Impact Assessment includes _____. So our trust needs to be limited, and focused. It needs to be very particular. Blind trust will get us into at least as much trouble as no trust at all. But without some degree of trust in our designated experts — the men and women who have devoted their lives to sorting out tough questions about the natural world we live in — we are paralyzed, in effect not knowing whether to make ready for the morning commute or not.

윗글의 빈칸에 들어갈 말로 가장 적절한 것을 고르시오.

① observations gathered from local native groups
② a collection of theoretical frameworks and assumptions
③ groundbreaking methodologies introduced by local scholars
④ anecdotal stories and cultural tales passed down generations
⑤ computer−generated information based on advanced algorithms

Scientists have no special purchase on moral or ethical decisions; a climate scientist is no more qualified to comment on health care reform than a physicist is to judge the causes of bee colony collapse. The very features that create expertise in a specialized domain lead to ignorance in many others. In some cases lay people — farmers, fishermen, patients, native peoples — may have relevant experiences that scientists can learn from. Indeed, in recent years, scientists have begun to recognize this: the Arctic Climate Impact Assessment includes observations gathered from local native groups. So our trust needs to be limited, and focused. It needs to be very particular. Blind trust will get us into at least as much trouble as no trust at all. But without some degree of trust in our designated experts — the men and women who have devoted their lives to sorting out tough questions about the natural world we live in — we are paralyzed, in effect not knowing whether to make ready for the morning commute or not.

윗글의 주제로 가장 적절한 것은?

① unparalleled expertise of scientists in every field
② role of native peoples in global scientific studies
③ necessity and limits of placing trust in experts
④ importance of including local insights in climate studies
⑤ challenges of trusting experts without considering local experiences

과학자들이 윤리적이고 도덕적인 결정에 대해 특별한 권위를 갖지 않는다고 언급하며 과학자들이 타 분야의 윤리적이거나 도덕적인 결정에 특별한 권한이 없다는 주장이 나오고 과학자들이 다른 분야에 대해 무지하다는 것을 강조하고 있으며, 때로는 비전문가들이 더 유용한 관찰과 경험을 제공할 수 있다는 내용의 글이다.

빈칸에 들어갈 말은 과학자들이 다른 분야와 상호작용하여 정보를 얻을 수 있는 경우를 나타내는 것이 적절하므로 빈칸에 들어갈 말로 가장 적절한 것은 ① '지역 원주민 그룹들로부터 수집된 관측'이다.

② 이론적 구조와 가정의 수집본
③ 지역 학자들에 의해 도입된 혁신적 방법론
④ 세대로 전해지는 일화와 문화 이야기
⑤ 고급 알고리즘을 기반으로 한 컴퓨터가 생성한 정보

🔁 아래의 프롬프트를 챗GPT에 입력해 보세요.
"위에 소개한 지문의 핵심 단어들을 모두 고르고 뜻도 알려줘."
"위에 제시된 지문을 핵심으로만 구성된 한 문장으로 요약해줘."

정답 ①

전문가에 대한 신뢰의 필요성과 한계를 다루며 전문가들이 특정 분야에서 뛰어난 지식을 가지고 있지만, 그 외 다른 분야에 대해서는 무지하다는 점을 지적한다. 이러한 사실 때문에 전문가에 대한 맹목적인 신뢰는 문제가 될 수 있음을 언급한다.

그럼에도 불구하고 우리는 전문가들이 우리를 지배하는 자연 세계에 대한 어려운 질문을 해결하기 위해 그들의 삶을 바쳤다는 사실을 인정해야 하며, 그들에게 어느 정도 신뢰를 가져야 함을 설명하는 내용의 글이다.

따라서 글의 주제로 가장 적절한 것은 ③ '전문가들에게 신뢰를 둘 필요성과 한계'이다.

① 각 분야의 과학자들의 비길 데 없는 전문 지식
② 지역 원주민들의 세계적인 과학 연구에서의 역할
④ 기후 연구에 지역적 통찰력을 포함하는 중요성
⑤ 지역적 경험을 고려하지 않고 전문가를 신뢰하는데의 문제점

정답 ③

PART 03

내용
일치

내용 일치/불일치(설명문)

CASE 01

난이도 ★★☆☆☆

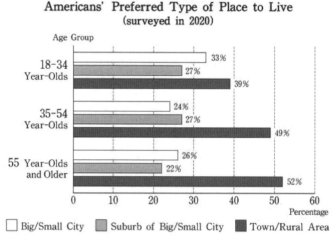

Americans' Preferred Type of Place to Live
(surveyed in 2020)

□ Big/Small City   ▨ Suburb of Big/Small City   ■ Town/Rural Area

Note: Percentages may not sum to 100% due to rounding.

　The above graph shows the percentages of Americans' preferred type of place to live by age group, based on a 2020 survey. ① In each of the three age groups, Town/Rural Area was the most preferred type of place to live. ② In the 18-34 year-olds group, the percentage of those who preferred Big/Small City was higher than that of those who preferred Suburb of Big/Small City. ③ In the 35-54 years-olds group, the percentage of those who preferred Suburb of Big/Small City exceeded that of those who preferred Big/Small City. ④ In the 55 year-olds and older group, the percentage of those who chose Big/Small City among the three preferred types of place to live was the lowest. ⑤ Each percentage of the three preferred types of place to live was higher than 20% across the three age groups.

위의 도표의 내용과 일치하지 <u>않는</u> 것은?

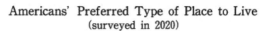

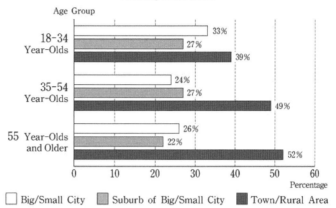

Americans' Preferred Type of Place to Live
(surveyed in 2020)

Note: Percentages may not sum to 100% due to rounding.

The above graph shows the percentages of Americans' preferred type of place to live by age group, based on a 2020 survey. ① In each of the three age groups, Town/Rural Area was the most preferred type of place to live. ② In the 18-34 year-olds group, the percentage of those(who preferred Big/Small City)was higher than that of those(who preferred Suburb of Big/Small City.)③ In the 35-54 years-olds group, the percentage of those(who preferred Suburb of Big/Small City) exceeded that of those(who preferred Big/Small City.) ④ In the 55 year-olds and older group, the percentage of those who chose Big/Small City among the three preferred types of place to live was the lowest. ⑤ Each percentage of the three preferred types of place to live was higher than 20% across the three age groups.

핵심 문장인 이유

'The above graph shows the percentages of Americans' preferred type of place to live by age group, based on a 2020 survey.'는 도표의 주제를 설명하는 문장이기에 핵심 문장에 해당한다.

본문 해설

"In the 55 year—olds and older group, the percentage of those who chose Big/Small City among the three preferred types of place to live was the lowest."에서 Big/Small City의 비율은 26%로 가장 낮은 것이 아닌, Suburb of Big/Small City가 22%로 가장 낮다.

문제 풀이 전략

low(낮은)의 최상급 the lowest(가장 낮은)의 의미를 알아야 하며, 해당 도표의 대상을 빠르게 파악하는 것이 중요하다. 도표 문제는 비교급/최상급이 자주 등장하므로 이와 관련된 표현에 익숙해져야 한다. 그래프가 복잡하게 보이더라도 침착하게 대입해서 비교하는 연습이 필요하다.

정답 ④

The above graph shows the percentages of Americans' preferred type of place to live by age group, based on a 2020 survey. In each of the three age ① groups, Town/Rural Area was the most preferred type of place to live. In the 18−34 year−olds group, the percentage of those ② who preferred Big/Small City was higher than that of those who preferred Suburb of Big/Small City. In the 35−54 years−olds group, the percentage of those who preferred Suburb of Big/Small City exceeded ③ that of those who preferred Big/Small City. In the 55 year−olds and older group, the percentage of those who chose Suburb of Big/Small City among the three preferred types of place to live ④ were the lowest. Each percentage of the three preferred types of place ⑤ to live was higher than 20% across the three age groups.

윗글의 밑줄 친 부분 중, 어법상 틀린 것은?

The above graph shows the percentages of Americans' preferred type of place to live by age group, based on a 2020 survey. In each of the three age groups, Town/Rural Area was the most preferred type of place to live. In the 18−34 year−olds group, (A) 대/소도시를 선호하는 사람들의 비율이 대/소도시의 교외를 선호하는 사람들의 비율보다 높았다. In the 35−54 years−olds group, the percentage of those who preferred Suburb of Big/Small City exceeded that of those who preferred Big/Small City. In the 55 year−olds and older group, the percentage of those who chose Suburb of Big/Small City among the three preferred types of place to live was the lowest. Each percentage of the three preferred types of place to live was higher than 20% across the three age groups.

밑줄 친 해석 (A)를 다음 〈조건〉을 참고하여 영작하시오.

〈조건〉
1. 원급을 사용하시오.
2. 대명사를 사용하시오.
3. 관계대명사를 사용하시오.
4. 단어 'so'를 반드시 사용하시오.
5. 완전한 문장으로 작성하시오.

수 일치를 묻는 문제이다. 주어는 'types'가 아닌 'the percentage'이므로 단수명사이다. 따라서 'was'가 적절하다.

① 'each of' 뒤에는 복수명사가 온다.
② 'those'는 'Americans'를 대신하므로 사람인 선행사에 주격관계대명사 'who'는 적절하다.
③ 단수명사 'the percentage'를 대신하므로 대명사 'that'은 적절하다.
⑤ 'place'를 수식하는 형용사적 용법의 'to live'는 적절하다.

🐢 아래의 프롬프트를 챗GPT에 입력해 보세요.
"단어 'each', 'each of'가 각각 들어간 예문을 6개 만들어줘."
"단어 'the percentage of'와 'percent of'가 각각 들어간 예문을 6개 만들어줘."
"명사를 수식하는 to부정사가 들어간 예문을 5개 만들어줘."

정답 ④

주어진 〈조건〉에 따르면 원급을 사용한 비교표현을 묻고 있다. as 원급 as 구문에서 부정문이 되면 비교급이 가능하다. 또한, 단어 'so'를 사용해야 하므로, not so(as) 원급 as로 나타낸다.
A is not as 원급 as B: "A는 B보다 ~하지 않다"는 표현에서 비교대상 A와 B를 적절하게 넣고 선행사 'those'에 주격 관계대명사 'who'를 사용하고, 'percentage'를 대신하는 대명사 that을 적절하게 활용하여 영작한다.

🐢 아래의 프롬프트를 챗GPT에 입력해 보세요.
"as 원급 as 구문을 사용한 예문을 비교급을 사용한 예문으로 변형한 예시를 5개 알려줘."

정답 the percentage of those who preferred Suburb of Big/Small City was not so high as that of those who preferred Big/Small City.

유형
08 내용 일치/불일치(설명문)

CASE **02**

기출문제
정복하기

2021년 수능
25번 문제

난이도 ★★☆☆☆

Online Shares of Retail Sales
in 2012 and in 2019

Note: Vacations, autos, gas, and tickets are excluded from retail sales.

    The graph above shows the online shares of retail sales for each of six countries in 2012 and in 2019. The online share of retail sales refers to the percentage of retail sales conducted online in a given country. ① For each country, its online share of retail sales in 2019 was larger than that in 2012. ② Among the six countries, the UK owned the largest online share of retail sales with 19.7% in 2019. ③ In 2019, the U.S. had the second largest online share of retail sales with 16.5%. ④ In 2012, the online share of retail sales in the Netherlands was larger than that in France, whereas the reverse was true in 2019. ⑤ In the case of Spain and Italy, the online share of retail sales in each country was less than 5.0% both in 2012 and in 2019.

위의 도표의 내용과 일치하지 <u>않는</u> 것은?

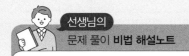

Online Shares of Retail Sales
in 2012 and in 2019

Note: Vacations, autos, gas, and tickets are excluded from retail sales.

   The graph above shows the online shares of retail sales for each of six countries in 2012 and in 2019. The online share of retail sales refers to the percentage of retail sales conducted online in a given country. ① For each country, its online share of retail sales in 2019 was larger than that in 2012. ② Among the six countries, the UK owned the largest online share of retail sales with 19.7% in 2019. ③ In 2019, the U.S. had the second largest online share of retail sales with 16.5%. ④ In 2012, the online share of retail sales in the Netherlands was larger than that in France, whereas the reverse was true in 2019. ⑤ In the case of Spain and Italy, the online share of retail sales in each country was less than 5.0% both in 2012 and in 2019.

핵심 문장인 이유

'The graph above shows the online shares of retail sales for each of six countries in 2012 and in 2019. The online share of retail sales refers to the percentage of retail sales conducted online in a given country.' 도표의 주제를 설명하는 문장이기에 핵심 문장에 해당한다.

본문 해설

"In the case of Spain and Italy, the online share of retail sales in each country was less than 5.0% both in 2012 and in 2019."에서 2019년 스페인은 5.4%로 5.0%보다 적지 않다.

문제 풀이 전략

상관접속사 both A and B: "A, B 둘 다"를 알아야 한다. A와 B는 서로 병렬구조이고 'Spain'과 'Italy'를 연결시킨다.

정답 ⑤

The graph above shows the online shares of retail sales for each of six ① countries in 2012 and in 2019. The online share of retail sales refers to the percentage of retail sales ② conducts online in a given country. For each country, its online share of retail sales in 2019 was larger than ③ that in 2012. Among the six countries, the UK owned the largest online share of retail sales with 19.7% in 2019. In 2019, the U.S. had the second largest online share of retail sales with 16.5%. In 2012, the online share of retail sales in the Netherlands was larger ④ than that in France, whereas the reverse was true in 2019. In the case of Spain and Italy, the online share of retail sales in each ⑤ country was less than 5.0% in 2012.

윗글의 밑줄 친 부분 중, 어법상 틀린 것은?

The graph above shows the online shares of retail sales for each of six countries in 2012 and in 2019. The online share of retail sales refers to the percentage of retail sales conducted online in a given country. For each country, its online share of retail sales in 2019 was larger than that in 2012. Among the six countries, the UK owned the largest online share of retail sales with 19.7% in 2019. In 2019, the U.S. had the second largest online share of retail sales with 16.5%. In 2012, the online share of retail sales in the Netherlands was larger than that in France, whereas the (A) reverse was true in 2019. In the case of Spain and Italy, the online share of retail sales in each country was less than 5.0% in 2012.

밑줄 친 (A)가 의미하는 내용을 다음 주어진 〈조건〉을 참고하여 영작하시오.

〈조건〉
1. 비교급을 사용하시오.
2. 대명사를 사용하시오.
3. 완전한 문장으로 완성하시오.

한 문장의 동사는 1개이다. 해당 문장의 동사는 'refers to'이다. 따라서 'conducts'는 'the percentage of retail sales'를 수식하는 분사 'conducted'가 되어야 한다.

① 'each of' 뒤에는 복수명사가 온다.
③ 단수명사 'online share of retail sales'를 대신하는 대명사 'that'은 적절하다.
④ 비교급을 사용한 문장에서 '~보다'의 의미를 가진 'than'은 적절하다.
⑤ 'each' 뒤에는 단수명사가 온다.

> ✍ 아래의 프롬프트를 챗GPT에 입력해 보세요.
> "단어 'each', 'each of'가 각각 들어간 예문을 6개 만들어줘."

정답 ②

밑줄 친 (A) reverse는 '반대'를 의미한다. 따라서 프랑스의 소매 판매 온라인 점유율이 더 높다는 걸 의미한다.

정답 the online share of retail sales in the France was larger than that in Netherlands

난이도 ★☆☆☆☆

Marjorie Kinnan Rawlings, an American author born in Washington, D.C. in 1896, wrote novels with rural themes and settings. While she was young, one of her stories appeared in *The Washington Post*. After graduating from university, Rawlings worked as a journalist while simultaneously trying to establish herself as a fiction writer. In 1928, she purchased an orange grove in Cross Creek, Florida. This became the source of inspiration for some of her writings which included *The Yearling* and her autobiographical book, *Cross Creek*. In 1939, The Yearling, which was about a boy and an orphaned baby deer, won the Pulitzer Prize for Fiction. Later, in 1946, *The Yearling* was made into a film of the same name. Rawlings passed away in 1953, and the land she owned at Cross Creek has become a Florida State Park honoring her achievements.

Marjorie Kinnan Rawlings에 관한 윗글의 내용과 일치하지 <u>않는</u> 것은?

① Washington, D.C.에서 태어난 미국 작가이다.

② 그녀의 이야기 중 하나가 *The Washington Post*에 실렸다.

③ 대학교를 졸업한 후 저널리스트로 일했다.

④ *The Yearling*이라는 소설은 다른 제목으로 영화화되었다.

⑤ Cross Creek에 소유했던 땅은 Florida 주립 공원이 되었다.

Marjorie Kinnan Rawlings, an American author born in Washington, D.C. in 1896, wrote novels with rural themes and settings. While she was young, one of her stories appeared in *The Washington Post*. After graduating from university, Rawlings worked as a journalist while simultaneously trying to establish herself as a fiction writer. In 1928, she purchased an orange grove in Cross Creek, Florida. This became the source of inspiration for some of her writings which included *The Yearling* and her autobiographical book, *Cross Creek*. In 1939, *The Yearling*, (which was about a boy and an orphaned baby deer) won the Pulitzer Prize for Fiction. Later, in 1946, *The Yearling* was made into a film of the same name. Rawlings passed away in 1953, and the land (she owned at Cross Creek)has become a Florida State Park honoring her achievements.

핵심 문장인 이유

'Marjorie Kinnan Rawlings, an American author born in Washington, D.C. in 1896, wrote novels with rural themes and settings.'는 이 글의 주된 설명 대상을 정의하고 있으므로 핵심 문장에 해당한다.

본문 해설

"Later, in 1946, The Yearling was made into a film of the same name." 이 문장에서는 The Yearling이라는 소설이 같은 이름의 영화로 만들어졌다고 했으므로 이 선택지는 지문 내용과 일치하지 않는다.

문제 풀이 전략

각 보기 문항의 핵심 단어를 영어로 빠르게 파악해서 찾는 연습이 중요하다. 예를 들어 ④에서 나오는 단어는 '소설, 다른 제목, 영화' 정도로 볼 수 있다. 이를 영어로 표현하자면 'novel, different title, film'이 될 수 있다. 이것을 머릿속으로 생각하면 어느 문장을 봐야 하는지 빠르게 파악할 수 있다.

정답 ④

Marjorie Kinnan Rawlings, an American author ① was born in Washington, D.C. in 1896, wrote novels with rural themes and settings. While she was young, one of her ② stories appeared in *The Washington Post*. After graduating from university, Rawlings worked as a journalist while simultaneously trying to establish ③ herself as a fiction writer. In 1928, she purchased an orange grove in Cross Creek, Florida. This became the source of inspiration for some of her writings ④ which included *The Yearling* and her autobiographical book, *Cross Creek*. In 1939, The Yearling, which was about a boy and an orphaned baby deer, won the Pulitzer Prize for Fiction. Later, in 1946, *The Yearling* was made into a film of the same name. Rawlings passed away in 1953, and the land she owned at Cross Creek has become a Florida State Park ⑤ honoring her achievements.

윗글의 밑줄 친 부분 중, 어법상 틀린 것은?

Marjorie Kinnan Rawlings, an American author born in Washington, D.C. in 1896, wrote novels with rural themes and settings. While she was young, one of her stories appeared in *The Washington Post*. After graduating from university, Rawlings worked as a journalist while simultaneously trying to establish herself as a fiction writer. In 1928, she purchased an orange grove in Cross Creek, Florida. This became the source of inspiration for some of her writings which included *The Yearling* and her autobiographical book, *Cross Creek*. In 1939, (A) 소년과 고아가 된 어린 사슴에 대한 이야기인 The Yearling은 소설 부문에서 퓰리처상을 수상했다. Later, in 1946, *The Yearling* was made into a film of the same name. Rawlings passed away in 1953, and the land she owned at Cross Creek has become a Florida State Park honoring her achievements.

밑줄 친 (A)를 다음 〈조건〉을 충족시켜 영작하시오.

> 〈조건〉
> 1. 계속적 용법을 사용하시오.
> 2. 'about', 'Pulitzer Prize for Fiction'을 사용하시오.

동사는 문장에 1개만 가능하다. 'was born'이 동사라면, 뒤에 나오는 'wrote' 때문에 한 문장의 동사가 2개가 된다.
따라서 'an American author'을 수식하는 구조로 만들어야 하기 때문에 'born'이 적절하다.

② 'One of 복수명사'를 묻는 문제이다. '~들 중에 하나'라는 의미로 복수명사 'stories'가 적절하다.

③ establish의 목적어가 주어와 동일하다. 따라서 재귀대명사 'herself'가 적절하다.

④ which가 이끄는 문장이 불완전(주어가 없음)하기 때문에 관계절로 볼 수 있고, 선행사 writings를 수식하므로 'which'가 적절하다.

⑤ 'honor'은 '~에게 영광을 베풀다(기리다)'는 의미로 쓰여 목적어 'her achievements'를 가진다.
   따라서 능동의 현재분사인 'honoring'이 적절하다.

> **아래의 프롬프트를 챗GPT에 입력해 보세요.**
> "재귀대명사가 강조용법이 아닌, 재귀용법으로 쓰인 예문을 5개 만들어줘."
> "주격관계대명사 which와 의문사 which가 들어간 예문을 각각 2개씩 만들어줘."

정답 ①

선행사를 The Yearling로 정하고, 계속적 용법을 사용해야 하므로 'that'이 아닌 'which'를 사용해야 한다. 계속적 용법을 사용해서 주어와 동사가 멀리 떨어지기 때문에 관계절이 끝나는 부분에도 ','를 표시해야 한다.
'고아가 된'은 수동의 의미를 가지기 때문에 'orphaned'를 사용해서 baby deer를 수식한다.

> **아래의 프롬프트를 챗GPT에 입력해 보세요.**
> "관계대명사 which가 삽입절에 사용된 예문을 5개 만들어줘."

정답 The Yearling, which was about a boy and an orphaned baby deer, won the Pulitzer Prize for Fiction.

내용 일치/불일치(설명문)   CASE 04

난이도 ★☆☆☆☆

Even though he won many Academy Awards, Miloš Forman was not a U.S. born filmmaker. Forman grew up in a small town near Prague. Orphaned when his parents died during World War II, he was raised by his relatives. In the 1950s, Forman studied film at the film school of the University of Prague. Throughout the late 1950s and early 1960s, Forman acted as either writer or assistant director on several films. Later, he emigrated to the U.S. and continued to make films. In 1975, he directed *One Flew over the Cuckoo's Nest*, which became only the second film in history to win Oscars in all the five major categories. Afterward, the movie *Amadeus*, a celebration of the genius of Mozart, which he also directed, swept eight Oscars including one for best director. With Jan Novák, Forman wrote his autobiography, *Turnaround: A Memoir*, which was published in 1994.

Miloš Forman에 관한 윗글의 내용과 일치하지 <u>않는</u> 것은?

① Prague 근교의 작은 마을에서 성장했다.

② Prague 대학교에서 영화를 공부했다.

③ 미국으로 이주한 후에도 계속 영화를 만들었다.

④ 영화 *Amadeus*로 오스카 최고 감독상을 수상했다.

⑤ *Turnaround: A Memoir*를 단독으로 집필했다.

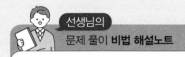

(Even though he won many Academy Awards,) Miloš Forman was not a U.S. born filmmaker.
①Forman grew up in a small town near Prague. (Orphaned when his parents died during World War II,) he was raised by his relatives. ②In the 1950s, Forman studied film at the film school of the University of Prague. Throughout the late 1950s and early 1960s, Forman acted as either writer or assistant director on several films. ③Later, he emigrated to the U.S. and continued to make films. In 1975, he directed *One Flew over the Cuckoo's Nest*, (which became only the second film in history to win Oscars in all the five major categories.) ④Afterward, the movie *Amadeus*, a celebration of the genius of Mozart, (which he also directed,) swept eight Oscars including one for best director. With Jan Novák, Forman wrote his autobiography, *Turnaround: A Memoir*, which was published in 1994.

핵심 문장인 이유

'Even though he won many Academy Awards, Miloš Forman was not a U.S. born filmmaker.'는 이 글의 주된 설명 대상을 정의하고 있으므로 핵심 문장에 해당한다.

본문 해설

"With Jan Novák, Forman wrote his autobiography, Turnaround: A Memoir…" 이 문장은 Forman이 그의 자서전을 Jan Novák와 함께 썼다는 내용이므로, 이 선택지는 지문의 내용과 일치하지 않는다.

문제 풀이 전략

각 보기 문항의 핵심 단어를 영어로 빠르게 파악해서 찾는 연습이 중요하다. 예를 들어 ⑤에서 나오는 단어는 '집필하다, 단독으로' 정도로 볼 수 있다. 이를 영어로 표현하자면 'write, alone.'이 될 수 있다. 이것을 머릿속으로 생각하면 어느 문장을 봐야 하는지 빠르게 파악할 수 있다

정답 ⑤

Even though he won many Academy Awards, Miloš Forman was not a U.S. born filmmaker. Forman grew up in a small town near Prague. ① Orphaned when his parents died during World War II, he ② was raised by his relatives. In the 1950s, Forman studied film at the film school of the University of Prague. Throughout the late 1950s and early 1960s, Forman acted as either writer or assistant director on several films. Later, he emigrated to the U.S. and ③ continued to make films. In 1975, he directed *One Flew over the Cuckoo's Nest*, ④ which became only the second film in history to win Oscars in all the five major categories. Afterward, the movie *Amadeus*, a celebration of the genius of Mozart, which he also directed, ⑤ sweeping eight Oscars including one for best director. With Jan Novák, Forman wrote his autobiography, *Turnaround: A Memoir*, which was published in 1994.

윗글의 밑줄 친 부분 중, 어법상 틀린 것은?

Even though he won many Academy Awards, Miloš Forman was not a U.S. born filmmaker. Forman grew up in a small town near Prague. (A) As Miloš Forman was orphaned when his parents died during World War II, he was raised by his relatives. In the 1950s, Forman studied film at the film school of the University of Prague. Throughout the late 1950s and early 1960s, Forman acted as either writer or assistant director on several films. Later, he emigrated to the U.S. and continued to make films. In 1975, he directed *One Flew over the Cuckoo's Nest*, which became only the second film in history to win Oscars in all the five major categories. Afterward, the movie *Amadeus*, a celebration of the genius of Mozart, which he also directed, swept eight Oscars including one for best director. With Jan Novák, Forman wrote his autobiography, *Turnaround: A Memoir*, which was published in 1994.

밑줄 친 (A)를 분사구문을 사용해서 변형하시오.

현재분사 'sweeping'이 된다면 해당 문장에 동사가 없게 된다. 따라서 시제에 맞춘 과거동사 'swept'가 적절하다.

① 분사구문에서 생략된 주어는 주절의 주어와 일치한다. 따라서 분사구문의 주어는 'Miloš Forman'이다. 'Miloš Forman'가 고아가 된 것이므로 수동의 의미를 가지는 과거분사 'orphaned'는 적절하다.

② 동사 'raise'는 '~을 기르다'라는 의미를 가진다. 위의 문장에서는 목적어가 없을뿐더러, '길러졌다'라는 의미가 되므로 수동태 구조 'was raised'가 적절하다.

③ 밑줄 친 부분 앞에 등위접속사(and)가 있다는 것은 병렬관계를 묻는 문제이다. 동사 'emigrated'와 병렬 구조를 이루고 있기 때문에 'continued'는 적절하다.

④ 계속적 용법의 관계대명사를 묻는 문제이다. 계속적 용법에서는 'that'을 사용할 수 없고, 선행사는 One Flew over the Cuckoo's Nest 이기 때문에 'which'가 적절하다.

> **아래의 프롬프트를 챗GPT에 입력해 보세요.**
> "'기르다'의 의미를 가지는 동사 raise와 과거분사 raised가 들어간 예문을 각각 2개 만들어줘."
> "등위접속사 and가 사용된 예문을 5개 만들어줘."

정답 ⑤

접속사 as가 생략되고, 부사절의 주어와 주절의 주어가 같으므로, 생략한다. 이 과정에서 주절의 주어는 'Miloš Forman'로 나타낸다. 부사절의 동사의 시제도 같으므로 'was'를 단순분사로 만들어 'being'이 된다. 이때 being이 문두에 위치할 때는 생략이 가능하다.

> **아래의 프롬프트를 챗GPT에 입력해 보세요.**
> "be동사가 있는 부사절과 분사구문으로 만든 예문을 각각 2개씩 만들어줘."

정답 Orphaned when his parents died during World War II, Miloš Forman was raised by his relatives.

내용 일치/불일치(실용문)   CASE 01

난이도 ★☆☆☆☆

Goldbeach SeaWorld Sleepovers

Do your children love marine animals? **A sleepover at Goldbeach SeaWorld will surely be an exciting overnight experience for them.** Join us for a magical underwater sleepover.

Participants
  - Children ages 8 to 12
  - Children must be accompanied by a guardian.

When: Saturdays 5 p.m. to Sundays 10 a.m. in May, 2022

Activities: guided tour, underwater show, and photo session with a mermaid

Participation Fee
  - $50 per person (dinner and breakfast included)

Note
  - Sleeping bags and other personal items will not be provided.
  - All activities take place indoors.
  - Taking photos is not allowed from 10 p.m. to 7 a.m.

For more information, you can visit our website at www.goldbeachseaworld.com.

Goldbeach SeaWorld Sleepovers에 관한 위의 안내문의 내용과 일치하는 것은?

① 7세 이하의 어린이가 참가할 수 있다.

② 평일에 진행된다.

③ 참가비에 아침 식사가 포함된다.

④ 모든 활동은 야외에서 진행된다.

⑤ 사진 촬영은 언제든지 할 수 있다.

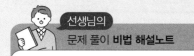
Goldbeach SeaWorld Sleepovers

Do your children love marine animals? A sleepover at Goldbeach SeaWorld will surely be an exciting overnight experience for them. Join us for a magical underwater sleepover.

Participants
①×
- Children ages 8 to 12

- Children must be accompanied by a guardian.

When: ②× Saturdays 5 p.m. to Sundays 10 a.m. in May, 2022

Activities: guided tour, underwater show, and photo session with a mermaid

Participation Fee
③○
- $50 per person (dinner and breakfast included)

Note

- Sleeping bags and other personal items will not be provided.
④×
- All activities take place indoors.
⑤×
- Taking photos is not allowed from 10 p.m. to 7 a.m.

For more information, you can visit our website at www.goldbeachseaworld.com.

핵심 문장인 이유

해당 문장은 'Goldbeach SeaWorld'에서의 'sleepover'이 아이들에게 흥미로운 경험이 될 것이라고 강조하면서 지문에서 가장 중요하고 매력적인 부분을 나타내며 독자의 관심을 끌기 위해 사용되므로 핵심 문장에 해당한다.

본문 해설

'dinner and breakfast included'에서 참가비에 저녁 식사 및 아침 식사가 포함된다고 했으므로, 안내문의 내용과 일치하는 것은 ③번이다.

문제 풀이 전략

선택지에 나온 정보를 먼저 읽고 하나씩 비교, 대조해가면서 문제를 푸는 것이 중요하다. 특히, 각 선택지의 주요한 내용들을 각 섹션별로 비교하여 일치, 불일치 여부를 ○, × 등으로 표시하여 푼다.

정답 ③

내용 일치/불일치(실용문)

난이도 ★☆☆☆☆

Green Tea Packaging Design Competition

Take the opportunity to design the packaging box for brand-new green tea products of TIIS Tea in the competition!

Deadline: December 2, 2019, 6:00 p.m.

Participants: Lokota County residents only

Details

· Our company name "TIIS Tea" should appear on the design.

· The competition theme is "Go Green with Green Tea."

· Entries (JPG format only) should be submitted by email to designmanager@ tiistea.com.

Evaluation Criteria

· Functionality   · Creativity   · Eco-friendliness

Awards

· 1st place: $1,000   · 2nd place: $500   · 3rd place: $250

  (The first-place winner's signature will be printed on the packaging box.)

Please visit www.tiistea.com to learn more about the competition.

Green Tea Packaging Design Competition에 관한 위의 안내문의 내용과 일치하지 <u>않는</u> 것은?

① 신제품 녹차를 위한 포장 상자 디자인 대회이다.

② Lokota County 주민들만 참가할 수 있다.

③ 출품작은 직접 방문하여 제출해야 한다.

④ 평가 기준에 창의성이 포함된다.

⑤ 1등 수상자의 서명이 포장 상자에 인쇄될 것이다.

Green Tea Packaging Design Competition

①○
Take the opportunity to design the packaging box for brand-new green tea products of TIIS Tea in the competition!

Deadline: December 2, 2019, 6:00 p.m.

②○
Participants: Lokota County residents only

Details

• Our company name "TIIS Tea" should appear on the design.

• The competition theme is "Go Green with Green Tea."

③×
• Entries (JPG format only) should be submitted by email to designmanager@tiistea.com.

Evaluation Criteria

• Functionality	④○ • Creativity	• Eco-friendliness

Awards

• 1st place: $1,000	• 2nd place: $500	• 3rd place: $250

⑤○
(The first-place winner's signature will be printed on the packaging box.)

Please visit www.tiistea.com to learn more about the competition.

핵심 문장인 이유

해당 문장은 TIIS Tea의 새로운 녹차 제품의 포장 디자인 경쟁에 참여할 수 있는 기회를 제공하는 내용을 담고 있다. 경쟁의 주요 내용을 간결하게 전달하여 관심을 끌고 참가자들에게 동기를 부여하는 핵심 문장에 해당한다.

본문 해설

"Entries (JPG format only) should be submitted by email to~"에서 출품작은 이메일로 제출해야 한다고 했으므로 일치하지 않는 것은 ③번이다.

문제 풀이 전략

선택지에 나온 정보를 먼저 읽고 하나씩 비교, 대조해가면서 문제를 푸는 것이 중요하다. 특히, 각 선택지의 주요한 내용들을 각 섹션별로 비교하여 일치, 불일치 여부를 ○, × 등으로 표시하여 푼다.

정답 ③

내용 일치/불일치(실용문)

CASE 02

난이도 ★☆☆☆☆

City of Sittka Public Bike Sharing Service

Are you planning to explore the city?
This is the eco-friendly way to do it!

Rent

· Register anywhere via our easy app.

· Payment can be made only by credit card.

Fee

· Free for the first 30 minutes

· One dollar per additional 30 minutes

Use

· Choose a bike and scan the QR code on the bike.

· Helmets are not provided.

Return

· Return the bike to the Green Zone shown on the app.

· Complete the return by pressing the OK button on the bike.

City of Sittka Public Bike Sharing Service에 관한 위의 안내문의 내용과 일치하지 <u>않는</u> 것은?

① 신용 카드 결제만 가능하다.

② 처음 30분은 무료이다.

③ 자전거의 QR 코드를 스캔해서 이용한다.

④ 헬멧이 제공된다.

⑤ 자전거의 OK 버튼을 눌러서 반납을 완료한다.

City of Sittka Public Bike Sharing Service

Are you planning to explore the city?

This is the eco-friendly way to do it!

Rent

- Register anywhere via our easy app.
  ① ○
- Payment can be made only by credit card.

Fee

- Free for the first 30 minutes
  ② ○
- One dollar per additional 30 minutes

Use

  ③ ○
- Choose a bike and scan the QR code on the bike.
  ④ ✕
- Helmets are not provided.

Return

- Return the bike to the Green Zone shown on the app.
  ⑤ ○
- Complete the return by pressing the OK button on the bike.

핵심 문장인 이유

해당 문장은 'Sittka'에서 공공 자전거 공유 서비스가 친환경에 도움이 되는 좋은 방법임을 소개하며 렌트 방법과 비용, 사용과 반납 등 여러 가지 정보들을 모두 아우르므로 핵심 문장에 해당한다.

본문 해설

"Helmets are not provided."에서 헬멧은 제공되지 않는다고 했으므로, 일치하지 않는 것은 ④번이다.

문제 풀이 전략

선택지에 나온 정보를 먼저 읽고 하나씩 비교, 대조해가면서 문제를 푸는 것이 중요하다. 특히, 각 선택지의 주요한 내용들을 각 섹션별로 비교하여 일치, 불일치 여부를 ○, ✕ 등으로 표시하여 푼다.

정답 ④

난이도 ★☆☆☆☆

2019 Badminton Challenge for Charity

Join the charity tournament event hosted by Cliffield Community Center! This event supports Salke Children's Hospital.

When & Where
- Saturday, November 23, 2:00 p.m.
- Cliffield Sports Center

How to Join the Tournament
- Make a two-member team.
- Pay your team's $100 entry fee as a donation.

Activities
- Challenge last year's champion team to a 3-point match.
- With an additional $20 donation, you can learn badminton skills from professional players.

※ Rackets and shuttlecocks will be provided.

Click here to register now!

2019 Badminton Challenge for Charity에 관한 위의 안내문의 내용과 일치하는 것은?

① Salke Children's Hospital이 주최한다.
② 3명이 한 팀을 구성해서 참가해야 한다.
③ 참가비는 한 사람당 100달러이다.
④ 20달러 추가 기부 시 배드민턴 기술을 배울 수 있다.
⑤ 라켓과 셔틀콕은 제공되지 않는다.

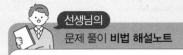

2019 Badminton Challenge for Charity

①×
Join the charity tournament event hosted by Cliffield Community Center! This event supports Salke Children's Hospital.

When & Where

- Saturday, November 23, 2:00 p.m.
- Cliffield Sports Center

How to Join the Tournament

②×
- Make a two-member team.
③×
- Pay your team's $100 entry fee as a donation.

Activities

- Challenge last year's champion team to a 3-point match.
④○
- With an additional $20 donation, you can learn badminton skills from professional players.

⑤×
※ Rackets and shuttlecocks will be provided.

Click here to register now!

핵심 문장인 이유

해당 문장은 독자들에게 해당 이벤트에 참여함으로써 자선 사업에 기여할 수 있는 기회를 제공하고자 하는 의도를 담고 있다. 독자의 관심을 끌고 참가 동기를 부여하므로 핵심 문장에 해당한다.

본문 해설

"With an additional $20 donation, you can learn badminton skills from professional players."에서 20달러를 추가 기부하면 전문 선수들에게 배드민턴 기술을 배울 수 있다고 하므로, 안내문의 내용과 일치하는 것은 ④번이다.

문제 풀이 전략

선택지에 나온 정보를 먼저 읽고 하나씩 비교, 대조해가면서 문제를 푸는 것이 중요하다. 특히, 각 선택지의 주요한 내용들을 각 섹션별로 비교하여 일치, 불일치 여부를 ○, × 등으로 표시하여 푼다.

정답 ④

내용 일치/불일치(실용문)

CASE 03

난이도 ★☆☆☆☆

Cornhill No Paper Cup Challenge

Cornhill High School invites you to join the "No Paper Cup Challenge."
This encourages you to reduce your use of paper cups. Let's save the earth together!

How to Participate

1) After being chosen, record a video showing you are using a tumbler.

2) Choose the next participant by saying his or her name in the video.

3) Upload the video to our school website within 24hours.

※ The student council president will start the challenge on December 1st, 2021.

Additional Information

• The challenge will last for two weeks.

• All participants will receive T-shirts.

If you have questions about the challenge, contact us at cornhillsc@chs.edu.

Cornhill No Paper Cup Challenge에 관한 위의 안내문의 내용과 일치하지 <u>않는</u> 것은?

① 참가자는 텀블러를 사용하는 자신의 동영상을 찍는다.

② 참가자가 동영상을 업로드할 곳은 학교 웹사이트이다.

③ 학생회장이 시작할 것이다.

④ 두 달 동안 진행될 예정이다.

⑤ 참가자 전원이 티셔츠를 받을 것이다

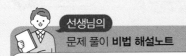
Cornhill No Paper Cup Challenge

Cornhill High School invites you to join the "No Paper Cup Challenge." This encourages you to reduce your use of paper cups. Let's save the earth together!

How to Participate

1) After being chosen, ①○ record a video showing you are using a tumbler.
2) Choose the next participant by saying his or her name in the video.
3) ②○ Upload the video to our school website within 24hours.
※ ③○ The student council president will start the challenge on December 1st, 2021.

Additional Information
· ④× The challenge will last for two weeks.
· ⑤○ All participants will receive T-shirts.

If you have questions about the challenge, contact us at cornhillsc@chs.edu.

핵심 문장인 이유

해당 문장은 해당 챌린지에 참여하도록 독자를 초대하는 내용을 전달한다. 핵심 주제, 주최자, 참가 대상 및 참여를 유도하는 요소를 포함하여 전체 문장 중에서 중요한 정보를 제공하는 역할을 하므로 핵심 문장에 해당한다.

본문 해설

"The challenge will last for two weeks." 문장에서 2주 동안 지속된다고 했으므로, 안내문의 내용과 일치하지 않는 것은 ④번이다.

문제 풀이 전략

선택지에 나온 정보를 먼저 읽고 하나씩 비교, 대조해가면서 문제를 푸는 것이 중요하다. 특히, 각 선택지의 주요한 내용들을 각 섹션별로 비교하여 일치, 불일치 여부를 ○, × 등으로 표시하여 푼다.

정답 ④

내용 일치/불일치(실용문)

난이도 ★☆☆☆☆

Flying Eagle Zipline Ride

Soar through the treetops over Lost Forest on our thrilling Flying Eagle Zipline! Feel the thrill of flying like an eagle!

- Age requirement: 13 years old and over
- Price: £20
- Zipline length: 500 metres
- Duration: 30 minutes (including safety instruction)
- Restrictions:
  - People with back problems or serious heart conditions
  - Weight: over 125 kg
  - Height: under 120 cm

※ We do not take responsibility for lost valuables.
※ No advanced reservations are necessary.

Please visit our website at www.flyingeaglezip.co.uk for more information.

Flying Eagle Zipline Ride에 관한 위의 안내문의 내용과 일치하지 <u>않는</u> 것은?

① 13세 이상부터 탈 수 있다.
② 집라인의 길이는 500미터이다.
③ 체중 제한이 있다.
④ 분실한 귀중품에 대해 책임을 지지 않는다.
⑤ 사전 예약이 필요하다.

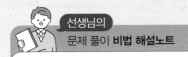

Flying Eagle Zipline Ride

Soar through the treetops over Lost Forest on our thrilling
Flying Eagle Zipline! Feel the thrill of flying like an eagle!

① ○
- Age requirement: 13 years old and over
- Price: £20
② ○
- Zipline length: 500 metres
- Duration: 30 minutes (including safety instruction)
- Restrictions:
  - People with back problems or serious heart conditions
    ③ ○
  - Weight: over 125 kg
  - Height: under 120 cm

④ ○
※ We do not take responsibility for lost valuables.
⑤ ×
※ No advanced reservations are necessary.

Please visit our website at www.flyingeaglezip.co.uk for more information.

핵심 문장인 이유

해당 문장은 집라인의 주요 내용을 간결하게 전달하고 있다. 집라인의 특징을 강조하여 독자의 관심을 끌고 참가 동기를 부여하기 위해 사용되었으므로 전략적인 접근을 가지는 핵심 문장이라고 볼 수 있다.

본문 해설

"No advanced reservations are necessary."에서 사전 예약은 불필요하다고 했으므로, 안내문의 내용과 일치하지 않는 것은 ⑤번이다.

문제 풀이 전략

선택지에 나온 정보를 먼저 읽고 하나씩 비교, 대조해가면서 문제를 푸는 것이 중요하다. 특히, 각 선택지의 주요한 내용들을 각 섹션별로 비교하여 일치, 불일치 여부를 ○, × 등으로 표시하여 푼다.

정답 ⑤

난이도 ★☆☆☆☆

Jason's Photography Class

Are you tired of taking pictures with your camera set to "Auto"? Do you want to create more professional-looking photos? **You won't want to miss this opportunity.**

- Date: Saturday, December 19
- Time: 1:30 p.m. – 5:30 p.m.
- Place: Thrombon Building, Room 2 on the first floor
- Tuition Fee: $50 (snacks provided)
- Level: Beginner
- Topics to Be Covered:
    - Equipment Selection
    - Lighting Techniques
    - Color Selection
    - Special Effects
- Class size is limited to eight, so don't delay!

Visit our web site at www.eypcap.com to register.

Jason's Photography Class에 관한 위의 안내문의 내용과 일치하는 것은?

① 오전에 시작된다.
② 3층에서 진행된다.
③ 중급자 수준이다.
④ 다루는 주제 중 하나는 특수 효과이다.
⑤ 수강 학생 수에는 제한이 없다.

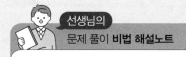
Jason's Photography Class

Are you tired of taking pictures with your camera set to "Auto"? Do you want to create more professional-looking photos? You won't want to miss this opportunity.

- Date: Saturday, December 19
①×
- Time: 1:30 p.m. – 5:30 p.m.
②×
- Place: Thrombon Building, Room 2 on the first floor
- Tuition Fee: $50 (snacks provided)
③×
- Level: Beginner
- Topics to Be Covered:
  - Equipment Selection
  - Lighting Techniques
  - Color Selection
④○
  - Special Effects
⑤×
- Class size is limited to eight, so don't delay!

Visit our web site at www.eypcap.com to register.

핵심 문장인 이유

해당 문장은 독자의 관심과 참여를 유도하며, 이번 사진 클래스와 관련된 중요한 정보를 전달할 것을 암시하므로 핵심 문장에 해당한다.

본문 해설

"Topics to Be Covered – Special Effects" 부분을 통해 다루는 주제 중 하나가 특수효과임을 알 수 있다. 따라서 안내문과 일치하는 것은 ④번이다.

문제 풀이 전략

선택지에 나온 정보를 먼저 읽고 하나씩 비교, 대조해가면서 문제를 푸는 것이 중요하다. 특히, 각 선택지의 주요한 내용들을 각 섹션별로 비교하여 일치, 불일치 여부를 ○, × 등으로 표시하여 푼다.

정답 ④

내용 일치/불일치(실용문) CASE **04**

난이도 ★☆☆☆☆

Wireless Charging Pad

- Instructions -

Wireless Smartphone Charging:

1. Connect the charging pad to a power source.

2. Place your smartphone on the charging pad with the display facing up.

3. **Place your smartphone on the center of the charging pad (or it will not charge).**

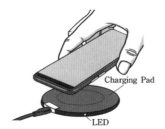

Charge Status LED:

· Blue Light: Your smartphone is charging. If there's a problem, the blue light will flash.

· White Light: Your smartphone is fully charged.

Caution:

· Do not place anything between your smartphone and the charging pad while charging.

· The charging pad is not water-resistant. Keep it dry.

Wireless Charging Pad 사용에 관한 위의 안내문의 내용과 일치하는 것은?

① 스마트폰의 화면을 아래로 향하게 두어야 한다.

② 스마트폰을 충전 패드 중앙에 놓지 않아도 된다.

③ LED 빛이 흰색이면 스마트폰이 완전히 충전되지 않은 것이다.

④ 스마트폰과 충전 패드 사이에 어떤 것도 놓지 않아야 한다.

⑤ 충전 패드는 방수가 된다.

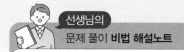

Wireless Charging Pad

- Instructions -

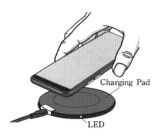

Charging Pad

LED

Wireless Smartphone Charging:

1. Connect the charging pad to a power source.
2. ①× Place your smartphone on the charging pad with the display facing up.
3. ②× Place your smartphone on the center of the charging pad (or it will not charge).

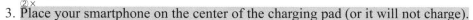

Charge Status LED:

- Blue Light: Your smartphone is charging. If there's a problem, the blue light will flash.
- ③× White Light: Your smartphone is fully charged.

Caution:

- ④○ Do not place anything between your smartphone and the charging pad while charging.
- ⑤× The charging pad is not water-resistant. Keep it dry.

핵심 문장인 이유

해당 문장은 (그렇지 않으면 충전되지 않을 것이다)를 덧붙여서 무선 충전 패드를 올바르게 사용하는 방법을 가장 중요하게 강조하고 있는 문장으로 핵심 문장에 해당한다.

본문 해설

"Do not place anything between your smartphone and the charging pad while charging." 문장에서 스마트폰과 충전 패드 사이에 아무것도 두지 않아야 함을 알 수 있다. 따라서 안내문과 일치하는 것은 ④번이다.

문제 풀이 전략

선택지에 나온 정보를 먼저 읽고 하나씩 비교, 대조해가면서 문제를 푸는 것이 중요하다. 특히, 각 선택지의 주요한 내용들을 각 섹션별로 비교하여 일치, 불일치 여부를 ○, × 등으로 표시하여 푼다.

정답 ④

PART 04

논리적
추론

빈칸 내용 추론하기

난이도 ★★★☆☆

People have always needed to eat, and they always will. Rising emphasis on self-expression values does not put an end to material desires. But prevailing economic orientations are gradually being reshaped. People who work in the knowledge sector continue to seek high salaries, but they place equal or greater emphasis on doing stimulating work and being able to follow their own time schedules. **Consumption is becoming progressively less determined by the need for sustenance and the practical use of the goods consumed.** People still eat, but a growing component of food's value is determined by its ＿＿＿＿＿＿ aspects. People pay a premium to eat exotic cuisines that provide an interesting experience or that symbolize a distinctive life-style. The publics of postindustrial societies place growing emphasis on "political consumerism," such as boycotting goods whose production violates ecological or ethical standards. Consumption is less and less a matter of sustenance and more and more a question of life-style — and choice.

윗글의 빈칸에 들어갈 말로 가장 적절한 것을 고르시오.

① quantitative

② nonmaterial

③ nutritional

④ invariable

⑤ economic

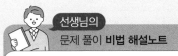
People have always needed to eat, and they always will. Rising emphasis on self-expression values does not put an end to material desires. But prevailing economic orientations are gradually being reshaped.//People who work in the knowledge sector continue to seek high salaries, but they place equal or greater emphasis/on doing stimulating work and being able to follow their own time schedules.//Consumption is becoming progressively less determined/by the need for sustenance and the practical use of the goods consumed.//People still eat, but a growing component of food's value is determined/by its _____ aspects.//People pay a premium/to eat exotic cuisines that provide an interesting experience or that symbolize a distinctive life-style. The publics of postindustrial societies place growing emphasis on "political consumerism,"/such as boycotting goods whose production violates ecological or ethical standards.//Consumption is less and less a matter of sustenance and more and more a question of life-style — and choice.//

핵심 문장인 이유

해당 문장은 이 지문의 중심 소재인 소비의 변화를 잘 드러내는 문장이다. 소비에 대한 인식의 전환을 강조하는 문장이므로 핵심 문장에 해당한다.

본문 해설

소비의 기준은 점점 생계나 물질적 필요보다는 라이프스타일과 선택에 중점을 둔다. 탈공업화 사회의 대중은 식품의 실질적 가치보다는 그것이 제공하는 경험이나 독특한 라이프스타일을 상징하는 흥미로운 경험이나 독특한 생활 방식의 표현, 생태적 또는 윤리적 기준의 준수와 같은 것으로 음식의 가치를 부여한다는 내용이므로, 빈칸에 들어갈 말로 가장 적절한 것은 ②번의 '비물질적인'이다.

① 양적인
③ 영양적인
④ 변함없는
⑤ 경제의

문제 풀이 전략

빈칸이 속한 문장에서 단서로 작용하는 단어를 찾는다. 종종 주변 단어들이 빈칸에 들어갈 적절한 내용을 힌트로 제공한다.

정답 ②

People have always needed to eat, and they always will. Rising emphasis on self-expression values does not put an end to material desires. But prevailing economic orientations are gradually being reshaped. People who work in the knowledge sector continue to seek high salaries, but they place equal or greater emphasis on doing stimulating work and being able to **(A)** [follow/break] their own time schedules. Consumption is becoming progressively less determined by the need for sustenance and the practical use of the goods consumed. People still eat, but a growing component of food's value is determined by its **(B)** [nonmaterial/material] aspects. People pay a premium to eat exotic cuisines that provide an interesting experience or that symbolize a distinctive life-style. The publics of postindustrial societies place growing emphasis on "political consumerism," such as **(C)** [supporting/boycotting] goods whose production violates ecological or ethical standards. Consumption is less and less a matter of sustenance and more and more a question of life-style — and choice.

윗글의 (A), (B), (C)의 각 괄호 안에서 문맥에 맞는 낱말로 가장 적절한 것은?

	(A)		(B)		(C)
①	follow	……	nonmaterial	……	supporting
②	follow	……	material	……	boycotting
③	follow	……	nonmaterial	……	boycotting
④	break	……	material	……	supporting
⑤	break	……	nonmaterial	……	supporting

People have always needed to eat, and they always will. Rising emphasis on self-expression values does not put an end to material desires. But prevailing economic orientations ① are gradually being reshaped. People who work in the knowledge sector continue to seek high salaries, but they place equal or greater emphasis on doing stimulating work and ② being able to follow their own time schedules. Consumption is becoming progressively less determined by the need for sustenance and the practical use of the goods ③ consumed. People still eat, but a growing component of food's value is determined by its nonmaterial aspects. People pay a premium to eat exotic cuisines that provide an interesting experience or ④ that symbolize a distinctive life-style. The publics of postindustrial societies place growing emphasis on "political consumerism," such as boycotting goods whose production ⑤ violate ecological or ethical standards. Consumption is less and less a matter of sustenance and more and more a question of life-style — and choice.

윗글의 밑줄 친 부분 중, 어법상 틀린 것은?

(A)에서는 지식 부문에서 일하는 사람들은 계속 높은 급여를 추구한다는 내용이 나온다. 접속사 but 뒤에 그들은 자극이 되는 일을 하는 것과 그들 자신의 시간 계획을 '따르는 것'에 동등한 또는 더 큰 중점을 둔다는 내용이 자연스러우므로 follow가 적절하다.

(B)에서는 바로 뒷 문장에서 사람들은 흥미로운 경험을 제공하거나 독특한 생활 방식을 상징하는 이국적인 요리를 먹고자 추가 요금을 낸다는 내용이 나오므로 사람들은 여전히 먹지만, 음식 가치의 증가하는 구성요소가 그것의 'nonmaterial(비물질적인)' 측면에 의해 결정된다는 것이 자연스럽다.

(C)에서는 탈공업화 사회의 대중은 생산이 생태적 또는 윤리적 기준을 위반하는 상품의 구매를 '거부하는 것(boycotting)'과 같은 '정치적 소비주의'에 점점 더 많은 중점을 둔다는 내용이 자연스럽다. 소비는 더 이상 생존의 문제가 아닌 생활 방식, 그리고 선택의 문제이기 때문이다.

> 🔧 **아래의 프롬프트를 챗GPT에 입력해 보세요.**
> "위에 소개한 지문의 핵심 단어들을 모두 고르고 뜻도 알려줘."

정답 ③

⑤ 소유격 관계대명사 whose가 앞에 나오는 선행사 goods의 production을 나타내므로 단수 주어인 production과 수일치를 시킨 단수 동사 violates가 적절하다.

① orientaions가 주어이므로 be동사 are은 적절하다.
② 앞선 emphasis on에 연결되어 동명사 형태이고 doing과 등위접속사 and에 의해 병렬구조로 연결된 being은 적절하다.
③ 소비된 상품이므로 goods를 수동으로 꾸며주는 과거분사 형태 consumed는 적절하다.
④ 앞선 exotic cuisines를 꾸며주는 주격 관계대명사 that이 등위접속사 or에 의해 병렬구조로 이루어져 있으므로 적절하다.

> 🔧 **아래의 프롬프트를 챗GPT에 입력해 보세요.**
> "whose가 쓰인 예시문장 3개 보여줘."
> "명사를 수식하는 현재분사와 과거분사 표현 예시를 3개씩 보여줘."
> "등위접속사의 종류와 그 쓰임을 알려줘."

정답 ⑤

빈칸 내용 추론하기

난이도 ★★★★☆

We understand that the segregation of our consciousness into present, past, and future is both a fiction and an oddly self-referential framework; your present was part of your mother's future, and your children's past will be in part your present. Nothing is generally wrong with structuring our consciousness of time in this conventional manner, and it often works well enough. In the case of climate change, however, the sharp division of time into past, present, and future has been desperately misleading and has, most importantly, hidden from view the extent of the responsibility of those of us alive now. **The narrowing of our consciousness of time smooths the way to divorcing ourselves from responsibility for developments in the past and the future with which our lives are in fact deeply intertwined.** In the climate case, it is not that _____.
It is that the realities are obscured from view by the partitioning of time, and so questions of responsibility toward the past and future do not arise naturally.

윗글의 빈칸에 들어갈 말로 가장 적절한 것을 고르시오.

① all our efforts prove to be effective and are thus encouraged

② sufficient scientific evidence has been provided to us

③ future concerns are more urgent than present needs

④ our ancestors maintained a different frame of time

⑤ we face the facts but then deny our responsibility

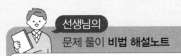

We understand that/the segregation (of our consciousness into present, past, and future) is both a fiction and an oddly self-referential framework;/your present was part of your mother's future, and your children's past will be in part your present.//Nothing is generally wrong with structuring our consciousness of time/in this conventional manner/ and it often works well enough//In the case of climate change, however, the sharp division (of time into past, present, and future) has been desperately misleading/and has, (most importantly,) hidden/from view [the extent of the responsibility]/ of [those] of us alive now.//The narrowing of/our consciousness/of time smooths the way to divorcing ourselves/from responsibility for developments in the past and the future with (which our lives are in fact deeply intertwined.) In the climate case,/ it is not that _____. It is that the realities are obscured from view/by the partitioning of time,/ and so questions of responsibility (toward the past and future) do not arise naturally.

핵심 문장인 이유

해당 문장은 핵심 키워드인 "responsibility(책임)", "interconnection(연관성)" 등을 통해 기후변화와 관련된 인식과 책임이라는 지문의 주제를 강조하므로 핵심 문장에 해당한다.

본문 해설

시간에 대한 의식을 현재, 과거, 미래로 분리하는 것은 허구이며 자기 지시적인 틀이지만 시간의식을 과거, 현재, 미래로 분리하는 것은 기후 변화 문제에서 매우 오해의 소지가 있으며, 우리가 현재 살아가는 책임을 숨기게 된다. 이러한 시간의 구분은 과거와 미래에 대한 책임을 인식하지 못하게 만든다는 내용의 글이다.

따라서 빈칸에 들어갈 말로 가장 적절한 것은 ⑤번의 '우리가 사실을 직면하면서도 우리의 책임을 부인하는'이다.

① 우리의 모든 노력이 효과적으로 밝혀지고 따라서 장려되는
② 충분한 과학적인 증거가 우리에게 제공되어온
③ 미래의 우려가 현재의 필요보다 더욱 긴급한
④ 우리의 조상들이 다른 시간적 틀을 유지한

문제 풀이 전략

지문에서 글쓴이가 전달하고자 하는 주요 의도나 메시지를 이해하고, 그것에 부합하는 내용을 빈칸으로 선택한다.

정답 ⑤

We understand that the segregation of our consciousness into present, past, and future is both a fiction and an oddly self-referential framework; your present was part of your mother's future, and your children's past will be in part your present. Nothing is generally wrong with ① structuring our consciousness of time in this conventional manner, and it often works well enough. In the case of climate change, however, the sharp division of time into past, present, and future ② has been desperately misleading and has, most importantly, hidden from view the extent of the responsibility of those of us alive now. The narrowing of our consciousness of time smooths the way to divorcing ourselves from responsibility for developments in the past and the future with ③ which our lives are in fact deeply intertwined. In the climate case, it is not ④ that we face the facts but then deny our responsibility. It is that the realities are obscured from view by the partitioning of time, and so questions of responsibility toward the past and future ⑤ does not arise naturally.

윗글의 밑줄 친 부분 중, 어법상 틀린 것은?

We understand that the segregation of our consciousness into present, past, and future is both a fiction and an oddly self-referential framework; your present was part of your mother's future, and your children's past will be in part your present. Nothing is generally wrong with structuring our consciousness of time in this conventional manner, and it often works well enough. In the case of climate change, however, the sharp division of time into past, present, and future has been desperately misleading and has, most importantly, hidden from view the extent of the responsibility of those of us alive now. The narrowing of our consciousness of time smooths the way to divorcing ourselves from responsibility for developments in the past and the future with which our lives are in fact deeply intertwined. In the climate case, it is not that we face the facts but then deny our responsibility. It is that the realities are obscured from view by the partitioning of time, and so questions of responsibility toward the past and future do not arise naturally.

윗글에서 필자가 주장하는 바로 가장 적절한 것은?
① 현재 우리의 책임 범위를 현실에서 숨겨야 한다.
② 시간 인식의 관습적인 구조는 기후 변화 문제에 적합하지 않다.
③ 현실을 직시하기 위해 기후변화에 대한 책임을 부정해야 한다.
④ 기후변화와 관련하여 시간 인식과 책임의 구분은 필수적이다.
⑤ 미래의 발전과 연관된 책임을 지기 위해 시간에 대한 우리의 의식을 좁혀야 한다.

⑤ 복수 주어 questions과 수일치를 시킨 복수 동사 do가 적절하다.

① our consciousness of time을 구성하거나 구조화하는 것을 나타내며, 이것이 generally wrong with의 주어 Nothing과 함께 주어의 동작이나 상태를 설명하는 현재분사구문으로 적절하다.

② 단수 주어 the sharp division와 수일치를 시킨 단수 동사로 has는 적절하다.

③ developments in the past and the future를 수식하는 관계절을 이끌며 이전 절의 주어 developments in the past and the future를 대신하여 사용되는 관계대명사 which는 적절하다.

④ we face ~ our responsibility라는 완전한 절을 이끌며 앞, 뒤 문장을 연결해주는 접속사 that은 적절하다.

🐱 아래의 프롬프트를 챗GPT에 입력해 보세요.
"that의 쓰임과 그 예시 알려줘."

정답 ⑤

기후변화 문제를 다룰 때 시간 인식을 과거, 현재, 미래로 세분화하는 관습적인 구조가 적합하지 않으며 시간의 세분화로 인해 현재와 미래의 책임 범위가 모호해져 현실적인 책임에 대한 인식이 가려진다는 내용의 글이다.

따라서 필자가 주장하는 바로 가장 적절한 것은 ②번의 '시간 인식의 관습적인 구조는 기후변화 문제에 적합하지 않다.'이다.

🐱 아래의 프롬프트를 챗GPT에 입력해 보세요.
"위에 소개한 지문의 핵심 단어들을 모두 고르고 뜻도 알려줘."
"위에 소개한 지문에서 필자의 주장을 영어 한 문장으로 알려줘."

정답 ②

빈칸 내용 추론하기

난이도 ★★★☆☆

More than just *having* territories, animals also *partition* them. And this insight turned out to be particularly useful for zoo husbandry. **An animal's territory has an internal arrangement that Heini Hediger compared to the inside of a person's house.** Most of us assign separate functions to separate rooms, but even if you look at a one-room house you will find the same internal specialization. In a cabin or a mud hut, or even a Mesolithic cave from 30,000 years ago, this part is for cooking, that part is for sleeping; this part is for making tools and weaving, that part is for waste. We keep _____. To a varying extent, other animals do the same. A part of an animal's territory is for eating, a part for sleeping, a part for swimming or wallowing, a part may be set aside for waste, depending on the species of animal.

윗글의 빈칸에 들어갈 말로 가장 적절한 것을 고르시오.

① an interest in close neighbors
② a neat functional organization
③ a stock of emergency supplies
④ a distance from potential rivals
⑤ a strictly observed daily routine

More than just *having* territories,/animals also *partition* them.//And this insight turned out to be/ particularly useful/for zoo husbandry.//An animal's territory has/an internal arrangement that Heini Hediger compared to the inside of a person's house.) Most of us/assign/separate functions/to separate rooms, but even if you look at a one-room house/you will find the same internal specialization.//In a cabin or a mud hut, or even a Mesolithic cave from 30,000 years ago, [this part is for cooking, that part is for sleeping; this part is for making tools and weaving, that part is for waste.]We keep _____. To a varying extent, other animals do the same.//A part (of an animal's territory) is [for eating,/a part for sleeping,/a part for swimming or wallowing, a part may be set aside for waste] depending on the species of animal.//

핵심 문장인 이유

해당 문장은 핵심 키워드인 동물의 "territory"라는 중요한 개념을 소개한다.
또한, 인간의 집 내부와 동물의 영역 간의 비교를 통해 지문 전체의 주제를 명확하게 반영하며 지문 내의 다른 세부 사항들에 대한 정보의 기반이 된다.

따라서 이 문장은 지문의 주요 아이디어를 전달하고 다른 세부 사항들과 연결시키기 때문에 핵심적인 문장에 해당한다.

본문 해설

동물들은 그들의 영역을 분할하는데 동물의 영역 안에는 기능에 따라 다양한 부분이 있으며, 이것은 인간의 집 내부의 구조와 비슷하다. 요리 공간, 수면 공간, 작업 공간, 폐기물을 위한 공간으로 나누어진다고 했으므로, 빈칸에 들어갈 말로 가장 적절한 것은 ②번의 '정돈된 기능적 체계'이다.

① 가까운 이웃에 대한 관심
③ 비상 대비용 공급물품들
④ 잠재적 경쟁자와의 거리
⑤ 엄격히 준수하는 일상적인 루틴

문제 풀이 전략

빈칸 전후의 문장들을 주의깊게 살펴야 한다. 주어진 문맥에서 빈칸에 들어갈 수 있는 내용을 추론하여 정답을 선택한다.

정답 ②

More than just having territories, animals also ① partition them. And this insight turned out to be particularly useful for zoo husbandry. An animal's territory has an internal arrangement that Heini Hediger compared to the ② inside of a person's house. Most of us assign separate ③ functions to separate rooms, but even if you look at a one-room house you will find the same internal specialization. In a cabin or a mud hut, or even a Mesolithic cave from 30,000 years ago, this part is for cooking, that part is for sleeping; this part is for making tools and weaving, that part is for waste. We keep a neat ④ chaotic organization. To a varying extent, other animals do the same. A part of an animal's ⑤ territory is for eating, a part for sleeping, a part for swimming or wallowing, a part may be set aside for waste, depending on the species of animal.

윗글의 밑줄 친 부분 중, 문맥상 낱말의 쓰임이 적절하지 <u>않은</u> 것은?

More than just having territories, animals also partition them. And this insight turned out to be particularly useful for zoo husbandry. An animal's territory has an internal arrangement that Heini Hediger compared to the inside of a person's house. Most of us assign separate functions to separate rooms, but even if you look at a one-room house you will find the same internal specialization. In a cabin or a mud hut, or even a Mesolithic cave from 30,000 years ago, this part is for cooking, that part is for sleeping; this part is for making tools and weaving, that part is for waste. We keep a neat functional organization. To a varying extent, other animals do the same. A part of an animal's territory is for eating, a part for sleeping, a part for swimming or wallowing, a part may be set aside for waste, depending on the species of animal.

윗글의 제목으로 가장 적절한 것은?

① The Historical Evolution of Human Living Spaces
② The Impact of Territory Partitioning on Zoo Husbandry
③ The Similarities between Human and Animal Living Styles
④ Heini Hediger: An Influential Figure in Animal Behaviour Studies
⑤ Understanding the Functional Organization of Animal Territories

동물들은 영역을 가지는데, 이 영역을 다시 세분화하여 사용하는 경향이 있다. 인간의 집과 비교하면 각 방마다 특정한 기능을 부여하는 것처럼, 동물들도 자신의 영역을 다양한 목적에 맞추어 사용한다. 다른 동물들도 마찬가지로 영역을 갖고 있으며, 이것은 종에 따라 음식, 수면, 수영 또는 뒹굴기에 사용되는 부분으로 나누어진다는 내용의 글이다.

따라서 ④번의 chaotic을 functional과 같은 낱말로 바꾸어야 한다.

> 아래의 프롬프트를 챗GPT에 입력해 보세요.
> "위에 소개한 지문의 핵심 단어들을 모두 고르고 뜻도 알려줘."
> "Heini Hediger의 대표적인 주장이 뭔지 알려줘."

정답 ④

동물들은 영역을 가지고 있을 뿐만 아니라 그것을 구획하는 경향이 있으며 동물의 영역은 인간의 집과 비슷한 내부 배열을 가지고 있고 다양한 기능에 따라 구분된다는 내용의 글이다. 따라서 글의 제목으로 가장 적절한 것은 ⑤번의 '동물 영역의 기능적 구성 이해하기'이다.

① 인간 거주 공간의 역사적 진화
② 동물원 경영에 영역 분할의 영향
③ 인간과 동물 거주 공간의 유사점
④ Heini Hediger: 동물 행동 연구에서 영향력 있는 인물

정답 ⑤

빈칸 내용 추론하기

난이도 ★★★☆☆

   In labor-sharing groups, people contribute labor to other people on a regular basis (for seasonal agricultural work such as harvesting) or on an irregular basis (in the event of a crisis such as the need to rebuild a barn damaged by fire). **Labor sharing groups are part of what has been called a "moral economy" since no one keeps formal records on how much any family puts in or takes out.** Instead, accounting is _____. The group has a sense of moral community based on years of trust and sharing. In a certain community of North America, labor sharing is a major economic factor of social cohesion. When a family needs a new barn or faces repair work that requires group labor, a barn-raising party is called. Many families show up to help. Adult men provide manual labor, and adult women provide food for the event. Later, when another family needs help, they call on the same people.

윗글의 빈칸에 들어갈 말로 가장 적절한 것을 고르시오.

① legally established
② regularly reported
③ socially regulated
④ manually calculated
⑤ carefully documented

   In labor-sharing groups, people contribute labor to other people on a regular basis (for seasonal agricultural work such as harvesting) or on an irregular basis (in the event of a crisis such as the need to rebuild a barn damaged by fire). Labor sharing groups are part of what has been called a "moral economy" since no one keeps/formal records/on how much any family puts in or takes out.// Instead, accounting is _____ . The group has a sense of moral community (based on years of trust and sharing.) In a certain community of North America, labor sharing is a major economic factor/of social cohesion.//When a family needs/a new barn or faces/repair work (that requires group labor,) a barn-raising party is called.//Many families show up to help.//Adult men provide manual labor, and adult women provide food for the event.//Later, when another family needs help, they call on the same people.//

핵심 문장인 이유

해당 문장은 "labor sharing groups"라는 핵심 키워드가 어떠한 원칙 아래에서 작동하는지를 명확하게 설명한다.

또한, "moral economy"라는 또 다른 핵심 키워드를 활용하여 노동 공유 그룹의 작동 원칙을 정의한다.
이러한 핵심 키워드들을 통해, 이 문장은 지문 내에서 노동 공유 그룹의 중심적인 원칙과 그 작동 방식을 설명하는 핵심 문장에 해당한다.

본문 해설

노동 공유 그룹에서는 사람들이 정기적 또는 비정기적으로 다른 사람들에게 노동을 제공하며, 이러한 노동 공유는 공식 기록 없이 사회적으로 조절된다. 신뢰와 나눔을 바탕으로 한 공동체에서 도움이 필요할 때마다 모여서 서로 도와주는 것이므로, 빈칸에 들어갈 말로 가장 적절한 것은 ③번의 '사회적으로 규제된다'이다.

① 법적으로 확립된다
② 정기적으로 보고된다
④ 수동으로 계산된다
⑤ 신중하게 문서화된다

문제 풀이 전략

빈칸이 포함된 문장은 주변 문맥과 일관성을 유지해야 한다. 특히, 역접의 접속사가 있지 않는 이상 뒤에 나오는 내용들과 의미적으로 상통하는지를 확인하는 것이 중요하다.

정답 ③

In labor-sharing groups, people contribute labor to other people on a regular basis (for seasonal agricultural work such as harvesting) or on an irregular basis (in the event of a crisis such as the need to rebuild a barn damaged by fire). Labor sharing groups are part of what has been called a "moral economy" since no one keeps formal records on how much any family puts in or takes out. Instead, accounting is socially regulated. The group has a sense of moral community based on years of trust and sharing. In a certain community of North America, labor sharing is a major economic factor of social cohesion. When a family needs a new barn or faces repair work that requires group labor, a barn-raising party is called. Many families show up to help. Adult men provide manual labor, and adult women provide food for the event. Later, when another family needs help, they call on the same people.

윗글의 내용을 한 문장으로 요약하고자 한다. 빈칸 (A), (B)에 들어갈 말로 가장 적절한 것은?

Labor-sharing groups operate within a "moral economy" without formal records, relying on ____(A)____ regulation and trust, exemplified by North American communities where collective efforts, such as barn-raisings, strengthen social ties and ensure ____(B)____ support.

	(A)		(B)
①	shared	·····	meaningful
②	social	·····	mutual
③	relevant	·····	personal
④	shared	·····	complete
⑤	social	·····	cultural

In labor-sharing groups, people contribute labor to other people on a regular basis (for seasonal agricultural work such as harvesting) or on an irregular basis (in the event of a crisis such as the need to rebuild a barn damaged by fire). ① Labor sharing groups are part of what has been called a "moral economy" since no one keeps formal records on how much any family puts in or takes out. ② Instead, accounting is socially regulated. ③ The group has a sense of moral community based on years of trust and sharing. ④ It would allow increasing opportunities for agricultural entrepreneurs, so that we could optimise agricultural output and production. ⑤ In a certain community of North America, labor sharing is a major economic factor of social cohesion. When a family needs a new barn or faces repair work that requires group labor, a barn-raising party is called. Many families show up to help. Adult men provide manual labor, and adult women provide food for the event. Later, when another family needs help, they call on the same people.

윗글에서 전체 흐름과 관계 <u>없는</u> 문장은?

노동 공유 그룹은 정기적으로(계절성 농업 노동) 또는 비정기적으로(위기 상황) 노동을 서로 기여한다. 이러한 그룹은 '도덕적 경제'로 불리며 상호 신뢰와 나눔에 기반한 도덕적 공동체 의식이 형성된다는 내용의 글이므로, 빈칸 (A), (B)에 들어갈 말로 가장 적절한 것은 ② '사회적 – 상호의'이다.

① 공유된   ……   유의미한
③ 관련 있는   ……   개인적인
④ 공유된   ……   완전한
⑤ 사회적   ……   문화의

📋 아래의 프롬프트를 챗GPT에 입력해 보세요.
"위에 소개한 지문을 영어 한 문장으로 요약해줘."
"위에 소개한 지문의 핵심 단어들을 모두 고르고 뜻도 알려줘."

정답 ②

노동 공유 그룹은 계절성 농업 작업과 위기 상황에서 노동을 서로 기여하며, 사회적으로 규제된 "도덕적 경제"를 형성하여 북미의 특정 지역 사회에서 사회적 결속력을 강화하는 주요 요소라는 내용의 글이다. 따라서 농업 기업가들에게 기회를 늘려 농산물 생산을 최적화하는 것이라는 내용의 ④번은 글의 전체 흐름과 관계가 없다.

정답 ④

흐름에 무관한 문장 찾기

CASE 01

난이도 ★★★☆☆

Since their introduction, information systems have substantially changed the way business is conducted. ① This is particularly true for business in the shape and form of cooperation between firms that involves an integration of value chains across multiple units. ② The resulting networks do not only cover the business units of a single firm but typically also include multiple units from different firms. ③ **As a consequence, firms do not only need to consider their internal organization in order to ensure sustainable business performance; they also need to take into account the entire ecosystem of units surrounding them.** ④ Many major companies are fundamentally changing their business models by focusing on profitable units and cutting off less profitable ones. ⑤ In order to allow these different units to cooperate successfully, the existence of a common platform is crucial.

윗글에서 전체 흐름과 관계 <u>없는</u> 문장은?

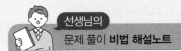

Since their introduction, information systems have substantially changed the way business is conducted. ① This is particularly true for business in the shape and form of cooperation between firms that involves an integration of value chains across multiple units. ② The resulting networks do not only cover the business units of a single firm but typically also include multiple units from different firms. ③ As a consequence, firms do not only need to consider their internal organization in order to ensure sustainable business performance; they also need to take into account the entire ecosystem of units surrounding them. ④ Many major companies are fundamentally changing their business models by focusing on profitable units and cutting off less profitable ones. ⑤ In order to allow these different units to cooperate successfully, the existence of a common platform is crucial.

핵심 문장인 이유

이 문장은 정보 시스템의 도입이 기업 간 협력과 가치 사슬 통합의 형태로 비즈니스를 변화시키는 방법에 대한 핵심 주제를 설명한다. 또한, 이 문장은 그들의 내부 조직뿐만 아니라 주위에 있는 사업부문들의 생태계를 고려해야 한다는 중요한 주장을 제시하므로 글 전체의 내용을 포괄하고 있다.

본문 해설

정보시스템의 도입 이후, 기업의 사업수행 방식의 변화를 설명하고 있다. 특히 가치 체인의 협력관계에 영향을 미치며, 기업을 둘러싸고 있는 전체 생태계에도 주의를 기울일 것을 주장하고 있다. 또한, 협력에 성공하기 위한 공동플랫폼의 중요성을 또한 강조한다. 정보시스템 등장으로 인한 기업의 변화와 이에 대한 대응 방법을 논하는 글로, 기업의 수익성을 논하는 내용의 문장은 전체 글에 어울리지 않는다.

문제 풀이 전략

문장 간 반복되는 주제를 정확하게 파악하고 이에 어긋나는 문장이 어떤 문장인지 체크해 보는 것이 중요하다.

🔖 아래의 프롬프트를 챗GPT에 입력해 보세요.

'이 글의 중심내용을 선정하고, 글의 일관성을 위해 필수적인 논리의 흐름을 제시하시오.'

정답 ④

Since their introduction, information systems have substantially changed the way business is conducted. This is particularly true for business in the shape and form of cooperation between firms that involves an integration of value chains across multiple units. The resulting networks do not only cover the business units of a single firm but typically also include multiple units from different firms. As a consequence, firms do not only need to consider their internal organization in order to ensure sustainable business performance; they also need to take into account _____ . In order to allow these different units to cooperate successfully, the existence of a common platform is crucial.

윗글의 빈칸에 들어갈 말로 가장 적절한 것은?

① the internal organization of a single firm

② the integration of value chains inside a unit

③ the development of new business models

④ the ability to communicate with each other

⑤ the entire ecosystem of units surrounding them

Since their introduction, information systems have substantially changed the way business is conducted. This is particularly true for business in the shape and form of cooperation between firms that involves an integration of value chains across multiple units. The resulting networks do not only cover the business units of a single firm but typically also include multiple units from different firms. As a consequence, firms do not only need to consider their internal organization in order to ensure sustainable business performance; they also need to take into account the entire ecosystem of units surrounding them. In order to allow these different units to cooperate successfully, the existence of a common platform is crucial.

윗글의 작성 목적으로 가장 적절한 것은?

① 정보 시스템의 기술적 특성과 작동 원리를 설명하기 위해

② 특정 기업이 정보 시스템을 효과적으로 사용하는 방법을 제시하기 위해

③ 정보 시스템의 비용 효율성과 수익성에 대해 주장하기 위해

④ 정보 시스템 도입이 기업 간의 협력과 가치 사슬 통합에 어떠한 영향을 미치는지 설명하기 위해

⑤ 기업 간 협력이 불필요하다는 주장을 반박하기 위해

이 글은 다양한 회사의 단위들이 어떻게 연결되는지에 초점을 맞추고 있다. 따라서 회사는 자신의 조직만을 고려하는 것이 아니라, 다른 회사의 사업부문(unit)들과의 네트워크 또한 이해하고 있어야 한다. '생태계'라는 개념은 이러한 비즈니스 네트워크의 상호 연결되고 상호 의존적인 특성을 잘 나타낸다. 단일 회사의 내부 조직, 사업부문 내의 가치 사슬의 통합, 새로운 비즈니스 모델의 개발, 서로 간의 의사소통 능력은 글의 전체적인 맥락을 고려할 때 빈칸에 부적절하다.

정답 ⑤

이 지문은 정보 시스템 도입이 기업 간의 협력과 가치 사슬 통합에 어떠한 영향을 미치는지 설명하고 있다.
정보 시스템의 기술적 특성이나 작동 원리, 특정 기업의 사례나 정보 시스템 사용법, 정보 시스템의 비용 효율성이나 수익성, 기업 간 협력의 필요성에 대한 주장은 언급되지 않았으므로 오답이다.

정답 ④

흐름에 무관한 문장 찾기

난이도 ★★★☆☆

In a highly commercialized setting such as the United States, it is not surprising that many landscapes are seen as commodities. In other words, they are valued because of their market potential. Residents develop an identity in part based on how the landscape can generate income for the community. ① This process involves more than the conversion of the natural elements into commodities. ② The landscape itself, including the people and their sense of self, takes on the form of a commodity. ③ Landscape protection in the US traditionally focuses on protecting areas of wilderness, typically in mountainous regions. ④ Over time, the landscape identity can evolve into a sort of "logo" that can be used to sell the stories of the landscape. ⑤ Thus, California's "Wine Country," Florida's "Sun Coast," or South Dakota's "Badlands" shape how both outsiders and residents perceive a place, and these labels build a set of expectations associated with the culture of those who live there.

윗글에서 전체 흐름과 관계 <u>없는</u> 문장은?

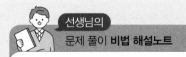
   In a highly commercialized setting such as the United States, it is not surprising that many landscapes are seen as commodities. In other words, they are valued because of their market potential. Residents develop an identity in part based on how the landscape can generate income for the community.① This process involves more than the conversion of the natural elements into commodities. ② The landscape itself, including the people and their sense of self, takes on the form of a commodity.③ Landscape protection in the US traditionally focuses on protecting areas of wilderness, typically in mountainous regions. ④ Over time, the landscape identity can evolve into a sort of "logo" that can be used to sell the stories of the landscape.⑤ Thus, California's "Wine Country," Florida's "Sun Coast," or South Dakota's "Badlands" shape how both outsiders and residents perceive a place, and these labels build a set of expectations associated with the culture of those who live there.

핵심 문장인 이유

미국에서 자연 경관이 가지는 시장가치를 설명하고 있는 글이다. 자연 경관과 이 자연 경관이 만들어 내는 시장가치에 대한 의미를 전반적으로 담고 있는 문장이 핵심 문장이다.

본문 해설

미국에서 자연 경관이 가지는 시장가치를 이야기하고 있다. ③번 문장은 미국의 자연 경관을 시장적 관점이 아닌 보호적 관점에서 논하고 있으므로 해당 문장이 관련 없는 문장이다.

문제 풀이 전략

경관의 상품화라는 주제를 찾아내어 글이 진행됨에 따라 구체화되는 논리를 파악하여야 한다.

> 🤖 아래의 프롬프트를 챗GPT에 입력해 보세요.
> "지문에서 "commodity"라는 단어의 의미와 그것이 문장 내에서 어떻게 사용되는지 설명하라."

정답 ③

In a highly commercialized setting such as the United States, it is not surprising that many landscapes are seen as commodities. In other words, they are valued because of their market potential. Residents develop an identity in part based on how the landscape can generate income for the community. This process involves more than the conversion of the natural elements into commodities. The landscape itself, including the people and their sense of self, takes on the form of a commodity. Over time, the landscape identity can evolve into a sort of "logo" that can be used to sell the stories of the landscape. Thus, California's "Wine Country," Florida's "Sun Coast," or South Dakota's "Badlands" shape how both outsiders and residents perceive a place, and these labels build a set of expectations associated with the culture of those who live there.

윗글의 제목으로 가장 적절한 것은?

① How to Create a Brand-New Identity in a Commercialized Setting

② What Is the Difference Between a Landform and a Commodity?

③ The Way the Landscape Generates Income for the Community

④ The Identity of the Landscape: From Natural Elements to Cultural Commodities

⑤ The Process of Converting Natural Element Into a Trademark

In a highly commercialized setting such as the United States, it is not surprising that many landscapes are seen as commodities. In other words, they are valued because of their market potential. Residents develop an identity in part based on how the landscape can generate income for the community. This process involves more than the conversion of the natural elements into commodities. The landscape itself, including the people and their sense of self, takes on the form of a commodity. Over time, the landscape identity can evolve into a sort of "logo" that can be used to _____. Thus, California's "Wine Country," Florida's "Sun Coast," or South Dakota's "Badlands" shape how both outsiders and residents perceive a place, and these labels build a set of expectations associated with the culture of those who live there.

윗글의 빈칸에 들어갈 말로 가장 적절한 것은?

① create a sense of self-esteem

② sell the stories of the landscape

③ provide an opportunity for community development

④ generate income for the community

⑤ be used as a means of communication

④번 제목은 풍경의 정체성과 그것이 어떻게 문화적 상품으로 전환되는지를 포괄하고 있어 지문의 핵심 주제를 가장 잘 반영한다.

① '새로운 정체성 창출'에 대한 방법론적 접근은 지문에 나타나지 않는다.
② 지문은 풍경과 상품 사이의 차이보다는 풍경이 어떻게 상품화되는지를 설명한다.
③ 지문의 일부 내용에는 부합하지만, 지문 전체의 주제를 포괄하기에는 좁은 범위에 집중된 표현이다.
⑤ 'Trademark'는 지문 내에서 직접적으로 언급되지 않았고, 상품화의 과정만을 강조하는 제목으로 지문의 주제를 완벽하게 포함하지는 않는다.

정답 ④

빈칸 전의 문장은 풍경의 정체성이 시간이 지남에 따라 "로고"와 같은 형태로 발전할 수 있다고 언급하고 있다. 이어지는 문장에서는 특정 지역들의 라벨(로고)이 외부인과 거주민 모두에게 어떻게 그 장소를 인식하게 하는지, 그리고 그러한 라벨들이 거기에 사는 사람들의 문화와 관련된 기대치를 형성하는 방법을 설명하며 특정 지역들의 라벨(로고)이 그 장소에 대한 이야기를 판매하는 방법을 설명하고 있다. 그러므로 빈칸에 들어갈 말로 'sell the stories of the landscape' 이 적절하다.

① create a sense of self-esteem: 지문에서는 풍경의 정체성이 개인의 자존감을 창출하는 것에 대해 언급하지 않았다.
③ provide an opportunity for community development: 빈칸 전후의 문맥에서는 커뮤니티 개발의 기회 제공에 대한 언급이 없다.
④ generate income for the community: 이 선지는 지문의 일부 내용과 관련이 있지만, 빈칸의 문맥에서는 "로고"가 직접적으로 커뮤니티에 대한 수익을 창출하는 것을 의미하지는 않는다.
⑤ be used as a means of communication: "로고"가 커뮤니케이션의 수단으로 사용될 수 있다는 아이디어는 빈칸 전후의 문맥과는 연관성이 낮다.

정답 ②

흐름에 무관한 문장 찾기 CASE 03

난이도 ★★★☆☆

Actors, singers, politicians and countless others recognise the power of the human voice as a means of communication beyond the simple decoding of the words that are used. **Learning to control your voice and use it for different purposes is, therefore, one of the most important skills to develop as an early career teacher.** ① The more confidently you give instructions, the higher the chance of a positive class response. ② There are times when being able to project your voice loudly will be very useful when working in school, and knowing that you can cut through a noisy classroom, dinner hall or playground is a great skill to have. ③ In order to address serious noise issues in school, students, parents and teachers should search for a solution together. ④ However, I would always advise that you use your loudest voice incredibly sparingly and avoid shouting as much as possible. ⑤ A quiet, authoritative and measured tone has so much more impact than slightly panicked shouting.

윗글에서 전체 흐름과 관계 없는 문장은?

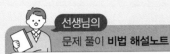
Actors, singers, politicians and countless others recognise the power of the human voice as a means of communication beyond the simple decoding of the words that are used. Learning to control your voice and use it for different purposes is, therefore, one of the most important skills to develop as an early career teacher. ① The more confidently you give instructions, the higher the chance of a positive class response. ② There are times when being able to project your voice loudly will be very useful when working in school, and knowing that you can cut through a noisy classroom, dinner hall or playground is a great skill to have. ③ In order to address serious noise issues in school, students, parents and teachers should search for a solution together. ④ However, I would always advise that you use your loudest voice incredibly sparingly and avoid shouting as much as possible. ⑤ A quiet, authoritative and measured tone has so much more impact than slightly panicked shouting.

핵심 문장인 이유

의사소통 수단으로서의 목소리를 사용하는 능력을 개발하는 것이 교사에게 중요한 역할을 하고 있다는 것을 설명하는 글이다. 이를 가장 잘 포함하는 문장이 핵심 문장이다.

본문 해설

목소리의 중요성을 글의 초반부에서 강조하고 있으며, 교사를 위한 목소리 사용법을 알려주고 있는 글이다. 소음 문제는 주제에서 벗어나는 토픽이므로 정답은 ③번이다.

문제 풀이 전략

먼저 글의 키워드를 파악한 후, 키워드 주제와 일관성이 떨어지는 문장을 찾는 것이 중요하다.

> 🔹 아래의 프롬프트를 챗GPT에 입력해 보세요.
> '이 글의 핵심 내용을 설명하고, 다른 문장이 이를 어떻게 뒷받침하는지 설명하시오.'

정답 ③

Actors, singers, politicians and countless others recognise the power of the human voice as a means of communication beyond the simple decoding of the words that are used. Learning to control your voice and use it for different purposes is, therefore, one of the most important skills to develop as an early career teacher. The more confidently you give instructions, the higher the chance of a positive class response. There are times when being able to project your voice loudly will be very useful when working in school, and knowing that you can cut through a noisy classroom, dinner hall or playground is a great skill to have. However, I would always advise that you use your loudest voice incredibly sparingly and avoid shouting as much as possible. A quiet, authoritative and measured tone has so much more impact than slightly panicked shouting.

윗글의 주제로 가장 적절한 것은?

① 초급 교사를 위한 효과적인 교실 관리 전략
② 목소리를 통한 효과적인 커뮤니케이션 방법
③ 학교 환경에서 목소리 사용의 중요성
④ 학생들의 긍정적인 반응을 이끌어 내는 방법
⑤ 초급 교사가 피해야 할 학급 관리 실수들

Actors, singers, politicians and countless others recognise the power of the human voice as a means of communication beyond the simple decoding of the words that are used.

(A) The more confidently you give instructions, the higher the chance of a positive class response. There are times when being able to project your voice loudly will be very useful when working in school, and knowing that you can cut through a noisy classroom, dinner hall or playground is a great skill to have.

(B) Learning to control your voice and use it for different purposes is, therefore, one of the most important skills to develop as an early career teacher.

(C) However, I would always advise that you use your loudest voice incredibly sparingly and avoid shouting as much as possible. A quiet, authoritative and measured tone has so much more impact than slightly panicked shouting.

제시문 뒤에 올 글의 순서로 가장 적절한 것은?

① (B)−(A)−(C)
② (C)−(B)−(A)
③ (A)−(B)−(C)
④ (B)−(C)−(A)
⑤ (A)−(C)−(B)

이 글은 교사가 학교 환경에서 목소리를 어떻게 사용해야 효과적인지에 대해 다루고 있다. 즉, 목소리의 통제, 목소리를 크게 내는 능력, 그리고 목소리 톤을 잘 사용하는 것이 중요하다는 내용을 포함한다. 이런 내용들로 보아 이 글의 주제는 '학교 환경에서 목소리 사용의 중요성'으로 볼 수 있다. 다른 선택지들은 모두 이 글의 주제를 부분적으로나 간접적으로 다루고 있지만, 핵심 주제를 정확하게 포착하지는 못하고 있다.

정답 ③

지문은 배우, 가수, 정치가 등 여러 직업군의 사람들이 목소리의 힘을 인식한다는 것으로 시작한다. 이어서 초보 교사로서 목소리를 제어하고 사용하는 것의 중요성(B), 그 목소리를 효과적으로 사용하는 법(A), 그리고 큰소리로 외치는 것보다 조용하고 권위 있는 음조의 중요성에 대한 조언(C) 순으로 진행하는 것이 가장 자연스러운 순서이다. 따라서 정답은 '(B) – (A) – (C)'이다.

정답 ①

흐름에 무관한 문장 찾기

난이도 ★★★☆☆

A variety of theoretical perspectives provide insight into immigration. Economics, which assumes that actors engage in utility maximization, represents one framework. ① **From this perspective, it is assumed that individuals are rational actors, i.e., that they make migration decisions based on their assessment of the costs as well as benefits of remaining in a given area versus the costs and benefits of leaving.** ② Benefits may include but are not limited to short-term and long-term monetary gains, safety, and greater freedom of cultural expression. ③ People with greater financial benefits tend to use their money to show off their social status by purchasing luxurious items. ④ Individual costs include but are not limited to the expense of travel, uncertainty of living in a foreign land, difficulty of adapting to a different language, uncertainty about a different culture, and the great concern about living in a new land. ⑤ Psychic costs associated with separation from family, friends, and the fear of the unknown also should be taken into account in cost-benefit assessments.

윗글에서 전체 흐름과 관계 <u>없는</u> 문장은?

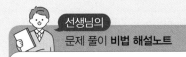
A variety of theoretical perspectives provide insight into immigration. Economics, which assumes that actors engage in utility maximization, represents one framework. ① From this perspective, it is assumed that individuals are rational actors, i.e., that they make migration decisions based on their assessment of the costs as well as benefits of remaining in a given area versus the costs and benefits of leaving. ② Benefits may include but are not limited to short-term and long-term monetary gains, safety, and greater freedom of cultural expression. ③ People with greater financial benefits tend to use their money to show off their social status by purchasing luxurious items. ④ Individual costs include but are not limited to the expense of travel, uncertainty of living in a foreign land, difficulty of adapting to a different language, uncertainty about a different culture, and the great concern about living in a new land. ⑤ Psychic costs associated with separation from family, friends, and the fear of the unknown also should be taken into account in cost-benefit assessments.

핵심 문장인 이유

이주에 대한 비용 평가가 중심 소재이며, 이어지는 문장에서 이를 부연하고 있다. 이를 가장 포괄적으로 담고 있는 문장이 핵심 문장이다.

본문 해설

이주를 경제학적으로 분석하여 이주를 하였을 때 들어가는 개인의 경제적, 사회적, 심리적 비용을 설명하는 글이다. 큰 경제적인 이득을 가진 사람이 사치품을 구매하여 개인의 사회적 지위를 드러낸다는 내용의 ③번 문장은 주제에서 벗어난다.

문제 풀이 전략

제시문에서 키워드를 찾아내어, 이를 가지고 다른 문장의 적절성을 평가해 나가는 것이 중요하다.

> 🤖 아래의 프롬프트를 챗GPT에 입력해 보세요.
>
> '지문의 각 문장에서 주요 키워드를 찾아 목록으로 작성하라.'
> '지문에서 "costs"와 "benefits"에 관련된 예시들을 나열하라.'

A variety of theoretical perspectives provide insight into immigration. Economics, which assumes that actors engage in utility maximization, represents one framework. From this perspective, it is assumed that individuals are rational actors, i.e., that they make migration decisions based on their _____ as well as benefits of remaining in a given area versus the costs and benefits of leaving. Benefits may include but are not limited to short−term and long−term monetary gains, safety, and greater freedom of cultural expression. Individual costs include but are not limited to the expense of travel, uncertainty of living in a foreign land, difficulty of adapting to a different language, uncertainty about a different culture, and the great concern about living in a new land. Psychic costs associated with separation from family, friends, and the fear of the unknown also should be taken into account in cost−benefit assessments.

윗글의 빈칸에 들어갈 말로 가장 적절한 것은?

① analysis of the cultural diversity

② anticipation of better living conditions

③ consideration of the social status

④ comparison of various perspectives

⑤ assessment of the costs

A variety of theoretical perspectives provide insight into immigration. Economics, which assumes that actors engage in utility maximization, represents one framework. From this perspective, it is assumed that individuals are rational actors, i.e., that they make migration decisions based on their assessment of the costs as well as benefits of remaining in a given area versus the costs and benefits of leaving. Benefits may include but are not limited to short−term and long−term monetary gains, safety, and greater freedom of cultural expression. Individual costs include but are not limited to the expense of travel, uncertainty of living in a foreign land, difficulty of adapting to a different language, uncertainty about a different culture, and the great concern about living in a new land. Psychic costs associated with separation from family, friends, and the fear of the unknown also should be taken into account in cost−benefit assessments.

윗글의 주제로 가장 적절한 것은?

① Theoretical perspectives on immigration

② Emotional challenges faced by immigrants

③ Factors influencing individuals' decisions to migrate

④ The benefits and costs of immigration: An economic perspective

⑤ The impact of immigration on cultural expression

지문의 내용을 주의 깊게 보면, 개인들이 이주 결정을 할 때 주어진 지역에 남아 있는 "비용"과 "혜택"을 기준으로 결정한다는 것을 알 수 있다. 여기서 '비용'과 '혜택'이라는 단어들이 반복적으로 언급되므로, 이는 중요한 키워드로 간주된다. 'assessment of the costs' 개인들은 이주 결정을 내릴 때 "비용"을 평가하므로, 이 선택지는 문맥에 가장 적합하다.

① 지문의 내용에는 문화적 다양성에 대한 분석이 언급되지 않는다. 따라서 이는 잘못된 선택이다.
② 이주의 동기 중 하나일 수 있지만, 지문에서 개인들이 이주 결정을 내릴 때 어떤 것을 기준으로 평가하는지에 대한 직접적인 답변이 아니다.
③ 지문 내에서 사회적 지위를 고려하는 것에 대한 언급이 전혀 없다.
④ 지문의 주요 내용은 개인들이 이주 결정을 내릴 때 고려하는 요인에 대한 것이며, 여러 관점의 비교에 대한 언급은 없다.

정답 ⑤

지문은 이주를 결정할 때 개인들이 고려하는 경제적 혜택과 비용에 중점을 둔다.

• ①은 넓은 범위의 주제를 포괄하지만, 지문의 핵심 내용인 '이주의 경제적 혜택과 비용'에 대한 구체적인 설명이 부족하다.
• ②는 지문에서 언급되는 'psychic costs'와 관련이 있지만, 지문의 전체 주제를 나타내지는 않는다.
• ③은 지문의 내용을 포괄적으로 다루지만, 지문의 주된 초점인 '경제적 관점'을 구체적으로 포함하고 있지 않다.
• ⑤는 지문에서 언급되는 'cultural expression'의 혜택과 관련이 있지만, 지문의 전체적인 주제를 반영하지는 않는다.

정답 ④

주어진 문장의 적합한 위치 찾기   CASE 01

난이도 ★★★☆☆

> There's a reason for that: traditionally, park designers attempted to create such a feeling by planting tall trees at park boundaries, building stone walls, and constructing other means of partition.

Parks take the shape demanded by the cultural concerns of their time. Once parks are in place, they are no inert stage — their purposes and meanings are made and remade by planners and by park users. Moments of park creation are particularly telling, however, for they reveal and actualize ideas about nature and its relationship to urban society. (①) **Indeed, what distinguishes a park from the broader category of public space is the representation of nature that parks are meant to embody.** (②) Public spaces include parks, concrete plazas, sidewalks, even indoor atriums. (③) Parks typically have trees, grass, and other plants as their central features. (④) When entering a city park, people often imagine a sharp separation from streets, cars, and buildings. (⑤) What's behind this idea is not only landscape architects' desire to design aesthetically suggestive park spaces, but a much longer history of Western thought that envisions cities and nature as antithetical spaces and oppositional forces.

글의 흐름으로 보아, 주어진 문장이 들어가기에 가장 적절한 곳을 고르시오.

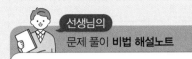
There's a reason for that: traditionally, park designers attempted to create such a feeling by planting tall trees at park boundaries, building stone walls, and constructing other means of partition.

Parks take the shape demanded by the cultural concerns of their time. Once parks are in place, they are no inert stage — their purposes and meanings are made and remade by planners and by park users. Moments of park creation are particularly telling, however, for they reveal and actualize ideas about nature and its relationship to urban society. (①) Indeed, what distinguishes a park from the broader category of public space is the representation of nature that parks are meant to embody. (②) Public spaces include parks, concrete plazas, sidewalks, even indoor atriums. (③) Parks typically have trees, grass, and other plants as their central features. (④) When entering a city park, people often imagine a sharp separation from streets, cars, and buildings. (⑤) What's behind this idea is not only landscape architects' desire to design aesthetically suggestive park spaces, but a much longer history of Western thought that envisions cities and nature as antithetical spaces and oppositional forces.

핵심 문장인 이유

'Indeed, what distinguishes a park from the broader category of public space is the representation of nature that parks are meant to embody.'는 공원이 다른 공공 공간과 어떻게 구분되는지를 명확히 설명하며, 이는 전체 지문의 주제인 공원의 기능과 목적에 대한 토론에 중요하기 때문에 핵심 문장에 해당한다.

본문 해설

주어진 문장은 도시 공원에 들어갈 때 사람들이 거리, 자동차, 건물로부터 명확히 분리된 느낌을 받는 이유에 대해 설명하며, 이는 도시와 자연을 대립적인 공간과 반대편 힘으로 상상하는 서양 사상의 긴 역사를 통해 이해할 수 있다는 내용과 잘 연결된다.

앞의 문장에서 'people often imagine a sharp separation~'이 주어진 문장의 'such a feeling'과 밀접한 관련이 있기 때문에 (⑤) 위치가 적절하다.

문제 풀이 전략

주어진 문장에서 연결사, 키워드를 파악한다. 이를 바탕으로 앞/뒤 문장을 예측하며 해결한다. 또한, 글의 흐름이 바뀌는 경우를 고려하며 읽어야 한다. 'separation(구분)'에 대한 이야기가 언급되고 이유가 나오는 게 자연스럽다.

정답 ⑤

Parks take the shape demanded by the cultural concerns of their time. Once parks are in place, they are no inert stage — their purposes and meanings are made and remade by planners and by park users.

(A) Public spaces include parks, concrete plazas, sidewalks, even indoor atriums. Parks typically have trees, grass, and other plants as their central features. When ① entering a city park, people often imagine a sharp separation from streets, cars, and buildings. There's a reason for that: traditionally, park designers attempted to create such a feeling by planting tall trees at park boundaries, building stone walls, and ② constructing other means of partition.

(B) Moments of park creation are particularly telling, however, for they reveal and actualize ideas about nature and its relationship to urban society. Indeed, ③ that distinguishes a park from the broader category of public space is the representation of nature ④ that parks are meant to embody.

(C) What's behind this idea is not only landscape architects' desire to design aesthetically suggestive park spaces, but a much longer history of Western thought ⑤ that envisions cities and nature as antithetical spaces and oppositional forces.

수능형

주어진 글 다음에 이어질 글의 순서로 가장 적절한 것을 고르시오.

① (A)－(C)－(B)

② (B)－(A)－(C)

③ (B)－(C)－(A)

④ (C)－(A)－(B)

⑤ (C)－(B)－(A)

내신형

윗글의 밑줄 친 부분 중, 어법상 틀린 것은?

(B) 단락이 먼저 오는 것이 적절하다. 이 단락은 공원의 창조와 그것이 도시 사회와 자연과의 관계에 대한 생각을 어떻게 구현하는지에 대한 개념을 도입한다.

(A) 단락은 공원이 일반적으로 가지는 특성과 도시 공원에 들어갈 때 사람들이 어떤 느낌을 받는지에 대해 구체적으로 설명하며, 공원 디자이너들이 그러한 느낌을 어떻게 창출하는지에 대한 이유를 제공한다.

마지막으로 (C) 단락은 이러한 아이디어의 배경에 대해 논의하며, 이것이 단순히 풍경 건축가들의 설계 욕구뿐만 아니라, 도시와 자연을 대립적인 공간으로 상상하는 서양 사상의 더 긴 역사와 연결되어 있다는 것을 설명한다.

정답 ②

'that'이 불완전한 문장을 이끌고 있다면, 관계대명사 that으로 봐야 한다. 하지만 선행사가 없기 때문에 선행사를 포함한 관계대명사 'what'이 적절하다.

① 현재분사 'entering'의 의미상 주어는 주절의 'people'이다. 서로 능동관계이므로 능동의 의미를 가지는 현재분사 entering이 적절하다.
② 등위접속사 'and' 병렬구조를 묻는 문제이다. 'by planting ~, building ~, and constructing'으로 동명사가 병렬구조를 가진다.
④ 'that'이 이끄는 절에서 'embody(~을 구현하다)'의 목적어가 없다. 'that'은 목적격 관계대명사로 적절하다.
⑤ 'envision(상상하다)'는 동사다. 주어가 없는 불완전한 문장을 이끄는 'that'은 주격 관계대명사로 적절하다.

> 🤖 아래의 프롬프트를 챗GPT에 입력해 보세요.
> "관계대명사 that, 관계대명사 what을 사용한 예문을 각각 2개씩 만들어줘."
> "동사지만 –ion 으로 끝나는 단어를 뜻과 함께 5개 알려줘."

정답 ③

주어진 문장의 적합한 위치 찾기   CASE 02

난이도 ★★★☆☆

It was not until relatively recent times that scientists came to understand the relationships between the structural elements of materials and their properties.

The earliest humans had access to only a very limited number of materials, those that occur naturally: stone, wood, clay, skins, and so on. (①) With time, they discovered techniques for producing materials that had properties superior to those of the natural ones; these new materials included pottery and various metals. (②) Furthermore, it was discovered that the properties of a material could be altered by heat treatments and by the addition of other substances. (③) At this point, materials utilization was totally a selection process that involved deciding from a given, rather limited set of materials, the one best suited for an application based on its characteristics. (④) This knowledge, acquired over approximately the past 100 years, has empowered them to fashion, to a large degree, the characteristics of materials. (⑤) Thus, tens of thousands of different materials have evolved with rather specialized characteristics that meet the needs of our modern and complex society, including metals, plastics, glasses, and fibers.

글의 흐름으로 보아, 주어진 문장이 들어가기에 가장 적절한 곳을 고르시오.

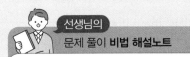
강조   It is not until A that B : A하고 나서야 B하다.

It was not until relatively recent times that scientists came to understand the relationships between
                              A   B
the structural elements of materials and their properties.

The earliest humans had access to only a very limited number of materials, those that occur
naturally: stone, wood, clay, skins, and so on. (①) With time, they discovered techniques for
producing materials that had properties superior to those of the natural ones; these new materials
included pottery and various metals. (②) Furthermore, it was discovered that the properties of
a material could be altered by heat treatments and by the addition of other substances. (③) At
this point, materials utilization was totally a selection process that involved deciding from a
given, rather limited set of materials, the one best suited for an application based on its
characteristics. (④) This knowledge, (acquired over approximately the past 100 years,) has
empowered them to fashion, to a large degree, the characteristics of materials. (⑤) Thus, tens of
thousands of different materials have evolved with rather specialized characteristics that meet the
needs of our modern and complex society, including metals, plastics, glasses, and fibers.

핵심 문장인 이유

이 지문의 주제는 초기의 자연 재료 사용에서 시작하여, 다양한 재료 개발과 그 특성 변경 기술의 발견을 통해 현대 사회의 요구에 부응하
는 수많은 특화된 소재들이 등장하게 된 과정이다.
이를 제시하는 "The earliest humans had access to only a very limited number of materials, those that occur naturally:
stone, wood, clay, skins, and so on."이 핵심 문장에 해당한다.

본문 해설

(④) 뒤에 오는 문장은 이러한 지식이 자재들의 특성을 가공하게 해주었다는 내용이다. 하지만 지식에 대한 구체적인 언급이 앞에 나오
지 않고 등장했다. 따라서 (④)에 주어진 문장이 말하는 물질의 구조적인 요소들과 성질 사이의 관계를 '지식'으로 접근해야 한다. 뒤에
이어지는 내용은 초기의 사람들이 물질의 제한적인 접근성을 가진 것이 뒷받침된다.

문제 풀이 전략

주어진 문장에서 연결사, 키워드를 파악한다. 이를 바탕으로 앞/뒤 문장을 예측하며 해결한다. 또한, 글의 흐름이 바뀌는 경우를 고려하며
읽어야 한다. 최근에 얻어진 지식이 언급되므로 이후의 내용도 얼마 지나지 않은 시간에서 일어나는 사건으로 접근해야 한다.

> 🔖 아래의 프롬프트를 챗GPT에 입력해 보세요.

"위의 제시한 문제를 해결할 때, 문맥을 자연스럽게 하는데 결정적인 키워드를 알려줘."
"'It is not until ～ that ～' 구문이 사용된 예문을 5개 알려줘."

정답 ④

The earliest humans had access to only a very limited number of materials, those that occur naturally: stone, wood, clay, skins, and so on. With time, they discovered techniques for producing materials that had properties superior to those of the natural ones; these new materials included pottery and various metals. Furthermore, it was discovered that the properties of a material could be altered by heat treatments and by the addition of other substances. At this point, materials utilization was totally a selection process that involved deciding from a given, rather limited set of materials, the one best suited for an application based on its characteristics. (A) 상대적으로 최근 시기가 되고 나서야 과학자들은 재료의 구조적 요소와 그것들의 성질 사이의 관계를 이해하게 되었다. This knowledge, acquired over approximately the past 100 years, has empowered them to fashion, to a large degree, the characteristics of materials. Thus, tens of thousands of different materials have evolved with rather specialized characteristics that meet the needs of our modern and complex society, including metals, plastics, glasses, and fibers.

수능형

윗글의 내용을 한 문장으로 요약하고자 한다. 빈칸 (A), (B)에 들어갈 말로 가장 적절한 것은?

Starting with ____(A)____ natural resources, early humans eventually learned to enhance these materials. This knowledge, especially over the last century, has led to the development of various ____(B)____ materials that meet the demands of our modern society.

	(A)		(B)
①	major	········	integrated
②	limited	········	specialized
③	processed	········	mixed
④	numerous	········	effective
⑤	discovered	········	replaced

내신형

밑줄 친 해석 (A)를 다음 〈조건〉을 참고하여 영작하시오.

〈조건〉
1. 강조구문을 사용하지 마시오.
2. 부정어구를 문두에 위치시키시오.
3. 단어 'not', 'until', 'and', 'of', 'come'을 사용하시오.
4. 완전한 문장으로 작성하시오.

글의 전개 방식은 초기의 인류는 주어진 천연자원에 제한적으로 사용할 수 있었고, 시간이 지남에 따라 과학자들이 자원(재료)의 구조와 특성을 이해하게 되어 지식을 쌓고 사회의 요구를 충족시키는 특화된 소재를 개발하게 되었다는 것이다. 따라서 'limited(제한된)', 'specialized(특화된)'이 적절하다.

> ✍️ 아래의 프롬프트를 챗GPT에 입력해 보세요.
> "위의 지문을 굉장히 짧은 영어 문장으로 요약해줘. 문장의 개수는 2개 정도로 해줘."

정답 ②

부정어구 'Not until relatively recent times'가 문두로 오게 되면 도치되어 문장의 어순이 바뀌게 된다. 'came'이 과거시제를 가진 일반 동사이기 때문에 조동사 'did'를 주어 'scientists' 앞에 위치시킨다. 조동사가 있으면 'came'은 원형인 'come'으로 바뀌어야 한다.

> ✍️ 아래의 프롬프트를 챗GPT에 입력해 보세요.
> "'Not until ~' 구문이 들어간 예문을 5개 알려줘."

정답 Not until relatively recent times did scientists come to understand the relationships between the structural elements of materials and their properties.

주어진 문장의 적합한 위치 찾기 (CASE 03)

난이도 ★★★★☆

I have still not exactly pinpointed Maddy's character since wickedness takes many forms.

Imagine I tell you that Maddy is bad. Perhaps you infer from my intonation, or the context in which we are talking, that I mean morally bad. Additionally, you will probably infer that I am disapproving of Maddy, or saying that I think you should disapprove of her, or similar, given typical linguistic conventions and assuming I am sincere. (①) However, you might not get a more detailed sense of the particular sorts of way in which Maddy is bad, her typical character traits, and the like, since people can be bad in many ways. (②) In contrast, if I say that Maddy is wicked, then you get more of a sense of her typical actions and attitudes to others. (③) **The word 'wicked' is more specific than 'bad'.** (④) But there is more detail nevertheless, perhaps a stronger connotation of the sort of person Maddy is. (⑤) In addition, and again assuming typical linguistic conventions, you should also get a sense that I am disapproving of Maddy, or saying that you should disapprove of her, or similar, assuming that we are still discussing her moral character.

글의 흐름으로 보아, 주어진 문장이 들어가기에 가장 적절한 곳을 고르시오.

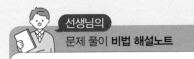
I have still not exactly pinpointed Maddy's character since wickedness takes many forms.

   Imagine I tell you that Maddy is bad. Perhaps you infer from my intonation, or the context in which we are talking, that I mean morally bad. Additionally, you will probably infer that I am disapproving of Maddy, or saying that I think you should disapprove of her, or similar, given typical linguistic conventions and assuming I am sincere. (①) However, you might not get a more detailed sense of the particular sorts of way in which Maddy is bad, her typical character traits, and the like, since people can be bad in many ways. (②) In contrast, if I say that Maddy is wicked, then you get more of a sense of her typical actions and attitudes to others. (③) The word 'wicked' is more specific than 'bad'. (④) But there is more detail nevertheless, perhaps a stronger connotation of the sort of person Maddy is. (⑤) In addition, and again assuming typical linguistic conventions, you should also get a sense that I am disapproving of Maddy, or saying that you should disapprove of her, or similar, assuming that we are still discussing her moral character.

핵심 문장인 이유

"The word 'wicked' is more specific than 'bad'." 이 문장은 지문에서 '나쁨(bad)'과 '악함(wicked)' 사이의 의미 차이를 중점적으로 다루고 있으며, 이를 통해 언어의 뉘앙스와 선택된 단어가 어떻게 그들의 의미를 특정하고 상황을 해석하는데 도움이 되는지를 설명하고 있어 핵심 문장에 해당한다.

본문 해설

"The word 'wicked' is more specific than 'bad'." 이후에 이 문장이 들어가면, '나쁨(bad)'보다 '악함(wicked)'이 더 구체적인 단어라는 이야기를 이어, '악함'이 여전히 다양한 형태를 가질 수 있어 Maddy의 성격을 정확히 규정하는 데에 한계가 있다는 내용이 잘 연결된다. 이후에 '악함'의 형태가 다양해서 한계가 있지만, Maddy라는 사람의 종류에 대한 세부사항이 있다고 연결하는 게 문맥상 옳다. 따라서 (④)이 적절하다.

문제 풀이 전략

주어진 문장에서 연결사, 키워드를 파악한다. 이를 바탕으로 앞/뒤 문장을 예측하며 해결한다. 또한, 글의 흐름이 바뀌는 경우를 고려하며 읽어야 한다. 주어진 문장에서 'still(여전히)'에 초점을 맞춰 앞에 내용과 맥락이 같다는 점을 파악해서 접근해야 한다.

🤖 아래의 프롬프트를 챗GPT에 입력해 보세요.
"위의 제시한 문제를 해결할 때, 문맥을 자연스럽게 하는데 결정적인 키워드를 알려줘."

정답 ④

Imagine I tell you that Maddy is bad. Perhaps you infer from my intonation, or the context in which we are talking, that I mean morally bad. Additionally, you will probably infer that I am disapproving of Maddy, or saying that I think you should disapprove of her, or similar, given typical linguistic conventions and assuming I am sincere. _____ⓐ_____, you might not get a more detailed sense of the particular sorts of way in which Maddy is bad, her typical character traits, and the like, since people can be bad in many ways. In contrast, if I say that Maddy is wicked, then you get more of a sense of her typical actions and attitudes to others. The word 'wicked' is more specific than 'bad'. I have still not exactly pinpointed Maddy's character since wickedness takes many forms. But there is more detail nevertheless, perhaps a stronger connotation of the sort of person Maddy is. _____ⓑ_____, and again assuming typical linguistic conventions, you should also get a sense that I am disapproving of Maddy, or saying that you should disapprove of her, or similar, assuming that we are still discussing her moral character.

수능형

윗글의 내용을 한 문장으로 요약하고자 한다. 빈칸 (A), (B)에 들어갈 말로 가장 적절한 것은?

It compares the _____(A)_____ of calling Maddy 'bad' versus 'wicked', emphasizing the latter's higher specificity yet varying _____(B)_____.

	(A)		(B)		(A)		(B)
①	implications	········	interpretations	②	meanings	········	personality
③	traits	········	flexibilities	④	appropriateness	········	integrations
⑤	attitudes	········	classifications				

내신형

윗글의 밑줄 친 (ⓐ), (ⓑ)에 알맞은 말로 가장 적절한 것은?

	(ⓐ)		(ⓑ)		(ⓐ)		(ⓑ)
①	Unfortunately	········	However	②	For instance	········	Exactly
③	For instance	········	Seemingly	④	Though	········	Nonetheless
⑤	Though	········	Moreover				

'bad'와 'wicked'로 부르는 것의 함축된 의미를 비교하고 있다. 'wicked' 더 구체적인 의미를 지니지만 여전히 다양한 의미를 가질 수 있어 이는 다양한 해석으로 이어질 수 있다. 따라서 'implications(함축)', 'interpretations(해석)'이 적절하다.

> 아래의 프롬프트를 챗GPT에 입력해 보세요.
> "단어 implication의 유의어를 쉬운 단어로 5개 알려줘."
> "단어 interpretation의 유의어를 쉬운 단어로 5개 알려줘."

정답 ①

"Maddy가 나쁘다"는 것에 대한 추론이나 그에 대한 비난을 할 수 있다는 아이디어를 제시하고, 다음에 나타나는 문장이 Maddy가 어떻게 나쁜지에 대한 더 구체적인 이해나 그녀의 일반적인 성격 특성을 파악하기는 어렵다는 새로운 관점을 제시하고 있으므로 'Though(그러나)'가 적절하다.

"there is more detail nevertheless, perhaps a stronger connotation of the sort of person Maddy is." 라는 문장은 Maddy의 성격에 대한 더 구체적인 정보를 제공하고 이어지는 문장에서 추가적인 통찰(Maddy를 비난하고 있다는 점과, 청자가 그녀를 비난해야 한다는 것을 느껴야 한다는 점)을 제공하므로 'Moreover(게다가)'가 적절하다.

> 아래의 프롬프트를 챗GPT에 입력해 보세요.
> "단어 Though의 유의어를 쉬운 단어로 5개 알려줘."
> "단어 Moreover의 유의어를 쉬운 단어로 5개 알려줘."

정답 ⑤

주어진 문장의 적합한 위치 찾기 CASE 04

난이도 ★★★★☆

> Thus, individuals of many resident species, confronted with the fitness benefits of control over a productive breeding site, may be forced to balance costs in the form of lower nonbreeding survivorship by remaining in the specific habitat where highest breeding success occurs.

Resident-bird habitat selection is seemingly a straightforward process in which a young dispersing individual moves until it finds a place where it can compete successfully to satisfy its needs. (①) Initially, these needs include only food and shelter. (②) However, eventually, the young must locate, identify, and settle in a habitat that satisfies not only survivorship but reproductive needs as well. (③) **In some cases, the habitat that provides the best opportunity for survival may not be the same habitat as the one that provides for highest reproductive capacity because of requirements specific to the reproductive period.** (④) Migrants, however, are free to choose the optimal habitat for survival during the nonbreeding season and for reproduction during the breeding season. (⑤) Thus, habitat selection during these different periods can be quite different for migrants as opposed to residents, even among closely related species.

글의 흐름으로 보아, 주어진 문장이 들어가기에 가장 적절한 곳을 고르시오.

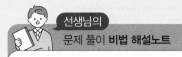
Thus, individuals of many resident species, confronted with the fitness benefits of control over a productive breeding site, may be forced to balance costs in the form of lower nonbreeding survivorship by remaining in the specific habitat where highest breeding success occurs.

Resident-bird habitat selection is seemingly a straightforward process in which a young dispersing individual moves until it finds a place where it can compete successfully to satisfy its needs. (①) Initially, these needs include only food and shelter. (②) However, eventually, the young must locate, identify, and settle in a habitat that satisfies not only survivorship but reproductive needs as well. (③) In some cases, the habitat that provides the best opportunity for survival may not be the same habitat as the one that provides for highest reproductive capacity because of requirements (specific to the reproductive period.) (④) Migrants, however, are free to choose the optimal habitat for survival during the nonbreeding season and for reproduction during the breeding season. (⑤) Thus, habitat selection during these different periods can be quite different for migrants as opposed to residents, even among closely related species.

핵심 문장인 이유

"In some cases, the habitat that provides the best opportunity for survival may not be the same habitat as the one that provides for highest reproductive capacity because of requirements specific to the reproductive period."
이 문장은 생존과 번식 사이에서의 복잡한 균형을 잡아야 하는 새들의 서식지 선택의 핵심적인 복잡성을 강조하고 있다. 이 문장은 번식과 생존이라는 두 가지 중요한 생물학적 목표 사이에서 생기는 상충 관계에 대한 통찰력을 제공하므로 핵심 문장에 해당한다.

본문 해설

"In some cases, ~"은 생존에 가장 이상적인 서식지와 번식 능력이 가장 높은 서식지가 다를 수 있음을 지적하고 있다. 이것은 번식 기간의 특정 요구사항 때문일 수 있다. 따라서 "In some cases, ~" 문장을 더욱 명확하게 만들기 위해 "thus(따라서)"를 사용한 주어진 문장은 (④)에 들어가는 것이 적절하다.

문제 풀이 전략

주어진 문장에서 연결사, 키워드를 파악한다. 이를 바탕으로 앞/뒤 문장을 예측하며 해결한다. 또한, 글의 흐름이 바뀌는 경우를 고려하며 읽어야 한다. 'thus(따라서)'가 이끄는 내용은 앞에 언급된 내용에 대한 결과를 명확하게 전달하기 위한 것임을 기억하자.

정답 ④

Resident-bird habitat selection is seemingly a straightforward process ① in which a young dispersing individual moves until it finds a place ② where it can compete successfully to satisfy its needs.

(A) Thus, individuals of many resident species, ③ confronted with the fitness benefits of control over a productive breeding site, may be forced to balance costs in the form of lower nonbreeding survivorship by remaining in the specific habitat where highest breeding success occurs.

(B) Migrants, however, are free to choose the optimal habitat for survival during the nonbreeding season and for reproduction during the breeding season. Thus, habitat selection during these different periods can be quite different for migrants as opposed to residents, even among ④ closely related species.

(C) Initially, these needs include only food and shelter. However, eventually, the young must locate, identify, and settle in a habitat ⑤ what satisfies not only survivorship but reproductive needs as well. In some cases, the habitat that provides the best opportunity for survival may not be the same habitat as the one that provides for highest reproductive capacity because of requirements specific to the reproductive period.

수능형

주어진 글 다음에 이어질 글의 순서로 가장 적절한 것을 고르시오.

① (A)-(C)-(B)　　　　　　　　② (B)-(A)-(C)

③ (B)-(C)-(A)　　　　　　　　④ (C)-(A)-(B)

⑤ (C)-(B)-(A)

내신형

윗글의 밑줄 친 부분 중, 어법상 틀린 것은?

주어진 문장은 새의 서식지 선택이 초기에는 단순하게 보일 수 있지만, 실제로는 더 복잡한 과정임을 시사한다.

(C)는 이 개념을 더욱 발전시키는데, 초기에는 음식과 보호만이 필요하지만, 결국에는 새가 생존과 번식 두 가지 요구사항을 모두 만족시키는 서식지를 찾아야 한다는 점을 강조한다.

(A)는 앞에서의 두 가지 요구사항을 구체화하고 확장한다. 번식하지 않는 시기 동안의 생존률이 낮아지는 비용과의 균형을 맞춰야 할 수 있다는 점을 보여준다.

(B)는 거주하는 새와 이주하는 새의 차이점을 보여주며, 이주하는 새들이 생존에 이상적인 서식지를 자유롭게 선택할 수 있고, 번식하지 않는 시기와 번식하는 시기에서의 서식지 선택이 크게 다를 수 있다는 점을 강조한다.

정답 ④

불완전한 문장을 이끌고 있지만 선행사가 있기 때문에 관계대명사 'that'이 적절하다.

① 선행사 "a straightforward process"를 수식하는 완전한 문장의 관계절이기 때문에 전치사+관계대명사 "in which"는 적절하다.
② 장소의 관한 선행사 "a place"를 수식하는 완전한 문장의 관계절이기 때문에 관계부사 "where"는 적절하다.
③ "individuals"와의 수식관계가 수동관계이므로 과거분사 "confronted"는 적절하다.
④ 분사 "related"를 수식할 수 있는 부사 "closely"는 적절하다.

🔁 아래의 프롬프트를 챗GPT에 입력해 보세요.
"관계부사가 사용된 예문을 5개 알려줘."
"전치사+관계대명사가 사용된 예문을 5개 알려줘."

정답 ⑤

CASE 01

난이도 ★★★☆☆

Time spent on on-line interaction with members of one's own, preselected community leaves less time available for actual encounters with a wide variety of people. If physicists, for example, were to concentrate on exchanging email and electronic preprints with other physicists around the world working in the same specialized subject area, they would likely devote less time, and be less receptive to new ways of looking at the world. Facilitating the voluntary construction of highly homogeneous social networks of scientific communication therefore allows individuals to filter the potentially overwhelming flow of information. **But the result may be the tendency to overfilter it, thus eliminating the diversity of the knowledge circulating and diminishing the frequency of radically new ideas.** In this regard, even a journey through the stacks of a real library can be more fruitful than a trip through today's distributed virtual archives, because it seems difficult to use the available "search engines" to emulate efficiently the mixture of predictable and surprising discoveries that typically result from a physical shelf-search of an extensive library collection.

↓

Focusing on on-line interaction with people who are engaged in the same specialized area can ___(A)___ potential sources of information and thus make it less probable for ___(B)___ findings to happen.

윗글의 내용을 한 문장으로 요약하고자 한다. 빈칸 (A) , (B)에 들어갈 말로 가장 적절한 것은?

(A)		(B)
① limit	……	unexpected
② limit	……	distorted
③ diversify	……	misleading
④ diversify	……	accidental
⑤ provide	……	novel

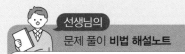
Time spent on on-line interaction with members of one's own, preselected community leaves less time available for actual encounters with a wide variety of people. If physicists, for example, were to concentrate on exchanging email and electronic preprints with other physicists around the world working in the same specialized subject area, they would likely devote less time, and be less receptive to new ways of looking at the world. Facilitating the voluntary construction of highly homogeneous social networks of scientific communication therefore allows individuals to filter the potentially overwhelming flow of information. But the result may be the tendency to overfilter it, thus eliminating the diversity of the knowledge circulating and diminishing the frequency of radically new ideas. In this regard, even a journey through the stacks of a real library can be more fruitful than a trip through today's distributed virtual archives, because it seems difficult to use the available "search engines" to emulate efficiently the mixture of predictable and surprising discoveries that typically result from a physical shelf-search of an extensive library collection.

⬇

Focusing on on-line interaction with people who are engaged in the same specialized area can ___(A)___ potential sources of information and thus make it less probable for ___(B)___ findings to happen.

핵심 문장인 이유

동질적인 집단 간의 커뮤니케이션은 다양한 분야와의 접촉을 저해하고, 정보나 아이디어를 접할 가능성을 줄인다는 주장이 이 글의 전체 구성논리이다. 따라서 논리와 키워드를 가장 잘 포함하고 있는 위의 문장이 핵심 문장이다.

본문 해설

동일 전문 분야에서만의 의사소통은 다양한 만남과 상호작용(potential sources)을 제한(limit)한다는 주장을 과학자들의 예를 들어서 설명하고 있다. 또한, 본인들만의 커뮤니티가 아닌, 다른 다양한 집단 등과 교류하면서 얻어지는 우연한 발견(unexpected)의 확률 또한 줄어들게 만든다고 주장하는 글이다.

문제 풀이 전략

먼저 동일 분야에서의 온라인 교류에 대한 작가의 관점을 파악하는 것이 중요하다. 그리고 그러한 행위의 특징이나 내용을 간략하게 정리하는 것이 중요하다.

> 🔊 아래의 프롬프트를 챗GPT에 입력해 보세요.
> "지문에서 핵심적인 5개의 어휘를 선정하시오. 그 단어들의 뜻을 정의하고, 지문에서 어떻게 사용되었는지 설명하시오."

Time spent on on-line interaction with members of one's own, preselected community leaves less time available for actual encounters with a wide variety of people. If physicists, for example, were to concentrate on exchanging email and electronic preprints with other physicists around the world working in the same specialized subject area, they would likely devote less time, and be less receptive to new ways of looking at the world. Facilitating the voluntary construction of highly homogeneous social networks of scientific communication therefore allows individuals to filter the potentially overwhelming flow of information. But the result may be the tendency to overfilter it, thus eliminating the diversity of the knowledge circulating and diminishing the frequency of radically new ideas. In this regard, even a journey through the stacks of a real library can be more fruitful than a trip through today's distributed virtual archives, because it seems difficult to use the available "search engines" to emulate efficiently the mixture of predictable and surprising discoveries that typically result from a physical shelf-search of an extensive library collection.

윗글의 내용과 일치하지 <u>않는</u> 것은?

① 온라인 상호작용이 증가하면 다양한 사람들과의 실제적인 만남에 할애할 수 있는 시간이 줄어든다.

② 예를 들어, 물리학자들이 특정 전문 분야의 다른 물리학자들과의 이메일과 전자 예고교환에 집중하게 되면, 새로운 관점을 받아들이는 데 덜 수용적이게 될 가능성이 있다.

③ 동질적인 사회 네트워크를 자발적으로 구축하는 것은 너무 많은 정보를 필터링하는 데 도움이 된다.

④ 실제 도서관에서의 탐색은 분산된 가상 아카이브를 통한 탐색보다 더욱 풍부한 결과를 가져올 수 있다.

⑤ 과도한 필터링의 결과로, 순환하는 지식의 다양성이 증가하고, 급진적인 새로운 아이디어의 빈도가 증가할 수 있다.

Time spent on on-line interaction with members of one's own, ① <u>preselected</u> community leaves less time available for actual encounters with a wide variety of people. If physicists, for example, were to concentrate on exchanging email and electronic preprints with other physicists around the world working in the same specialized subject area, they would likely devote less time, and be less ② <u>receptive</u> to new ways of looking at the world. Facilitating the voluntary construction of highly homogeneous social networks of scientific communication therefore allows individuals to ③ <u>filter</u> the potentially overwhelming flow of information. But the result may be the tendency to overfilter it, thus eliminating the ④ <u>consistency</u> of the knowledge circulating and diminishing the frequency of radically new ideas. In this regard, even a journey through the stacks of a real library can be more ⑤ <u>fruitful</u> than a trip through today's distributed virtual archives, because it seems difficult to use the available "search engines" to emulate efficiently the mixture of predictable and surprising discoveries that typically result from a physical shelf-search of an extensive library collection.

윗글의 밑줄 친 부분 중, 문맥상 낱말의 쓰임이 적절하지 <u>않은</u> 것은?

지문에 따르면, 과도한 필터링으로 인해 지식의 다양성이 사라지고, 급진적인 새로운 아이디어가 덜 나오게 될 수 있다고 말하고 있다. 따라서 ⑤번 선택지는 지문의 내용과 상충된다.

정답 ⑤

지문에서는 온라인 상호작용이 많아짐에 따라 정보나 지식의 다양성이 감소될 수 있다는 포인트를 설명하고 있다. 즉, 온라인에서 너무 특정한 정보나 지식에만 집중하게 되면 그 외의 다양한 정보나 지식에 대한 접근이 줄어들게 된다. 이러한 문맥에서 "consistency(일관성)"는 부적절하며, 올바른 표현은 'diversity'가 된다.

정답 ④

유형

13 문단 요약하기

CASE 02

기출문제
정복하기

2019년 9월
평가원
40번 문제

난이도 ★★★☆☆

Perceptions of forest use and the value of forests as standing timber vary considerably from indigenous peoples to national governments and Western scientists. These differences in attitudes and values lie at the root of conflicting management strategies and stimulate protest groups such as the Chipko movement. For example, the cultivators of the Himalayas and Karakoram view forests as essentially a convertible resource. That is, under increasing population pressure and growing demands for cultivable land, the conversion of forest into cultivated terraces means a much higher productivity can be extracted from the same area. Compensation in the form of planting on terrace edges occurs to make up for the clearance. This contrasts with the national view of the value of forests as a renewable resource, with the need or desire to keep a forest cover over the land for soil conservation, and with a global view of protection for biodiversity and climate change purposes, irrespective of the local people's needs.

⬇

For indigenous peoples forests serve as a source of ____(A)____ resources, while national and global perspectives prioritize the ____(B)____ of forests, despite the local needs.

윗글의 내용을 한 문장으로 요약하고자 한다. 빈칸 (A) , (B)에 들어갈 말로 가장 적절한 것은?

	(A)	(B)
①	transformable	preservation
②	transformable	practicality
③	consumable	manipulation
④	restorable	potential
⑤	restorable	recovery

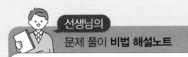
Perceptions of forest use and the value of forests as standing timber vary considerably from indigenous peoples to national governments and Western scientists. These differences in attitudes and values lie at the root of conflicting management strategies and stimulate protest groups such as the Chipko movement. For example, the cultivators of the Himalayas and Karakoram view forests as essentially a convertible resource. That is, under increasing population pressure and growing demands for cultivable land, the conversion of forest into cultivated terraces means a much higher productivity can be extracted from the same area. Compensation in the form of planting on terrace edges occurs to make up for the clearance. This contrasts with the national view of the value of forests as a renewable resource, with the need or desire to keep a forest cover over the land for soil conservation, and with a global view of protection for biodiversity and climate change purposes, irrespective of the local people's needs.

⬇

For indigenous peoples forests serve as a source of _____(A)_____ resources, while national and global perspectives prioritize the _____(B)_____ of forests, despite the local needs.

핵심 문장인 이유

숲의 사용과 가치에 대한 관점의 차이를 나타내는 글이다. 지역의 토착민과 국가적, 세계적 관점의 차이를 드러내는 글로 이를 가장 잘 담고 있는 해당 문장이 핵심 문장이다.

본문 해설

숲에 대한 지역민들과 다른 집단 간의 태도와 가치의 차이가 있음을 보여주며, 경작자들은 숲을 바꿀 수 있는 (transformable)자원으로 바라보는 반면, 외부의 다른 집단은 숲의 보호(preservation)를 우선 시 한다는 것을 알려주는 글이다.

문제 풀이 전략

각각의 주장에 대하여, 지역민과 외부 집단의 견해가 가지는 특징을 분류하는 과정이 필요하다.

> 🔖 **아래의 프롬프트를 챗GPT에 입력해 보세요.**
> "Convertible"라는 단어를 이 글의 관점을 바탕으로 설명하라"

정답 ①

Perceptions of forest use and the value of forests as standing timber vary considerably from indigenous peoples to national governments and Western scientists. These differences in attitudes and values lie at the root of conflicting management strategies and stimulate protest groups such as the Chipko movement.

(A) That is, under increasing population pressure and growing demands for cultivable land, the conversion of forest into cultivated terraces means a much higher productivity can be extracted from the same area. Compensation in the form of planting on terrace edges occurs to make up for the clearance.

(B) This contrasts with the national view of the value of forests as a renewable resource, with the need or desire to keep a forest cover over the land for soil conservation, and with a global view of protection for biodiversity and climate change purposes, irrespective of the local people's needs.

(C) For example, the cultivators of the Himalayas and Karakoram view forests as essentially a convertible resource.

주어진 글 다음에 이어질 글의 순서로 가장 적절한 것을 고르시오.

① (B)−(A)−(C)　　　　　　② (A)−(C)−(B)
③ (B)−(C)−(A)　　　　　　④ (A)−(B)−(C)
⑤ (C)−(A)−(B)

Perceptions of forest use and the value of forests as standing timber vary considerably from indigenous peoples to national governments and Western scientists. These differences in attitudes and values lie at the root of conflicting management strategies and stimulate protest groups such as the Chipko movement. For example, the cultivators of the Himalayas and Karakoram view forests as essentially a convertible resource. That is, under increasing population pressure and growing demands for cultivable land, the conversion of forest into cultivated terraces means a much higher productivity can be extracted from the same area. Compensation in the form of planting on terrace edges occurs to make up for the clearance. This contrasts with the national view of the value of forests as a renewable resource, with the need or desire to keep a forest cover over the land for soil conservation, and with a global view of protection for biodiversity and climate change purposes, irrespective of the local people's needs.

윗글의 주제로 가장 적절한 것은?

① The Chipko Movement and Its Impact on Forest Conservation

② The Influence of Western Science on Forest Management

③ Differences in Forest Value Perceptions and Their Effect on Management Strategies

④ The Role of Indigenous Peoples in Soil Conservation

⑤ Conversion of Forests into Cultivated Terraces: A Case Study of the Himalayas and Karakoram

(C)는 제시문에서 나온 "indigenous peoples"에 관한 언급을 구체적으로 예시를 들어 설명하고 있다. 지문에서 "Perceptions of forest use"에 대해 언급하면서 다양한 그룹 간의 차이점을 지적했고, 그 중 하나의 그룹인 "indigenous peoples"의 관점을 "cultivators of the Himalayas and Karakoram"을 예로 들어 구체화하고 있다.

(A)는 (C)에서 제시된 "convertible resource"라는 개념을 좀 더 구체적으로 설명한다. "convertible resource"가 무엇인지 자세히 설명하며, 이는 (C)에서 제시된 관점의 연장선에 있다.

(B)는 (A)에서 설명한 지역 주민들의 관점과는 대조적으로, 국가나 글로벌 차원에서 숲을 어떻게 바라보는지를 설명하고 있다. 이 문장은 이전에 제시된 지역 주민들의 숲 사용에 대한 관점과 국가나 글로벌 차원의 관점 사이의 차이점을 부각시킨다.

정답 ⑤

이 지문은 숲을 이용하고, 숲의 가치를 어떻게 인식하는지에 대한 관점이 원주민부터 국가 정부와 서양 과학자들 사이에서 어떻게 다른지를 중점으로 논하고 있다. 이런 차이점이 어떻게 충돌하는 관리 전략의 근본이 되는지, 그리고 항의 그룹들을 어떻게 자극하는지를 설명하고 있다.

또한, 히말라야와 카라코람의 농부들이 숲을 어떻게 변환 가능한 자원으로 보는지, 그리고 이것이 국가적인 시각과 세계적인 시각과 어떻게 대비되는지를 설명하고 있다. 따라서 이 지문의 주제는 "숲 가치 인식의 차이와 그것이 관리 전략에 미치는 영향"이 될 수 있다. 선택지 중에서 이 내용을 가장 잘 반영하는 것은 ③번이다.

정답 ③

문단 요약하기

난이도 ★★★☆☆

A striving to demonstrate individual personality through designs should not be surprising. Most designers are educated to work as individuals, and design literature contains countless references to 'the designer'. Personal flair is without doubt an absolute necessity in some product categories, particularly relatively small objects, with a low degree of technological complexity, such as furniture, lighting, small appliances, and housewares. In larger-scale projects, however, even where a strong personality exercises powerful influence, the fact that substantial numbers of designers are employed in implementing a concept can easily be overlooked. The emphasis on individuality is therefore problematic — rather than actually designing, many successful designer 'personalities' function more as creative managers. **A distinction needs to be made between designers working truly alone and those working in a group.** In the latter case, management organization and processes can be equally as relevant as designers' creativity.

↓

Depending on the ___(A)___ of a project, the capacity of designers to ___(B)___ team-based working environments can be just as important as their personal qualities.

윗글의 내용을 한 문장으로 요약하고자 한다. 빈칸 (A), (B)에 들어갈 말로 가장 적절한 것은?

(A)	(B)	(A)	(B)
① size ····· coordinate		② cost ····· systematize	
③ size ····· identify		④ cost ····· innovate	
⑤ goal ····· investigate			

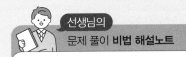
A striving to demonstrate individual personality through designs should not be surprising. Most designers are educated to work as individuals, and design literature contains countless references to 'the designer'. Personal flair is without doubt an absolute necessity in some product categories, particularly relatively small objects, with a low degree of technological complexity, such as furniture, lighting, small appliances, and housewares. In larger-scale projects, however, even where a strong personality exercises powerful influence, the fact that substantial numbers of designers are employed in implementing a concept can easily be overlooked. The emphasis on individuality is therefore problematic —rather than actually designing, many successful designer 'personalities' function more as creative managers. A distinction needs to be made between designers working truly alone and those working in a group. In the latter case, management organization and processes can be equally as relevant as designers' creativity.

⬇

Depending on the _____(A)_____ of a project, the capacity of designers to _____(B)_____ team-based working environments can be just as important as their personal qualities.

핵심 문장인 이유

디자인을 하는 대상의 규모가 크다면 조직관리 능력이 디자이너의 개인적 역량보다 중요한 것처럼 규모에 따라 필요한 역량이 달라질 수 있음을 주장하는 글이다. 키워드와 글의 주장을 가장 잘 반영하는 해당 문장이 핵심 문장이다.

본문 해설

디자이너는 개인의 개성을 보여주어야 하며 낮은 복잡성을 가진 작은 물건의 경우 개인의 재능이 중요하다는 통념을 먼저 제시하고 있다. 그러나 프로젝트의 규모가 커지면(size) 많은 수의 디자이너가 참여하며 이 조직을 관리하는 능력(coordinate)이 중요하다는 사실을 보여주는 글이다.

문제 풀이 전략

대조되는 두 가지 개념의 특징을 잘 찾아서 분류하는 것이 중요하다.

> 🐾 **아래의 프롬프트를 챗GPT에 입력해 보세요.**
> "글에서 대조되는 관점 2가지를 알려주고, 내용을 정리해줘."

정답 ①

A striving to demonstrate individual personality through designs should not be surprising. Most designers are educated to work as individuals, and design literature contains countless references to 'the designer'. Personal flair is without doubt an absolute necessity in some product categories, particularly relatively small objects, with a low degree of technological complexity, such as furniture, lighting, small appliances, and housewares. In larger-scale projects, however, even where a strong personality exercises powerful influence, the fact that substantial numbers of designers are employed in implementing a concept can easily be overlooked. The emphasis on individuality is therefore problematic—rather than actually designing, many successful designer 'personalities' function more as _____. A distinction needs to be made between designers working truly alone and those working in a group. In the latter case, management organization and processes can be equally as relevant as designers' creativity.

윗글의 빈칸에 들어갈 어휘로 가장 적절한 것은?

① accounting managers
② human resources managers
③ software engineers
④ sales directors
⑤ creative managers

A striving to demonstrate individual personality through designs should not be surprising. Most designers are educated to work as individuals, and design literature contains countless references to 'the designer'. Personal flair is without doubt an absolute necessity in some product categories, particularly relatively small objects, with a low degree of technological complexity, such as furniture, lighting, small appliances, and housewares. In larger-scale projects, however, even where a strong personality exercises powerful influence, the fact that substantial numbers of designers are employed in implementing a concept can easily be overlooked. The emphasis on individuality is therefore problematic —rather than actually designing, many successful designer 'personalities' function more as creative managers. A distinction needs to be made between designers working truly alone and those working in a group. In the latter case, management organization and processes can be equally as relevant as designers' creativity.

윗글을 읽고 추론할 수 있는 정보는?

① 개인적인 특징은 모든 디자인 분야에서 결정적으로 중요하다.
② 대규모 프로젝트에서는 대부분의 디자인이 개별 디자이너에 의해 수행된다.
③ 규모와 상관없이 디자인은 주로 디자이너의 개인적인 능력에 초점을 맞춘다.
④ 성공적인 디자이너는 그들이 디자인을 하는 것보다 창의적인 관리자로서 역할을 하는 경우가 많다.
⑤ 모든 디자이너는 반드시 그룹 내에서 작업해야 한다.

개인으로 일하는 디자이너와 그룹에서 일하는 디자이너를 구별해야 하며, 후자의 경우에서 관리 조직과 과정이 디자이너의 창의성만큼 중요하다는 점을 강조하고 있다.

이 맥락에서, 성공한 디자이너들이 '창의적인 관리자'로서의 역할을 수행한다는 것은 그들이 디자인의 창조적인 측면뿐만 아니라 프로젝트 관리, 팀 협업, 리소스 할당 등의 관리적 측면도 동시에 다룬다는 것을 의미하므로 정답은 ⑤번이 되어야 한다.

정답 ⑤

④는 글에서 명시적으로 언급된 내용으로, 많은 성공적인 디자이너가 실제로 디자인을 하는 것보다 창의적인 관리자로서의 역할을 하는 것을 포함하고 있다.

- ①은 일부 상품 카테고리, 특히 상대적으로 작은 물건에 대해 이야기하고 있지만, 모든 디자인 분야에서 결정적으로 중요하다고는 말하고 있지 않다.
- ②는 글에서 대규모 프로젝트에서는 많은 디자이너들이 참여하여 개념을 구현하는 사실이 종종 간과될 수 있다고 언급한 내용과 일치하지 않는다.
- ③은 규모에 따라 디자이너에게 요구되는 역량이 다르다는 글의 주장과 다르다.
- ⑤는 글에서 언급되지 않았다. 디자이너가 반드시 그룹 내에서 작업해야 한다는 주장은 이 글에서 볼 수 없다.

정답 ④

난이도 ★★★☆☆

After the United Nations environmental conference in Rio de Janeiro in 1992 made the term "sustainability" widely known around the world, the word became a popular buzzword by those who wanted to be seen as pro-environmental but who did not really intend to change their behavior. It became a public relations term, an attempt to be seen as abreast with the latest thinking of what we must do to save our planet from widespread harm. **But then, in a decade or so, some governments, industries, educational institutions, and organizations started to use the term in a serious manner.** In the United States a number of large corporations appointed a vice president for sustainability. Not only were these officials interested in how their companies could profit by producing "green" products, but they were often given the task of making the company more efficient by reducing wastes and pollution and by reducing its carbon emissions.

↓

While the term "sustainability," in the initial phase, was popular among those who ___(A)___ to be eco-conscious, it later came to be used by those who would ___(B)___ their pro-environmental thoughts.

윗글의 내용을 한 문장으로 요약하고자 한다. 빈칸 (A), (B)에 들어갈 말로 가장 적절한 것은?

   (A)   (B)

① pretended ······ actualize

② pretended ······ disregard

③ refused ······ realize

④ refused ······ idealize

⑤ attempted ······ mask

After the United Nations environmental conference in Rio de Janeiro in 1992 made the term "sustainability" widely known around the world, the word became a popular buzzword by those who wanted to be seen as pro-environmental but who did not really intend to change their behavior. It became a public relations term, an attempt to be seen as abreast with the latest thinking of what we must do to save our planet from widespread harm. But then, in a decade or so, some governments, industries, educational institutions, and organizations started to use the term in a serious manner. In the United States a number of large corporations appointed a vice president for sustainability. Not only were these officials interested in how their companies could profit by producing "green" products, but they were often given the task of making the company more efficient by reducing wastes and pollution and by reducing its carbon emissions.

⬇

While the term "sustainability," in the initial phase, was popular among those who ＿＿(A)＿＿ to be eco-conscious, it later came to be used by those who would ＿＿(B)＿＿ their pro-environmental thoughts.

핵심 문장인 이유

시간이 지남에 따라 '지속가능성'이라는 어휘를 사용한 주체가 바뀐 현상에 대하여 설명한 글이다. '지속가능성'이라는 어휘의 사용자 변화를 가장 잘 반영한 해당 문장이 핵심 문장이다.

본문 해설

처음 '지속가능성'을 사용한 집단은 단지 환경보호를 옹호하는 척하며(pretend) 홍보용으로 이 용어를 사용하여 실제로 행동으로 옮기지는 않았으나 시간이 흐른 후, 일부 조직들이 이러한 용어를 진지하게 사용하여 실제로 환경보호를 위한 조치를 취하는(actualize) 등의 실천을 하고 있는 현상을 설명하는 글이다.

문제 풀이 전략

서로 다른 시기에 용어를 사용한 집단에서의 차이점을 명확하게 구분하여야 한다. 처음에는 용어만 사용하며 실천에 옮기지 않았지만, 나중에 이 용어를 사용한 집단은 실제로 환경보호를 실천하였다는 요지를 정확하게 찾아야 한다.

🤖 **아래의 프롬프트를 챗GPT에 입력해 보세요.**

'이 글에서 대조되고 있는 내용과 그 세부적 내용을 나눠서 정리해줘.'

정답 ①

After the United Nations environmental conference in Rio de Janeiro in 1992 made the term "sustainability" widely known around the world, the word became a popular buzzword by those who wanted to be seen as pro−environmental but who did not really intend to change their behavior.

(A) In the United States a number of large corporations appointed a vice president for sustainability.

(B) Not only were these officials interested in how their companies could profit by producing "green" products, but they were often given the task of making the company more efficient by reducing wastes and pollution and by reducing its carbon emissions.

(C) It became a public relations term, an attempt to be seen as abreast with the latest thinking of what we must do to save our planet from widespread harm. But then, in a decade or so, some governments, industries, educational institutions, and organizations started to use the term in a serious manner.

제시문 다음에 올 글의 순서로 가장 적절한 것은?

① (A)−(B)−(C)
② (C)−(B)−(A)
③ (B)−(C)−(A)
④ (C)−(A)−(B)
⑤ (A)−(C)−(B)

After the United Nations environmental conference in Rio de Janeiro in 1992 made the term "sustainability" widely known around the world, the word became a popular buzzword by those who wanted to be seen as pro−environmental but who did not really intend to change their behavior. It became a public relations term, an attempt to be seen as abreast with the latest thinking of what we must do to save our planet from widespread harm. But then, in a decade or so, some governments, industries, educational institutions, and organizations started to use the term in a serious manner. In the United States a number of large corporations appointed a vice president for sustainability. Not only were these officials interested in how their companies could profit by producing "green" products, but they were often given the task of making the company more efficient by reducing wastes and pollution and by reducing its carbon emissions.

What responsibilities are assigned to vice presidents of sustainability in large U.S. corporations in the text?

① They were tasked with increasing the company's carbon emissions.

② They were tasked with making the company more efficient by reducing wastes, pollution, and its carbon emissions.

③ They were tasked with expanding the company's physical footprint.

④ They were tasked with creating public relations campaigns about sustainability.

⑤ They were tasked with decreasing the company's investment in renewable energy.

제시문에서 '지속가능성'이라는 용어가 처음으로 널리 알려진 이후, 이 용어가 홍보 용어로 쓰이게 되고 친환경적 사고와 보조를 맞추고 있는 것처럼 보이게 해당 용어를 사용한 것(C)을 설명하고, 이후 달라진 용어의 사용에 대한 언급을 한다. 그 다음에는 이 용어를 진지하게 사용한 것의 예시로 미국의 여러 대기업들이 지속가능성 부사장을 임명했음(A)을 언급하며, 마지막으로 이들 부사장들이 자사의 '녹색' 제품 생산 및 폐기물, 오염, 탄소 배출 감소에 대한 업무를 맡았음(B)을 설명하는 글의 흐름이 가장 자연스럽다.

정답 ④

미국의 대형 기업에서 지정된 지속가능성 부사장들에게 주어진 책임은 무엇인가?

① 그들은 회사의 탄소 배출을 증가시키는 일을 맡았다.
② 그들은 폐기물, 오염, 그리고 자신의 탄소 배출을 줄이는 방법으로 회사를 더 효율적으로 만드는 일을 맡았다.
③ 그들은 회사의 물리적 영향력을 확장하는 일을 맡았다.
④ 그들은 지속가능성에 대한 캠페인을 만드는 일을 맡았다.
⑤ 그들은 회사의 재생 에너지 투자를 줄이는 일을 맡았다.

원문에서, '지속가능성 부서의 부사장들은 종종 회사를 더 효율적으로 만드는 일, 즉 폐기물, 오염, 그리고 탄소 배출을 줄이는 일을 맡게 되었다'고 언급하고 있다.

다른 선택지에서, 지속가능성에 대한 캠페인을 만드는 것이 지속가능성 부사장의 역할의 일부일 수 있지만, 주어진 원문에서 이것이 그들의 업무 중 하나였다고 명시적으로 언급되지 않았다. 재생 에너지 투자를 줄이는 것 또한 지속가능성의 전반적인 목표와 반대되므로, 이 역시 잘못된 선택지이다.

정답 ②

문단 내 글의 순서 파악하기 　CASE 01

난이도 ★★★☆☆

The growing complexity of computer software has direct implications for our global safety and security, particularly as the physical objects upon which we depend — things like cars, airplanes, bridges, tunnels, and implantable medical devices — transform themselves into computer code.

(A) As all this code grows in size and complexity, so too do the number of errors and software bugs. According to a study by Carnegie Mellon University, commercial software typically has twenty to thirty bugs for every thousand lines of code — 50 million lines of code means 1 million to 1.5 million potential errors to be exploited.

(B) This is the basis for all malware attacks that take advantage of these computer bugs to get the code to do something it was not originally intended to do. As computer code grows more elaborate, software bugs flourish and security suffers, with increasing consequences for society at large.

(C) Physical things are increasingly becoming information technologies. Cars are "computer we ride in," and airplanes are nothing more than "flying Solaris boxes attached to bucketfuls of industrial control system."

주어진 글 다음에 이어질 글의 순서로 가장 적절한 것을 고르시오.

① (A)-(C)-(B)　　　　　　　　　　② (B)-(A)-(C)

③ (B)-(C)-(A)　　　　　　　　　　④ (C)-(A)-(B)

⑤ (C)-(B)-(A)

The growing complexity of computer software has direct implications for our global safety and security, particularly as the physical objects (upon which we depend) — things like cars, airplanes, bridges, tunnels, and implantable medical devices — transform themselves into computer code.

(A) As all this code grows in size and complexity, so too do the number of errors and software bugs. According to a study by Carnegie Mellon University, commercial software typically has twenty to thirty bugs for every thousand lines of code — 50 million lines of code means 1 million to 1.5 million potential errors to be exploited.

(B) This is the basis for all malware attacks (that take advantage of these computer bugs to get the code to do something it was not originally intended to do.) As computer code grows more elaborate, software bugs flourish and security suffers, with increasing consequences for society at large.

(C) Physical things are increasingly becoming information technologies. Cars are "computer we ride in," and airplanes are nothing more than "flying Solaris boxes attached to bucketfuls of industrial control system."

핵심 문장인 이유

"The growing complexity of computer software has direct implications for our global safety and security" 문장은 컴퓨터 프로그램이 점점 더 복잡해지는 것이 우리의 안전과 보안에 직접적인 영향을 미치고 있다는 걸 의미한다. 이는 프로그램이 복잡해질수록 안전과 보안 문제가 더 중요해진다는 내용이므로 핵심 문장에 해당한다.

본문 해설

(C)는 주어진 문장이 이야기하는 컴퓨터 코드의 복잡성이 증가하고 있는 현상을 더욱 구체화하고 확장한다. 주어진 문장에서 "physical objects"가 (C)의 "physical things"로 연결된다.

(A)는 이 변화의 결과로서 소프트웨어의 크기와 복잡성이 증가함에 따라 오류와 소프트웨어 버그의 수가 늘어나고 있다는 점을 지적한다. 이는 컴퓨터 코드의 복잡성 증가에 따른 구체적인 문제를 지적하며, 특정 연구를 통해 이를 뒷받침한다.

(B)는 이런 문제들이 어떻게 사회에 영향을 미치는지에 대해 논의한다. 컴퓨터 코드가 점점 더 복잡해짐에 따라 소프트웨어 버그가 증가하고 보안이 악화되며, 이는 전체 사회에 점점 더 심각한 "consequence(결과)"를 초래하고 있다는 점을 강조한다.

문제 풀이 전략

연결고리를 찾는 것이 중요하다. 주로 맨 앞과 끝의 문장의 비중이 크다. 문단이 서로 유기적으로 연결되기 위해서는 언급된 내용이 다른 방식으로 서술되기 때문이다. 각 문단마다 핵심을 옆에 적고 연결 관계를 고려해 보는 것도 좋다.

정답 ④

The growing complexity of computer software has direct implications for our global safety and security, particularly as the physical objects upon which we depend — things like cars, airplanes, bridges, tunnels, and implantable medical devices — transform themselves into computer code. (①) Physical things are increasingly becoming information technologies. (②) Cars are "computer we ride in," and airplanes are nothing more than "flying Solaris boxes attached to bucketfuls of industrial control system." As all this code grows in size and complexity, so too do the number of errors and software bugs. (③) According to a study by Carnegie Mellon University, commercial software typically has twenty to thirty bugs for every thousand lines of code — 50 million lines of code means 1 million to 1.5 million potential errors to be exploited. (④) As computer code grows more elaborate, software bugs flourish and security suffers, with increasing consequences for society at large. (⑤)

수능형

윗글의 주제로 가장 적절한 것은?

① Increasing software complexity's impact on privacy
② Positive vision of physical objects transforming into complex computer code
③ Software capability as a breeding ground for malware threats
④ The need to improve system vulnerability
⑤ The societal consequences of escalating software bugs due to code complexity

내신형

글의 흐름으로 보아, 주어진 문장이 들어가기에 가장 적절한 곳을 고르시오.

This is the basis for all malware attacks that take advantage of these computer bugs to get the code to do something it was not originally intended to do.

"As all this code grows in size and complexity, so too do the number of errors and software bugs." 문장은 컴퓨터 코드의 크기와 복잡성의 증가가 오류와 소프트웨어 버그의 증가로 이어진다는 내용을 담고 있다.

또한, 마지막 문장인 "As computer code grows more elaborate, software bugs flourish and security suffers, with increasing consequences for society at large." 문장은 컴퓨터 소프트웨어의 복잡성 증가에 따른 사회적 영향을 강조한다.

따라서 복잡성으로 인한 버그 증가와 그로 인한 사회적 결과를 의미하는 ⑤번이 정답이다.

정답 ⑤

주어진 문장은 악성 소프트웨어가 소프트웨어 버그를 어떻게 이용하는지에 대해 설명하고 있다. 따라서 (④) 앞부분에서 상업용 소프트웨어에서 잠재적인 오류 수에 대한 설명이 언급된 이후에 (④)에서 논리적으로 이어져야 한다.

정답 ④

문단 내 글의 순서 파악하기 CASE 02

난이도 ★★★☆☆

Experts have identified a large number of measures that promote energy efficiency. **Unfortunately many of them are not cost effective. This is a fundamental requirement for energy efficiency investment from an economic perspective**.

(A) And this has direct repercussions at the individual level: households can reduce the cost of electricity and gas bills, and improve their health and comfort, while companies can increase their competitiveness and their productivity. Finally, the market for energy efficiency could contribute to the economy through job and firms creation.

(B) There are significant externalities to take into account and there are also macroeconomic effects. For instance, at the aggregate level, improving the level of national energy efficiency has positive effects on macroeconomic issues such as energy dependence, climate change, health, national competitiveness and reducing fuel poverty.

(C) However, the calculation of such cost effectiveness is not easy: it is not simply a case of looking at private costs and comparing them to the reductions achieved.

주어진 글 다음에 이어질 글의 순서로 가장 적절한 것을 고르시오.

① (A) - (C) - (B)　　　　　　　② (B) - (A) - (C)

③ (B) - (C) - (A)　　　　　　　④ (C) - (A) - (B)

⑤ (C) - (B) - (A)

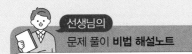
Experts have identified a large number of measures that promote energy efficiency. Unfortunately many of them are not cost effective. This is a fundamental requirement for energy efficiency investment from an economic perspective.

(A) And this has direct repercussions at the individual level: households can reduce the cost of electricity and gas bills, and improve their health and comfort, while companies can increase their competitiveness and their productivity. Finally, the market for energy efficiency could contribute to the economy through job and firms creation.

(B) There are significant externalities to take into account and there are also macroeconomic effects. For instance, at the aggregate level, improving the level of national energy efficiency has positive effects on macroeconomic issues such as energy dependence, climate change, health, national competitiveness and reducing fuel poverty.

(C) However, the calculation (of such cost effectiveness) is not easy: it is not simply a case of looking at private costs and comparing them to the reductions achieved.

핵심 문장인 이유

"Unfortunately many of them are not cost effective. This is a fundamental requirement for energy efficiency investment from an economic perspective." 문장은 에너지 효율성을 증진시키는 많은 방안들이 비용 효과적이지 않다는 문제점을 시작으로 글이 전개되기 때문에 핵심 문장에 해당한다.

본문 해설

주어진 문단에서 비용 효율성을 "a fundamental requirement(근본적인 요구사항)"라고 강조하고 있다. 다음에 이어질 내용은 비용 효율성일 것이다.

(C)에서는 "비용 효율성의 한계점(the calculation of such cost effectiveness is not easy)"에 대해 언급하고 있다.
(B)에서는 "외부성(externalities)"과 "거시경제적인 효과(macroeconomic effects)"를 언급하며 단순한 비교만으로는 계산이 어렵다는 비용 효율성의 한계점을 좀 더 구체적으로 설명하고 있다. 다음에 이어지는 내용은 거시경제성에 대한 설명이 이어질 것이다.
(A)에서는 국가가 가지는 거시경제성이 개인에게 긍정적인 효과가 있다는 내용이다.

문제 풀이 전략

연결고리를 찾는 것이 중요하다. 주로 맨 앞과 끝의 문장의 비중이 크다. 문단이 서로 유기적으로 연결되기 위해서는 언급된 내용이 다른 방식으로 서술되기 때문이다. 각 문단마다 핵심을 옆에 적고 연결 관계를 고려해 보는 것도 좋다.

정답 ⑤

Experts have identified a large number of measures that promote energy efficiency. Unfortunately many of them are not cost ① effective. This is a fundamental requirement for energy efficiency investment from an economic perspective. However, the calculation of such cost effectiveness is not ② easy: it is not simply a case of looking at private costs and comparing them to the reductions achieved. There are significant externalities to take into account and there are also ③ macroeconomic effects. For instance, at the aggregate level, improving the level of national energy efficiency has positive effects on macroeconomic issues such as energy dependence, climate change, health, national competitiveness and reducing fuel ④ abundance. And (A) this has direct repercussions at the individual level: households can reduce the cost of electricity and gas bills, and improve their health and comfort, while companies can increase their competitiveness and their productivity. Finally, the market for energy ⑤ efficiency could contribute to the economy through job and firms creation.

수능형

윗글의 밑줄 친 부분 중, 문맥상 낱말의 쓰임이 적절하지 <u>않은</u> 것은?

내신형

윗글의 밑줄 친 (A)가 가리키는 말을 본문에서 찾아 쓰시오.

➡ _____

국가의 에너지 효율성을 향상시키는 것은 긍정적인 영향력을 가지기 때문에 연료의 '풍족함'을 감소시키는 것은 적절하지 않다. 따라서 'abundance' → 'poverty'로 해야 한다.

> 아래의 프롬프트를 챗GPT에 입력해 보세요.
> "'abundance'의 유의어와 반의어를 3개씩 알려줘."

정답 ④

거시경제 문제에 긍정적인 영향을 미치는 주체가 'National energy efficiency improvement'이다. 가정에서 전기와 가스 비용을 줄이는 긍정적인 효과를 언급하고 있으므로, 대명사 'this'는 'National energy efficiency improvement'를 가리킨다.

정답 National energy efficiency improvement

문단 내 글의 순서 파악하기   CASE 03

난이도 ★★★☆☆

> **Recently, a number of commercial ventures have been launched that offer social robots as personal home assistants, perhaps eventually to rival existing smart-home assistants**.

(A) They might be motorized and can track the user around the room, giving the impression of being aware of the people in the environment. Although personal robotic assistants provide services similar to those of smart-home assistants, their socal presence offers an opportunity that is unique to social robots.

(B) Personal robotic assistants are devices that have no physical manipulation or locomotion capabilities. Instead, they have a distinct social presence and have visual features suggestive of their ability to interact socially, such as eyes, ears, or a mouth.

(C) For instance, in addition to playing music, a social personal assistant robot would express its engagement with the music so that users would feel like they are listening to the music together with the robot. These robots can be used as surveillance devices, acts as communicative intermediates, engage in richer games, tell stories, or be used to provide encouragement or incentives.

주어진 글 다음에 이어질 글의 순서로 가장 적절한 것을 고르시오.

① (A)－(C)－(B)　　　　　　② (B)－(A)－(C)
③ (B)－(C)－(A)　　　　　　④ (C)－(A)－(B)
⑤ (C)－(B)－(A)

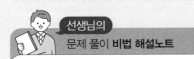
Recently, a number of commercial ventures have been launched that offer social robots as personal home assistants, perhaps eventually to rival existing smart-home assistants.

(A) They might be motorized and can track the user around the room, giving the impression of being aware of the people in the environment. Although personal robotic assistants provide services similar to those of smart-home assistants, their socal presence offers an opportunity that is unique to social robots.

(B) Personal robotic assistants are devices that have no physical manipulation or locomotion capabilities. Instead, they have a distinct social presence and have visual features suggestive of their ability to interact socially, such as eyes, ears, or a mouth.

(C) For instance, in addition to playing music, a social personal assistant robot would express its engagement with the music so that users would feel like they are listening to the music together with the robot. These robots can be used as surveillance devices, acts as communicative intermediates, engage in richer games, tell stories, or be used to provide encouragement or incentives.

핵심 문장인 이유

"Recently, a number of commercial ventures have been launched that offer social robots as personal home assistants, perhaps eventually to rival existing smart-home assistants." 이 문장은 사회적 로봇이 상업적인 차원에서의 상호작용을 언급하고, 글의 주제인 로봇의 특성과 기능에 대해 맥락을 제공할 수 있으므로 핵심 문장에 해당한다.

본문 해설

주어진 문단에서 로봇이 개인용 가정 도우미의 역할을 함으로써 경쟁력을 가진다는 내용이다. 따라서 이어질 내용은 로봇의 특성과 기능에 대한 소개로 예상해 볼 수 있다.

(B)에서는 신체 조작이나 이동 능력이 없다는 내용으로 개인용 로봇 도우미의 물리적 특징을 언급하고 있다. 물리적 특징 대신, 상호작용할 수 있는 능력을 통해 사회적 존재감을 가진다는 내용을 언급한다. 따라서 주어진 문단에 바로 이어지는 것이 자연스럽다.
(A)에서는 (B)에서 언급한 로봇이 사회적 존재감을 어떤 식으로 가지는지 구체적으로 설명하고 있고, 스마트홈 도우미와 비교하며 차이점(an opportunity that is unique to social robots)을 제시한다. 따라서 (B) 다음에 이어지는 것이 자연스럽다.
(C)에서는 'For instance' 표현을 사용하여, 스마트홈 도우미와의 차이점을 구체적으로 설명하고 있다. 따라서 (A) 다음에 이어지는 것이 자연스럽다.

문제 풀이 전략

연결고리를 찾는 것이 중요하다. 주로 맨 앞과 끝의 문장의 비중이 크다. 문단이 서로 유기적으로 연결되기 위해서는 언급된 내용이 다른 방식으로 서술되기 때문이다. 각 문단마다 핵심을 옆에 적고 연결 관계를 고려해 보는 것도 좋다.

정답 ②

Recently, a number of commercial ventures have been launched ① <u>that</u> offer social robots as personal home assistants, perhaps eventually to rival existing smart-home assistants. Personal robotic assistants are devices ② <u>that</u> have no physical manipulation or locomotion capabilities. Instead, they have a distinct social presence and have visual features suggestive of their ability to interact socially, such as eyes, ears, or a mouth. They might be motorized and can track the user around the room, giving the impression of being aware of the people in the environment. Although personal robotic assistants provide services ③ <u>that</u> are similar to those of smart-home assistants, their socal presence offers an opportunity ④ <u>that</u> is unique to social robots. For instance, in addition to playing music, a social personal assistant robot would express its engagement with the music so ⑤ <u>that</u> users would feel like they are listening to the music together with the robot. These robots can be used as surveillance devices, acts as communicative intermediates, engage in richer games, tell stories, or be used to provide encouragement or incentives.

수능형

윗글의 제목으로 가장 적절한 것은?

① Transforming Home Assistance: The Advent of Social Robots
② Virtual Assistants: The Dominance of Smart Homes
③ Innovation in Personal Healthcare: Role of AI Devices
④ Digital Assistants: A Threat to Privacy?
⑤ Internet of Things: Transforming Modern Living

내신형

윗글의 밑줄 친 ①~⑤ 중, 성격이 <u>다른</u> 하나는?

기존의 스마트홈 도우미와 달리 사회적 존재감을 가진 로봇의 등장을 주제로 하고 있으므로, 'Transforming Home Assistance: The Advent of Social Robots(홈 어시스턴스의 변화: 사회적 로봇의 등장)'이 가장 적절하다.

> 🎓 **아래의 프롬프트를 챗GPT에 입력해 보세요.**
> "이 글의 주제를 영어로 아주 간략하게 적어줘."

정답 ①

---

①~④는 주격관계대명사 'that'이다. ⑤는 'so that~(~하도록)'의 의미를 가지는 목적의 부사절 접속사 'that'이다. 주격관계대명사가 이끄는 절은 주어가 없지만, 접속사가 이끄는 절은 완전한 구조를 가진다.

> 🎓 **아래의 프롬프트를 챗GPT에 입력해 보세요.**
> "접속사 that과 주격관계대명사 that이 사용된 문장을 각 5개씩 알려줘."
> "접속사와 관계대명사의 차이를 알려줘."
> "'so that ~' 구문이 사용된 예문을 5개 알려줘."

정답 ⑤

유형 **14**

문단 내 글의 순서 파악하기   CASE 04

기출문제
정복하기

2019년 9월
평가원
36번 문제

난이도 ★★★☆☆

Most of us have a general, rational sense of what to eat and when — there is no shortage of information on the subject.

(A) ***Emotional eating* is a popular term used to describe eating that is influenced by emotions, both positive and negative**. Feelings may affect various aspects of your eating, including your motivation to eat, your food choices, where and with whom you eat, and the speed at which you eat. Most overeating is prompted by feelings rather than physical hunger.

(B) Yet there is often a disconnect between what we know and what we do. We may have the facts, but decisions also involve our feelings. Many people who struggle with difficult emotions also struggle with eating problems.

(C) Individuals who struggle with obesity tend to eat in response to emotions. However, people who eat for emotional reasons are not necessarily overweight. People of any size may try to escape an emotional experience by preoccupying themselves with eating or by obsessing over their shape and weight.

주어진 글 다음에 이어질 글의 순서로 가장 적절한 것을 고르시오.

① (A)-(C)-(B)   ② (B)-(A)-(C)
③ (B)-(C)-(A)   ④ (C)-(A)-(B)
⑤ (C)-(B)-(A)

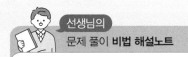
Most of us have a general, rational sense of what to eat and when — there is no shortage of information on the subject.

(A) ***Emotional eating* is a popular term used to describe eating** that is influenced by emotions, both positive and negative. Feelings may affect various aspects of your eating, including your motivation to eat, your food choices, where and with whom you eat, and the speed at which you eat. Most overeating is prompted by feelings rather than physical hunger.

(B) Yet there is often a disconnect between what we know and what we do. We may have the facts, but decisions also involve our feelings. Many people who struggle with difficult emotions also struggle with eating problems.

(C) Individuals who struggle with obesity tend to eat in response to emotions. However, people who eat for emotional reasons are not necessarily overweight. People of any size may try to escape an emotional experience by preoccupying themselves with eating or by obsessing over their shape and weight.

핵심 문장인 이유

"Emotional eating is a popular term used to describe eating that is influenced by emotions, both positive and negative."
이 문장은 감정적인 식사가 무엇인지 정의하고 있으며, 이후의 문단들이 더 자세히 설명하고 확장하는 데 기반을 제공하기 때문에 핵심 문장에 해당한다.

본문 해설

주어진 문단에서 먹는 행위에 대해 이성적인 감정이 있다고 언급한다. 그 말은 즉, 대상에 대한 정보가 충분하기 때문에 이성적으로 행동할 수 있다는 걸 의미한다.

(B)에서는 'Yet(그러나)'을 사용하여 지식과 실제 행동 사이의 차이를 언급하며 감정에 어려움을 겪는 사람들이 'eating problem'를 겪는다고 한다. 따라서 주어진 문단 다음에 (B)가 오는 것이 적절하다.
(A)에서는 'eating problem'을 감정과 연관시킨 'emotional eating'을 소개하며 감정과 식사 사이의 연결을 구체화한다.
(C)에서는 감정적 식사가 비만에만 국한되지 않고 모든 체형의 사람들에게 영향을 미칠 수 있다고 언급한다. 이는 (A)의 내용을 확장시킨다. 따라서 'emotional eating'를 언급한 (A) 뒤에 오는 것이 적절하다.

문제 풀이 전략

연결고리를 찾는 것이 중요하다. 주로 맨 앞과 끝의 문장의 비중이 크다. 문단이 서로 유기적으로 연결되기 위해서는 언급된 내용이 다른 방식으로 서술되기 때문이다. 각 문단마다 핵심을 옆에 적고 연결 관계를 고려해 보는 것도 좋다.

정답 ②

Most of us have a general, rational sense of what to eat and when — there is no shortage of information on the subject. Yet there is often a disconnect between what we know and what we do. We may have the facts, but decisions also involve our feelings. Many people who ① struggle with difficult emotions also struggle with eating problems. *Emotional eating* is a popular term ② used to describe eating that is influenced by emotions, both positive and negative. Feelings may affect various aspects of your eating, including your motivation to eat, your food choices, where and with ③ whom you eat, and the speed at ④ which you eat. Most overeating is prompted by feelings rather than physical hunger. Individuals who struggle with obesity tend to eat in response to emotions. However, people who eat for emotional reasons are not necessarily overweight. People of any size may try to escape an emotional experience by preoccupying ⑤ them with eating or by obsessing over their shape and weight.

윗글의 밑줄 친 부분 중, 어법상 틀린 것은?

Most of us have a general, rational sense of what to eat and when — there is no shortage of information on the subject. (①) We may have the facts, but decisions also involve our feelings. Many people who struggle with difficult emotions also struggle with eating problems. (②) *Emotional eating* is a popular term used to describe eating that is influenced by emotions, both positive and negative. (③) Feelings may affect various aspects of your eating, including your motivation to eat, your food choices, where and with whom you eat, and the speed at which you eat. (④) Most overeating is prompted by feelings rather than physical hunger. Individuals who struggle with obesity tend to eat in response to emotions. (⑤) People of any size may try to escape an emotional experience by preoccupying themselves with eating or by obsessing over their shape and weight.

글의 흐름으로 보아, 주어진 문장이 들어가기에 가장 적절한 곳을 고르시오.

However, people who eat for emotional reasons are not necessarily overweight.

'preoccupy(몰두하다)'의 목적어가 의미상의 주어인 'people'과 같기 때문에 'them' → 'themselves'으로 고쳐야 한다.

① 관계절의 동사는 선행사 수의 일치시킨다. 선행사가 'Many people'로 복수명사이기 때문에 'struggle'은 옳다.

② 'a popular term'을 수식하는 과거분사 'used'는 옳다.

③ 'You eat with whom'을 간접의문문의 어순으로 나타내면 'with whom you eat'이 옳다.

④ 'You eat at the speed'에서 'the speed'가 선행사로 된다. 그러므로 the speed를 수식하는 관계절이 오려면 'the speed'를 대신하고 'you eat'을 연결시켜 주는 관계대명사 'which'를 사용해야 한다.

> 🔁 아래의 프롬프트를 챗GPT에 입력해 보세요.
> "현재분사와 과거분사의 차이점을 알려줘."
> "간접의문문이 사용된 예문 5개를 알려줘."

정답 ⑤

주어진 문장은 감정적인 이유로 먹는 사람들이 반드시 과체중이지는 않다는 내용이다. (⑤) 뒤에 문장은 모든 체형의 사람들이 자신의 체형과 체중에 집착함으로써 감정적인 것에서 벗어나려고 노력하는 내용이 있다. 이는 과체중에서 벗어나려는 시도로 해석할 수 있다. 따라서 주어진 문장의 위치는 (⑤)이 적절하다.

정답 ⑤

PART
05

장문 독해

유형 15 장문 독해(기본편)

기출문제 정복하기

2022년 수능 41~42번 문제

난이도 ★★☆☆☆

Classifying things together into groups is something we do all the time, and it isn't hard to see why. Imagine trying to shop in a supermarket where the food was arranged in random order on the shelves: tomato soup next to the white bread in one aisle, chicken soup in the back next to the 60-watt light bulbs, one brand of cream cheese in front and another in aisle 8 near the cookies. The task of finding what you want would be (a) <u>time-consuming</u> and extremely difficult, if not impossible.

In the case of a supermarket, someone had to (b) <u>design</u> the system of classification. But there is also a ready-made system of classification embodied in our language. The word "dog," for example, groups together a certain class of animals and distinguishes them from other animals. Such a grouping may seem too (c) <u>abstract</u> to be called a classification, but this is only because you have already mastered the word. As a child learning to speak, you had to work hard to (d) <u>learn</u> the system of classification your parents were trying to teach you. Before you got the hang of it, you probably made mistakes, like calling the cat a dog. If you hadn't learned to speak, the whole world would seem like the (e) <u>unorganized</u> supermarket; you would be in the position of an infant, for whom every object is new and unfamiliar. **In learning the principles of classification, therefore, we'll be learning about the structure that lies at the core of our language**.

1. 윗글의 제목으로 가장 적절한 것은?

① Similarities of Strategies in Sales and Language Learning
② Classification: An Inherent Characteristic of Language
③ Exploring Linguistic Issues Through Categorization
④ Is a Ready-Made Classification System Truly Better?
⑤ Dilemmas of Using Classification in Language Education

2. 밑줄 친 (a)~(e) 중에서 문맥상 낱말의 쓰임이 적절하지 <u>않은</u> 것은?

① (a)　　　　② (b)　　　　③ (c)　　　　④ (d)　　　　⑤ (e)

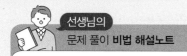
Classifying things together into groups is something we do all the time, and it isn't hard to see why. Imagine trying to shop in a supermarket (where the food was arranged in random order on the shelves: tomato soup next to the white bread in one aisle, chicken soup in the back next to the 60-watt light bulbs, one brand of cream cheese in front and another in aisle 8 near the cookies.) The task of finding what you want would be (a) time-consuming and extremely difficult, if not impossible.

In the case of a supermarket, someone had to (b) design the system of classification. But there is also a ready-made system of classification embodied in our language. The word "dog," for example, groups together a certain class of animals and distinguishes them from other animals. Such a grouping may seem too (c) abstract to be called a classification, but this is only because you have already mastered the word. As a child learning to speak, you had to work hard to (d) learn the system of classification your parents were trying to teach you. Before you got the hang of it, you probably made mistakes, like calling the cat a dog. If you hadn't learned to speak, the whole world would seem like the (e) unorganized supermarket; you would be in the position of an infant, for whom every object is new and unfamiliar. In learning the principles of classification, therefore, we'll be learning about (the structure that lies at the core of our language.)

핵심 문장인 이유

"In learning the principles of classification, therefore, we'll be learning about the structure that lies at the core of our language." 이 문장은 언어를 배우는 과정에서 분류 체계의 중요성을 강조하는 요지를 집약하고 있으므로 핵심 문장에 해당한다.

본문 해설

1. 언어 내에서의 분류 시스템이 어떻게 작동하는지, 그리고 그것이 어떻게 언어 학습과 일상생활에 중요한 역할을 하는지에 대한 내용을 잘 요약해주기 때문에 ② Classification: An Inherent Characteristic of Language이 제목으로 가장 적절하다.

2. 이미 만들어진 분류체계를 구체적으로 'dog'라는 단어로 설명한다. 특정 부류의 동물들을 함께 분류하여 다른 동물들과 구별한다. 특정 단어를 숙달했기 때문에 추상적으로 보이는 것이 아니라 명백하게 보이는 것이 적절하다. 따라서 'abstract' → 'obvious'로 바꾸는 것이 적절하다.

문제 풀이 전략

1. 키워드를 중심으로 제시된 예시의 핵심 내용을 파악해야 한다.

2. 지문에 나오는 소재나 문제에 대해 긍정적인지 부정적인지를 우선적으로 파악해야 한다.

Classifying things together into groups is something we do all the time, and it isn't hard to see why. (①) Imagine trying to shop in a supermarket where the food was arranged in random order on the shelves: tomato soup next to the white bread in one aisle, chicken soup in the back next to the 60-watt light bulbs, one brand of cream cheese in front and another in aisle 8 near the cookies. The task of finding what you want would be time-consuming and extremely difficult, if not impossible. (②)

In the case of a supermarket, someone had to design the system of classification. (③) The word "dog," for example, groups together a certain class of animals and distinguishes them from other animals. Such a grouping may seem too obvious to be called a classification, but this is only because you have already mastered the word. (④) As a child learning to speak, you had to work hard to learn the system of classification your parents were trying to teach you. Before you got the hang of it, you probably made mistakes, like calling the cat a dog. If you hadn't learned to speak, the whole world would seem like the unorganized supermarket; you would be in the position of an infant, for whom every object is new and unfamiliar. (⑤) In learning the principles of classification, therefore, we'll be learning about the structure that lies at the core of our language.

수능형

윗글의 내용을 한 문장으로 요약하고자 한다. 빈칸 (A), (B)에 들어갈 말로 가장 적절한 것은?

Classification systems, like those we learn through language, bring order and ____(A)____ to our world. Without them, navigating life would be as chaotic as searching for groceries in an ____(B)____ supermarket.

(A)	(B)		(A)	(B)
① adapting	········ structured		② coming	········ increased
③ understanding	········ disordered		④ referring	········ unorganized
⑤ contributing	········ specialized			

내신형

글의 흐름으로 보아, 주어진 문장이 들어가기에 가장 적절한 곳을 고르시오.

But there is also a ready-made system of classification embodied in our language.

이 지문은 언어를 통해 배우는 분류 체계가 세상을 이해하는데 도움을 준다는 것이고, 분류 체계가 없을 경우 우리의 삶을 무질서한 슈퍼마켓에 비유하여 정보를 쉽게 찾거나 이해하지 못한다는 내용이다. 따라서 'understanding(이해)', 'disordered(무질서한)'가 정답이다.

> 🔖 아래의 프롬프트를 챗GPT에 입력해 보세요.
>
> "위의 지문을 굉장히 짧은 영어 문장으로 요약해줘. 문장의 개수는 2개 정도로 해줘."

정답 ③

주어진 문장은 언어 속에 이미 만들어진 분류체계가 있다는 내용이다. 따라서 뒤에 이어질 내용은 언어(단어)로 인해 분류체계가 이루어진다는 내용이 와야 하므로, (③)이 가장 적절하다. (③)뒤에 이어지는 내용은 단어 'dog'를 사용하여 분류체계가 이루어진다는 구체적인 내용을 담고 있기 때문이다.

정답 ③

장문 독해(기본편)

CASE 02

난이도 ★★★☆☆

In many mountain regions, rights of access to water are associated with the possession of land — until recently in the Andes, for example, land and water rights were (a) underlined combined so water rights were transferred with the land. **However, through state land reforms and the development of additional sources of supply, water rights have become separated from land, and may be sold at auction.** This therefore (b) favours those who can pay, rather than ensuring access to all in the community. The situation arises, therefore, where individuals may hold land with no water. In Peru, the government grants water to communities separately from land, and it is up to the community to allocate it. Likewise in Yemen, the traditional allocation was one measure (*tasah*) of water to one hundred '*libnah*' of land. This applied only to traditional irrigation supplies — from runoff, wells, etc., where a supply was (c) guaranteed. Water derived from the capture of flash floods is not subject to Islamic law as this constitutes an certain source, and is therefore free for those able to collect and use it. However, this traditional allocation per unit of land has been bypassed, partly by the development of new supplies, but also by the (d) decrease in cultivation of a crop of substantial economic importance. This crop is harvested throughout the year and thus required more than its fair share of water. The economic status of the crop (e) ensures that water rights can be bought or bribed away from subsistence crops.

1. 윗글의 제목으로 가장 적절한 것은?

① Water Rights No Longer Tied to Land

② Strategies for Trading Water Rights

③ Water Storage Methods: Mountain vs. Desert

④ Water Supplies Not stable in Mountain Regions

⑤ Unending Debates: Which Crop We Should Grow

2. 밑줄 친 (a)~(e) 중에서 문맥상 낱말의 쓰임이 적절하지 <u>않은</u> 것은?

① (a)   ② (b)   ③ (c)   ④ (d)   ⑤ (e)

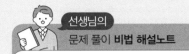
   In many mountain regions, rights of access to water are associated with the possession of land —
until recently in the Andes, for example, land and water rights were (a) combined so water rights
were transferred with the land. However, (through state land reforms and the development of
additional sources of supply,) water rights have become separated from land, and may be sold at
auction. This therefore (b) favours those who can pay, rather than ensuring access to all in the
community. The situation arises, therefore, where individuals may hold land with no water. In Peru,
the government grants water to communities separately from land, and it is up to the community to
allocate it. Likewise in Yemen, the traditional allocation was one measure (*tasah*) of water to one
hundred '*libnah*' of land. This applied only to traditional irrigation supplies — from runoff, wells,
etc., where a supply was (c) guaranteed. Water derived from the capture of flash floods is not
subject to Islamic law as this constitutes an certain source, and is therefore free for those able to
collect and use it. However, this traditional allocation per unit of land has been bypassed, partly by
the development of new supplies, but also by the (d) decrease in cultivation of a crop of substantial
economic importance. This crop is harvested throughout the year and thus required more than its
fair share of water. The economic status of the crop (e) ensures that water rights can be bought or
bribed away from subsistence crops.

핵심 문장인 이유

"However, through state land reforms and the development of additional sources of supply, water rights have become
separated from land, and may be sold at auction." 이 문장은 물에 대한 접근 권리가 이전의 전통적인 방식에서 경제적 지위에 기
초한 방식으로 변화하고 있다는 내용을 나타내므로 핵심 문장에 해당한다.

본문 해설

1. 많은 산악 지역에서는 물에 대한 접근 권리가 토지 소유와 연결되어 있었다. 하지만 국가의 토지 개혁과 새로운 공급원의 발전으로 인
   해 물 권리는 토지에서 분리되게 되었다. 따라서 ① Water Rights No Longer Tied to Land이 제목으로 가장 적절하다.

2. ④ 뒤에 오는 내용을 살펴보면, 작물이 일년 내내 수확되므로 물이 공정하게 배분되는 것보다 더 많이 필요로 되고, 이로 인해 작물의
   경제적 지위로 인해 물에 대한 권리를 살 수 있도록 보장한다. 이는 작물의 재배 감소가 아닌 증가로 인해 이러한 상황이 만들어진 걸로
   볼 수 있다. 따라서 'decrease' → 'increase'로 바꾸는 것이 적절하다.

문제 풀이 전략

1. 키워드를 중심으로 제시된 예시의 핵심 내용을 파악해야 한다.

2. 지문에 나오는 소재나 문제에 대해 긍정적인지 부정적인지를 우선적으로 파악해야 한다.

In many mountain regions, rights of access to water are associated with the possession of land — until recently in the Andes, for example, land and water rights were combined so water rights were transferred with the land. However, through state land reforms and the development of additional sources of supply, Ⓐ water rights have become separated from land, and may be sold at auction. (①) This therefore favours those who can pay, rather than ensuring access to all in the community. (②) The situation arises, therefore, where individuals may hold land with no water. In Peru, the government grants water to communities separately from land, and it is up to the community to allocate it. (③) Likewise in Yemen, the traditional allocation was one measure (*tasah*) of water to one hundred '*libnah*' of land. This applied only to traditional irrigation supplies — from runoff, wells, etc., where a supply was guaranteed. (④) Water derived from the capture of flash floods is not subject to Islamic law as this constitutes an certain source, and is therefore free for those able to collect and use it. (⑤) This crop is harvested throughout the year and thus required more than its fair share of water. The economic status of the crop ensures that water rights can be bought or bribed away from subsistence crops.

수능형

글의 흐름으로 보아, 주어진 문장이 들어가기에 가장 적절한 곳을 고르시오.

However, this traditional allocation per unit of land has been bypassed, partly by the development of new supplies, but also by the increase in cultivation of a crop of substantial economic importance.

내신형

윗글의 밑줄 친 Ⓐ의 용법과 같은 것을 고르시오.

① I have already finished my homework.

② He has just cleaned the house.

③ She has gone to that new restaurant.

④ They have known each other since they were children.

⑤ I have visited France twice.

예멘을 예로 들어, 전통적으로 물 공급이 보장된 전통적인 농업 공급원에서만 물의 할당이 정해졌다. 그러나 (⑤)뒤에 이어지는 내용은 작물의 경제적 지위로 인해 물을 공정하게 배분받는 것보다 더 많이 필요하게 되었다는 내용이 등장하므로, 기존의 전통적인 물 공급으로 이루어질 수 없는 내용이 등장한다. 따라서 주어진 문장은 (⑤)이 적절하다.

정답 ⑤

밑줄 친 ⓐ 'She has gone to that new restaurant.(그녀는 그 새 식당으로 갔다)'는 완료시제 용법(완료, 계속, 경험, 결과) 중 '결과'이다.

① 'already(이미)'는 '완료'의 의미를 가진다.
② 'just(막)'는 '완료'의 의미를 가진다.
④ 'since'는 '계속'의 의미를 가진다.
⑤ 'twice(두 번)'은 '경험'의 의미를 가진다.

⚙ 아래의 프롬프트를 챗GPT에 입력해 보세요.
"완료시제 용법(완료, 계속, 경험, 결과) 예문을 각 5개씩 알려줘."

정답 ③

유형

15

장문 독해(기본편)

기출문제
정복하기

2022년 9월
평가원
41~42번 문제

CASE 03

난이도 ★★★☆☆

In studies examining the effectiveness of vitamin C, researchers typically divide the subjects into two groups. One group (the experimental group) receives a vitamin C supplement, and the other (the control group) does not. Researchers observe both groups to determine whether one group has fewer or shorter colds than the other. The following discussion describes some of the pitfalls inherent in an experiment of this kind and ways to (a) avoid them. In sorting subjects into two groups, researchers must ensure that each person has an (b) equal chance of being assigned to either the experimental group or the control group. This is accomplished by randomization; that is, the subjects are chosen randomly from the same population by flipping a coin or some other method involving chance. **Randomization helps to ensure that results reflect the treatment and not factors that might influence the grouping of subjects**. Importantly, the two groups of people must be similar and must have the same track record with respect to colds to (c) rule out the possibility that observed differences in the rate, severity, or duration of colds might have occurred anyway. If, for example, the control group would normally catch twice as many colds as the experimental group, then the findings prove (d) nothing. In experiments involving a nutrient, the diets of both groups must also be (e) different, especially with respect to the nutrient being studied. If those in the experimental group were receiving less vitamin C from their usual diet, then any effects of the supplement may not be apparent.

1. 윗글의 제목으로 가장 적절한 것은?

① Perfect Planning and Faulty Results: A Sad Reality in Research
② Don't Let Irrelevant Factors Influence the Results!
③ Protect Human Subjects Involved in Experimental Research!
④ What Nutrients Could Better Defend Against Colds?
⑤ In−depth Analysis of Nutrition: A Key Player for Human Health

2. 밑줄 친 (a)~(e) 중에서 문맥상 쓰임이 적절하지 <u>않은</u> 것은?

① (a)　　　　② (b)　　　　③ (c)　　　　④ (d)　　　　⑤ (e)

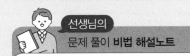
　　In studies examining the effectiveness of vitamin C, researchers typically divide the subjects into two groups. One group (the experimental group) receives a vitamin C supplement, and the other (the control group) does not. Researchers observe both groups to determine whether one group has fewer or shorter colds than the other. The following discussion describes some of the pitfalls inherent in an experiment of this kind and ways to (a) <u>avoid</u> them. In sorting subjects into two groups, researchers must ensure that each person has an (b) <u>equal</u> chance of being assigned to either the experimental group or the control group. This is accomplished by randomization; that is, the subjects are chosen randomly from the same population by flipping a coin or some other method involving chance. Randomization helps to ensure that results reflect the treatment and not factors that might influence the grouping of subjects. Importantly, the two groups of people must be similar and must have the same track record with respect to colds to (c) <u>rule out</u> the possibility that observed differences in the rate, severity, or duration of colds might have occurred anyway. If, for example, the control group would normally catch twice as many colds as the experimental group, then the findings prove (d) <u>nothing</u>. In experiments involving a nutrient, the diets of both groups must also be (e) <u>different</u>, especially with respect to the nutrient being studied. If those in the experimental group were receiving less vitamin C from their usual diet, then any effects of the supplement may not be apparent.

> **핵심 문장인 이유**

"Randomization helps to ensure that results reflect the treatment and not factors that might influence the grouping of subjects." 이 문장은 연구 설계에 근본적인 중요성을 가지는 무작위화에 대해 설명하고 있으므로 핵심 문장에 해당한다.

> **본문 해설**

1. 이 지문은 연구 설계에서 관련성이 없는 요인들이 결과에 어떻게 영향을 미칠 수 있는지, 그리고 이를 어떻게 피해야 하는지에 대해 설명하고 있다. 따라서 제목은 ② Don't Let Irrelevant Factors Influence the Results!(무관한 요인들이 결과에 영향을 미치게 하지 마라!)가 가장 적절하다.

2. 두 집단의 식단이 'different(다른)'이면 다른 식단 요소들도 감기의 발생과 지속에 영향을 줄 수 있다. 이는 비타민 C가 실제로 감기에 미치는 영향을 정확히 알아내지 못하게 하므로, 다른 모든 변수들은 가능한 한 'similar(비슷한)'하게 되어야 한다.

> **문제 풀이 전략**

1. 키워드를 중심으로 제시된 예시의 핵심 내용을 파악해야 한다.

2. 지문에 나오는 소재나 문제에 대해 긍정적인지 부정적인지를 우선적으로 파악해야 한다.

In studies examining the effectiveness of vitamin C, researchers typically divide the subjects into two groups. One group (the experimental group) receives a vitamin C supplement, and the other (the control group) does not. Researchers observe both groups ① <u>determine</u> whether one group has fewer or shorter colds than ② <u>the other</u>. The following discussion describes some of the pitfalls inherent in an experiment of this kind and ways to avoid ③ <u>them</u>. In sorting subjects into two groups, researchers must ensure that each person has an equal chance of ④ <u>being assigned</u> to either the experimental group or the control group. This is accomplished by randomization; that is, the subjects are chosen randomly from the same population by flipping a coin or some other method involving chance. Randomization helps to ensure that results reflect the treatment and not factors that might influence the grouping of subjects. Importantly, the two groups of people must be similar and must have the same track record with respect to colds to rule out the possibility that observed differences in the rate, severity, or duration of colds might have occurred anyway. If, for example, the control group would normally catch twice as many colds as the experimental group, then the findings prove nothing. In experiments involving a nutrient, the diets of both groups must also be similar, especially with respect to the nutrient ⑤ <u>being studied</u>. If those in the experimental group were receiving less vitamin C from their usual diet, then any effects of the supplement may not be apparent.

수능형

윗글의 밑줄 친 부분 중, 어법상 틀린 것은?

내신형

윗글의 내용을 한 문장으로 요약하고자 한다. 빈칸 (A), (B)에 들어갈 말로 가장 적절한 것은?

Researchers must ensure equal chance of assignment to the control or experimental group via randomization, to prevent ___(A)___ factors from skewing the results. It's critical that both groups have similar diets, especially in terms of the nutrient being examined, to ___(B)___ assess the effects of the supplement.

	(A)	(B)		(A)	(B)
①	influenced	properly	②	unrelated	precisely
③	unexpected	widely	④	independent	specifically
⑤	unprecedented	practically			

문장의 동사 'observe(관찰하다)'가 지각동사라서 원형부정사가 와야 한다는 실수를 유도하는 문제이다. 문장의 목적어 'both groups'가 'determine whether one group has fewer or shorter colds than the other.'한다는 건 의미상 적절하지 않다. 따라서 to 부정사 부사적용법(목적)인 'to determine ~ '이 적절하다.

② 두 개의 집단 중에서 먼저 언급된 집단을 제외하면 나머지 한 집단밖에 없으므로 'the other'은 적절하다.

③ 복수명사 'pitfalls'를 대신하는 명사 'them'은 적절하다.

④ 'an equal chance'를 수식하는 관계가 수동이고, 전치사 of의 목적어로 동명사 수동태인 'being assigned'는 적절하다.

⑤ 'the nutrient'와의 관계가 수동이므로 'being studied'는 적절하다.

정답 ①

연구자들은 집단을 설정하는 과정에서 연구결과를 왜곡하는 걸 방지해야 하므로 관련 없는 요인들을 방지해야 한다. 또한, 두 집단이 비슷한 식단을 유지해야 평가를 정확하게 할 수 있다는 점을 강조하므로 'unrelated'와 'precisely'가 적절하다.

> 아래의 프롬프트를 챗GPT에 입력해 보세요.
> "'irrelevant', 'accurately' 의 유의어를 각각 알려줘."

정답 ②

유형 15

기출문제
정복하기

2022년 6월
평가원
41~42번 문제

장문 독해(기본편)

CASE 04

난이도 ★★★☆☆

The right to privacy may extend only to the point where it does not restrict someone else's right to freedom of expression or right to information. The scope of the right to privacy is (a) similarly restricted by the general interest in preventing crime or in promoting public health. However, when we move away from the property-based notion of a right(where the right to privacy would protect, for example, images and personality), to modern notions of private and family life, we find it (b) easier to establish the limits of the right. This is, of course, the strength of the notion of privacy, in that it can adapt to meet changing expectations and technological advances.

In sum, what is privacy today? The concept includes a claim that we should be unobserved, and that certain information and images about us should not be (c) circulated without our permission. Why did these privacy claims arise? They arose because powerful people took offence at such observation. Furthermore, privacy incorporated the need to protect the family, home, and correspondence from arbitrary (d) interference and, in addition, there has been a determination to protect honour and reputation. How is privacy protected? Historically, privacy was protected by restricting circulation of the damaging material. But if the concept of privacy first became interesting legally as a response to reproductions of images through photography and newspapers, more recent technological advances, such as data storage, digital images, and the Internet, (e) pose new threats to privacy. **The right to privacy is now being reinterpreted to meet those challenges**.

1. 윗글의 제목으로 가장 적절한 것은?

① Side Effects of Privacy Protection Technologies
② The Legal Domain of Privacy Claims and Conflicts
③ The Right to Privacy: Evolving Concepts and Practices
④ Who Really Benefits from Looser Privacy Regulations?
⑤ Less Is More: Reduce State Intervention in Privacy!

2. 밑줄 친 (a)~(e) 중에서 문맥상 낱말의 쓰임이 적절하지 <u>않은</u> 것은?

① (a)　　② (b)　　③ (c)　　④ (d)　　⑤ (e)

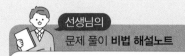
The right to privacy may extend only to the point where it does not restrict someone else's right to freedom of expression or right to information. The scope of the right to privacy is (a) similarly restricted by the general interest in preventing crime or in promoting public health. However, when we move away from the property-based notion of a right(where the right to privacy would protect, for example, images and personality), to modern notions of private and family life, we find it (b) easier to establish the limits of the right. This is, of course, the strength of the notion of privacy, in that it can adapt to meet changing expectations and technological advances.

In sum, what is privacy today? The concept includes a claim that we should be unobserved, and that certain information and images about us should not be (c) circulated without our permission. Why did these privacy claims arise? They arose because powerful people took offence at such observation. Furthermore, privacy incorporated the need to protect the family, home, and correspondence from arbitrary (d) interference and, in addition, there has been a determination to protect honour and reputation. How is privacy protected? Historically, privacy was protected by restricting circulation of the damaging material. But if the concept of privacy first became interesting legally as a response to reproductions of images through photography and newspapers, more recent technological advances, such as data storage, digital images, and the Internet, (e) pose new threats to privacy. The right to privacy is now being reinterpreted to meet those challenges.

핵심 문장인 이유

"The right to privacy is now being reinterpreted to meet those challenges." 이 문장은 개인정보보호에 대한 현대적인 문제의 변화와 이해를 요약하고 있으므로 핵심 문장에 해당한다.

본문 해설

1. 이 글은 개인정보보호가 시간이 지나며 어떻게 변화해 왔고, 최근 기술 발전에 따른 새로운 도전과 그에 대응하는 방법을 다루고 있다. 따라서 ③ The Right to Privacy: Evolving Concepts and Practices이 제목으로 가장 적절하다.

2. 이미지와 인격을 보호하는 것이 주요 목표인 'property-based notion of a right'와 'modern notions of private and family life'를 비교하는 부분이다. 현대 개념에서 privacy는 더 모호해진다. 따라서 개인정보보호의 경계를 설정하는 것이 더 어려워지므로 'easier' → 'more difficult'로 바꾸는 것이 적절하다.

문제 풀이 전략

1. 키워드를 중심으로 제시된 예시의 핵심 내용을 파악해야 한다.

2. 지문에 나오는 소재나 문제에 대해 긍정적인지 부정적인지를 우선적으로 파악해야 한다.

정답 1 ③　2 ②

The right to privacy may extend only to the point where it does not restrict someone else's right to freedom of expression or right to information. The scope of the right to privacy is similarly restricted by the general interest in preventing crime or in promoting public health. (①)   (A)   , when we move away from the property−based notion of a right(where the right to privacy would protect, for example, images and personality), to modern notions of private and family life, we find it more difficult to establish the limits of the right. (②) This is, of course, the strength of the notion of privacy, in that it can adapt to meet changing expectations and technological advances.

In sum, what is privacy today? (③) Why did these privacy claims arise? They arose because powerful people took offence at such observation.   (B)   , privacy incorporated the need to protect the family, home, and correspondence from arbitrary interference and, in addition, there has been a determination to protect honour and reputation. How is privacy protected? Historically, privacy was protected by restricting circulation of the damaging material. (④) But if the concept of privacy first became interesting legally as a response to reproductions of images through photography and newspapers, more recent technological advances, such as data storage, digital images, and the Internet, pose new threats to privacy. (⑤) The right to privacy is now being reinterpreted to meet those challenges.

수능형

글의 흐름으로 보아, 주어진 문장이 들어가기에 가장 적절한 곳을 고르시오.

The concept includes a claim that we should be unobserved, and that certain information and images about us should not be circulated without our permission.

내신형

윗글의 밑줄 친 (A), (B)에 들어갈 표현이 바르게 짝지어진 것을 고르시오.

	(A)	(B)		(A)	(B)
①	However	Besides	②	For instance	What's more
③	Thus	Shortly	④	By contrast	For example
⑤	Unfortunately	For example			

오늘날의 사생활의 개념을 묻는 질문에 대한 답이다. 뒤에 이어지는 'Why did these privacy claims arise?'에 대한 답으로는 'They arose because powerful people took offence at such observation.'가 등장한다. 따라서 주어진 문장을 (③)에 위치시켜야 글의 구조가 논리적이다.

정답 ③

(A) 뒤에 이어지는 내용은 privacy의 개념을 현대적으로 접근하고 있어서 기존의 privacy와 달라진 점을 언급하려 한다. 따라서 역접의 의미를 가지는 'However'가 적절하다.

(B) 뒤에 이어지는 내용은 개인정보보호가 임의적인 간섭으로부터 보호하는 필요성을 포함하고 있다는 추가적인 사실을 강조하고 있다. 앞부분에서는 개인적 관찰이나 침해에 대해 불편함을 느낀다고 미리 언급했기 때문에 추가적인 정보를 제공할 때 사용하는 'Besides'가 적절하다.

> 🙋 아래의 프롬프트를 챗GPT에 입력해 보세요.
> "'However', 'Besides'의 유의어를 각각 알려줘."

정답 ①

장문 독해(심화편)

CASE 01

난이도 ★★★☆☆

(A)

"Hailey, be careful!" Camila yelled uneasily, watching her sister carrying a huge cake to the table. "Don't worry, Camila," Hailey responded, smiling. Camila relaxed only when Hailey had safely placed the cake on the party table. "Dad will be here shortly. **What gift did (a) you buy for his birthday?**" Camila asked out of interest. "Dad will be surprised to find out what it is!" Hailey answered with a wink.

(B)

"Dad, these glasses can help correct your red-green color blindness," said Hailey. He slowly put them on, and stared at the birthday presents on the table. Seeing vivid red and green colors for the first time ever, he started to cry. "Incredible! Look at those wonderful colors!" He shouted in amazement. Hailey told him in tears, "Dad, I'm glad you can now finally enjoy the true beauty of rainbows and roses. Red represents love and green represents health. You deserve both." Camila nodded, seeing how happy (b) her gift of the glasses had made their dad.

(C)

"Happy birthday! You're fifty today, Dad. We love you!" Camila said before (c) her sister handed him a small parcel. When he opened it, he discovered a pair of glasses inside. "Hailey, Dad doesn't have eyesight problems," Camila said, puzzled. "Actually Camila, I recently found out he has long been suffering from color blindness. He's kept it a secret so as not to worry us," Hailey explained.

(D)

"I bet (d) you bought a wallet or a watch for him," Camila said. In reply, Hailey answered, "No. I bought something much more personal. By the way, there's something (e) you should know about Dad..." They were suddenly interrupted by the doorbell ringing. It was their dad and they were overjoyed to see him. "My lovely ladies, thank you for inviting me to your place for my birthday." He walked in joyfully, hugging his daughters. They all walked into the dining room, where he was greeted with a rainbow-colored birthday cake and fifty red roses.

1. 주어진 글 (A)에 이어질 내용을 순서에 맞게 배열한 것으로 가장 적절한 것은?

① (B)-(D)-(C)
② (C)-(B)-(D)
③ (C)-(D)-(B)
④ (D)-(B)-(C)
⑤ (D)-(C)-(B)

2. 밑줄 친 (a)~(e) 중에서 가리키는 대상이 나머지 넷과 <u>다른</u> 것은?

① (a)
② (b)
③ (c)
④ (d)
⑤ (e)

3. 윗글에 관한 내용으로 적절하지 <u>않은</u> 것은?

① Hailey는 생일 케이크를 테이블로 무사히 옮겨 놓았다.
② 아버지는 생일 선물로 받은 안경을 직접 써 보았다.
③ Hailey는 아버지가 색맹이라는 사실을 최근에 알게 되었다.
④ Hailey와 Camila는 아버지의 집을 방문하였다.
⑤ 아버지는 자신의 나이와 똑같은 수의 장미를 받았다.

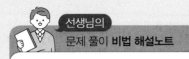
(A)

"Hailey, be careful!" Camila yelled uneasily, watching her sister carrying a huge cake to the table. "Don't worry, Camila," Hailey responded, smiling. Camila relaxed only when Hailey had safely placed the cake on the party table. "Dad will be here shortly. What gift did (a) you buy for his birthday?" Camila asked out of interest. "Dad will be surprised to find out what it is!" Hailey answered with a wink.

(B)

"Dad, these glasses can help correct your red-green color blindness," said Hailey. He slowly put them on, and stared at the birthday presents on the table. Seeing vivid red and green colors for the first time ever, he started to cry. "Incredible! Look at those wonderful colors!" He shouted in amazement. Hailey told him in tears, "Dad, I'm glad you can now finally enjoy the true beauty of rainbows and roses. Red represents love ① and green represents health ②. You deserve both ①+②." Camila nodded, (seeing how happy (b) her gift of the glasses had made their dad.)

(C)

"Happy birthday! You're fifty today, Dad. We love you!" Camila said before (c) her sister handed him a small parcel. When he opened it, he discovered a pair of glasses inside. "Hailey, Dad doesn't have eyesight problems," Camila said, puzzled. "Actually Camila, I recently found out he has long been suffering from color blindness. He's kept it a secret (so as not to worry us,)" Hailey explained.

(D)

"I bet (d) you bought a wallet or a watch for him," Camila said. In reply, Hailey answered, "No. I bought something (much more personal.) By the way, there's something (e) you should know about Dad..." They were suddenly interrupted by the doorbell ringing. It was their dad and they were overjoyed to see him. "My lovely ladies, thank you for inviting me to your place for my birthday." He walked in joyfully, hugging his daughters. They all walked into the dining room, (where he was greeted with a rainbow-colored birthday cake and fifty red roses.)

핵심 문장인 이유

"What gift did you buy for his birthday?" 이 문장은 처음 제시된 문단 (A)에서 다음 문단으로 이어질 때 필요한 내용을 담고 있다. 생일을 축하하는 배경이 제시되므로, 핵심 문장에 해당한다.

본문 해설

1. (A)에서 Camila가 Hailey의 선물에 대해 질문했으므로 다음에 이어질 내용은 선물에 대한 이야기가 이어질 것이다. 따라서 (D)에서 대사 "I bet you bought a wallet or a watch for him."가 이어지는 것이 적절하다. 바로 이어서 (B)가 오기에는 생일 선물에 대한 구체적인 언급이 나타나 어색하다. 따라서 (D)에 이어서 (C)가 이어져야 한다. (C)에서 아버지가 색맹이라는 사실을 언급하고 있다. 이어서 그에 맞는 선물인 안경을 쓰고 언급하는 (B)가 마지막으로 오는 것이 적절하다.
2. (a)~(d)는 Hailey이다. (e)는 Hailey가 대답을 이어 나가며 말하는 것이므로 'Camila'를 가리킨다.
3. Hailey와 Camila는 아버지의 집을 방문한 것이 아니라 아버지를 맞이하고 있으므로 ④번은 글의 내용과 일치하지 않는다.

문제 풀이 전략

장문 독해 지문은 시간적인 여유가 없는 상태에서 집중도가 흐트러질 수 있다. 주의해야 할 점은 각 문항마다 지문을 다시 보는 것이 아니라, 문항의 키워드를 정확히 확인하고 이를 상기시키며 지문을 읽어 나가야 한다.

정답 1 ⑤ 2 ⑤ 3 ④

"Hailey, be careful!" Camila yelled uneasily, watching her sister carrying a huge cake to the table. "Don't worry, Camila," Hailey responded, smiling. Camila relaxed only when Hailey had safely placed the cake on the party table. "Dad will be here shortly. What gift did you buy for his birthday?" Camila asked out of interest. "Dad will be surprised to find out ① what it is!" Hailey answered with a wink.

"I bet you bought a wallet or a watch for him," Camila said. In reply, Hailey answered, "No. I bought something much more personal. By the way, there's something you should know about Dad..." They were ② suddenly interrupted by the doorbell ringing. It was their dad and they were overjoyed to see him. "My lovely ladies, thank you for inviting me to your place for my birthday." He walked in joyfully, Ⓐ hugging his daughters. They all walked into the dining room, ③ in which he was greeted with a rainbow-colored birthday cake and fifty red roses.

"Happy birthday! You're fifty today, Dad. We love you!" Camila said before her sister handed him a small parcel. When he opened it, he discovered a pair of glasses inside. "Hailey, Dad doesn't have eyesight problems," Camila said, puzzled. "Actually Camila, I recently found out he has long been suffering from color blindness. He's kept it a secret so as not to worry us," Hailey explained.

"Dad, these glasses can help correct your red-green color blindness," said Hailey. He slowly ④ put on them, and stared at the birthday presents on the table. Seeing vivid red and green colors for the first time ever, he started to cry. "Incredible! Look at those wonderful colors!" He shouted in amazement. Hailey told him in tears, "Dad, I'm glad you can now finally enjoy the true beauty of rainbows and roses. Red represents love and green represents health. You deserve both." Camila nodded, ⑤ seeing how happy her gift of the glasses had made their dad.

수능형

윗글의 밑줄 친 부분 중, 어법상 틀린 것은?

내신형

다음 보기 중, 밑줄 친 Ⓐ를 부사절로 올바르게 변형한 것은?

① and he hugged his daughters.

② although he had hugged his daughters.

③ because he hugged his daughters.

④ after he had hugged his daughters.

⑤ while he had hugged his daughters.

이어동사는 목적어가 대명사일 때, 동사(put) 뒤에 바로 와야 한다.

① 간접의문문의 어순 '의문사＋주어＋동사'의 구조를 가진다.
② 과거분사 interrupted를 수식하는 부사 'suddenly'이다.
③ 장소 선행사 'room'을 수식하는 '전치사＋관계대명사'이고 뒤에 이끄는 절이 완전하다.
⑤ 'Camila nodded'가 완전한 문장이므로 뒤에는 분사구문이 온다. 또한, 주어 'Camila'와 'seeing'의 관계는 능동이다.

> 🔁 아래의 프롬프트를 챗GPT에 입력해 보세요.
> "영문법에서 소개하는 이어동사에 대해 설명해줘."
> "관계부사를 '전치사＋관계대명사'로 나타낸 예문을 5개 알려줘."

정답 ④

밑줄 친 ⓐhugging his daughters는 연속동작의 분사구문이다. 따라서 부사절로 바꿀 경우, 적절한 접속사는 'and'가 된다. 분사구문의 주어가 나타나지 않았으므로, 주절의 주어(He)와 같다. 또한 과거시제를 나타내는 동사 'walked'와 시제가 일치하기 때문에 'hugged'가 적절하다.

> 🔁 아래의 프롬프트를 챗GPT에 입력해 보세요.
> "분사구문을 부사절로 바꾸는 구체적인 방법을 알려주고 예문도 5개 정도 알려줘."

정답 ①

난이도 ★★☆☆☆

(A)

In the gym, members of the taekwondo club were busy practicing. Some were trying to kick as high as they could, and some were striking the sparring pad. Anna, the head of the club, was teaching the new members basic moves. Close by, her friend Jane was assisting Anna. **Jane noticed that Anna was glancing at the entrance door of the gym. She seemed to be expecting someone.** At last, when Anna took a break, Jane came over to (a) <u>her</u> and asked, "Hey, are you waiting for Cora?"

(B)

Cora walked in like a wounded soldier with bandages on her face and arms. Surprised, Anna and Jane simply looked at her with their eyes wide open. Cora explained, "I'm sorry I've been absent. I got into a bicycle accident, and I was in the hospital for two days. Finally, the doctor gave me the okay to practice." Anna said excitedly, "No problem! We're thrilled to have you back!" Then, Jane gave Anna an apologetic look, and (b) <u>she</u> responded with a friendly pat on Jane's shoulder.

(C)

Anna answered the question by nodding uneasily. In fact, Jane knew what her friend was thinking. Cora was a new member, whom Anna had personally invited to join the club. Anna really liked (c) <u>her</u>. Although her budget was tight, Anna bought Cora a taekwondo uniform. When she received it, Cora thanked her and promised, "I'll come to practice and work hard every day." However, unexpectedly, she came to practice only once and then never showed up again.

(D)

Since Cora had missed several practices, Anna wondered what could have happened. Jane, on the other hand, was disappointed and said judgingly, "Still waiting for her, huh? I can't believe (d) <u>you</u> don't feel disappointed or angry. Why don't you forget about her?" Anna replied, "Well, I know most newcomers don't keep their commitment to the club, but I thought that Cora would be different. She said she would come every day and practice." Just as Jane was about to respond to (e) <u>her</u>, the door swung open. There she was!

1. 주어진 글 (A)에 이어질 내용을 순서에 맞게 배열한 것으로 가장 적절한 것은?

① (B)−(D)−(C)   ② (C)−(B)−(D)

③ (C)−(D)−(B)   ④ (D)−(B)−(C)

⑤ (D)−(C)−(B)

2. 밑줄 친 (a)~(e) 중에서 가리키는 대상이 나머지 넷과 <u>다른</u> 것은?

① (a)   ② (b)   ③ (c)   ④ (d)   ⑤ (e)

3. 윗글에 관한 내용으로 적절하지 <u>않은</u> 것은?

① Anna는 신입 회원에게 태권도를 가르쳤다.

② Anna와 Jane은 Cora를 보고 놀라지 않았다.

③ Anna는 Cora에게 태권도 도복을 사 주었다.

④ Cora는 여러 차례 연습에 참여하지 않았다.

⑤ Anna는 Cora를 대다수의 신입 회원과 다를 것이라 생각했다.

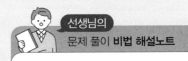

(A)

In the gym, members of the taekwondo club were busy practicing. Some were trying to kick as high as they could, and some were striking the sparring pad. Anna, the head of the club, was teaching the new members basic moves. Close by, her friend Jane was assisting Anna. Jane noticed that Anna was glancing at the entrance door of the gym. She seemed to be expecting someone. At last, when Anna took a break, Jane came over to (a) her and asked, "Hey, are you waiting for Cora?"

(B)

Cora walked in like a wounded soldier with bandages on her face and arms. Surprised, Anna and Jane simply looked at her with their eyes wide open. Cora explained, "I'm sorry I've been absent. I got into a bicycle accident, and I was in the hospital for two days. Finally, the doctor gave me the okay to practice." Anna said excitedly, "No problem! We're thrilled to have you back!" Then, Jane gave Anna an apologetic look, and (b) she responded with a friendly pat on Jane's shoulder.

(C)

Anna answered the question by nodding uneasily. In fact, Jane knew what her friend was thinking. Cora was a new member, (whom Anna had personally invited to join the club.) Anna really liked (c) her. Although her budget was tight, Anna bought Cora a taekwondo uniform. When she received it, Cora thanked her and promised, "I'll come to practice and work hard every day." However, unexpectedly, she came to practice only once and then never showed up again.

(D)

Since Cora had missed several practices, Anna wondered what could have happened. Jane, on the other hand, was disappointed and said judgingly, "Still waiting for her, huh? I can't believe (d) you don't feel disappointed or angry. Why don't you forget about her?" Anna replied, "Well, I know most newcomers don't keep their commitment to the club, but I thought that Cora would be different. She said she would come every day and practice." Just as Jane was about to respond to (e) her, the door swung open. There she was!

핵심 문장인 이유

"Jane noticed that Anna was glancing at the entrance door of the gym. She seemed to be expecting someone." 이 문장은 Anna가 누군가를 기다리는 내용을 언급한다. 따라서 글의 전반적인 전개를 암시하는 문장이므로 핵심 문장에 해당한다.

본문 해설

1. (A)에서 마지막 부분에 Cora를 기다리고 있냐는 질문이 등장한다. 따라서 (C)의 첫 질문에 응답하는 내용이 나오므로 (C)가 이어지는 게 자연스럽다. Cora가 연습에 잦은 결석이 있다는 내용이 있기 때문에 (D)에서 Cora가 여러 번의 연습에 빠졌다는 내용이 바로 이어져야 한다. (B)에서 Cora가 마침내 등장하는 내용과 연습을 못 온 이유를 설명하므로 (B)가 마지막에 오는 것이 적절하다.

2. (c)는 주어가 Anna이기 때문에 목적어 'her'은 Cora이다. 나머지는 모두 Anna를 가리킨다.

3. 'Surprised, Anna and Jane simply looked at her with their eyes wide open'이라는 표현은 눈이 휘둥그레진 상태로 놀란 것을 의미한다. 따라서 ②는 글의 내용과 일치하지 않는다.

문제 풀이 전략

장문 독해 지문은 시간적인 여유가 없는 상태에서 집중도가 흐트러질 수 있다. 주의해야 할 점은 각 문항마다 지문을 다시 보는 것이 아니라, 문항의 키워드를 정확히 확인하고 이를 상기시키며 지문을 읽어 나가야 한다.

정답 **1** ③ **2** ③ **3** ②

In the gym, members of the taekwondo club were busy practicing. Some were trying to kick as ① high as they could, and some were striking the sparring pad. Anna, the head of the club, was teaching the new members basic moves. Close by, her friend Jane was assisting Anna. Jane noticed that Anna was glancing at the entrance door of the gym. She seemed to be ② expecting someone. At last, when Anna took a break, Jane came over to her and asked, "Hey, are you waiting for Cora?"

Anna answered the question by nodding uneasily. In fact, Jane knew ③ that her friend was thinking. Cora was a new member, whom Anna had personally invited to join the club. Anna really liked her.

_____(A)_____ her budget was tight, Anna bought Cora a taekwondo uniform. When she received it, Cora thanked her and promised, "I'll come to practice and work hard every day." _____(B)_____, unexpectedly, she came to practice only once and then never showed up again.

Since Cora had missed several practices, Anna wondered ④ what could have happened. Jane, on the other hand, was disappointed and said judgingly, "Still waiting for her, huh? I can't believe you don't feel disappointed or angry. Why don't you forget about her?" Anna replied, "Well, I know most newcomers don't keep their commitment to the club, but I thought that Cora would be different. She said she would come every day and practice." Just as Jane was about ⑤ to respond to her, the door swung open. There she was!

Cora walked in like a wounded soldier with bandages on her face and arms. Surprised, Anna and Jane simply looked at her with their eyes wide open. Cora explained, "I'm sorry I've been absent. I got into a bicycle accident, and I was in the hospital for two days. Finally, the doctor gave me the okay to practice." Anna said excitedly, "No problem! We're thrilled to have you back!" Then, Jane gave Anna an apologetic look, and she responded with a friendly pat on Jane's shoulder.

수능형

윗글의 밑줄 친 부분 중, 어법상 틀린 것은?

내신형

윗글의 밑줄 친 (A), (B)에 들어갈 표현이 바르게 짝지어진 것을 고르시오.

	(A)	(B)		(A)	(B)
①	Since	⋯⋯ In addition	②	Otherwise	⋯⋯ In other words
③	When	⋯⋯ Shortly	④	If	⋯⋯ For example
⑤	Even though	⋯⋯ However			

'that'이 이끄는 문장이 불완전하다. 수식하는 선행사도 없기 때문에 관계대명사 that도 아니다. 의문사 'what'을 사용한 간접의문문으로 나타나야 한다.

① 'as 원급 as'에서 원급은 형용사/부사의 원래 형태이다. 따라서 'high'는 적절하다.
② to 부정사의 진행형에서 현재분사 'expecting'의 의미상의 주어는 'She'이다. 따라서 능동관계이기 때문에 적절하다.
④ 간접의문문에서 '의문사=주어'인 경우이다.
⑤ 'be about to ~ (막 ~하려 하다)'이다. to는 전치사가 아닌, 부정사이다.

아래의 프롬프트를 챗GPT에 입력해 보세요.
"간접의문문에서 의문사와 주어가 같은 예문을 5개 알려줘."

정답 ③

(A)가 이끄는 부사절에서는 Anna의 예산이 빠듯한 내용이지만, 주절에서는 태권도 도복을 사 주었다는 내용이므로 부사절과 주절의 맥락이 다르다. 따라서 양보접속사 'Even though'가 적절하다. (B) 앞의 문장은 매일 연습하러 오겠다는 내용이지만, 뒤에 오는 문장은 한 번만 오고 그 뒤로는 오지 않았다는 내용이다. 따라서 역접의 의미를 가지는 'However'가 적절하다.

아래의 프롬프트를 챗GPT에 입력해 보세요.
"양보접속사를 5개 정도 알려줘."

정답 ⑤

장문 독해(심화편)

난이도 ★★☆☆☆

(A)

In this area, heavy snow in winter was not uncommon. Sometimes it poured down for hours and hours and piled up very high. Then, no one could go out. Today too, because of the heavy snow, Mom was doing her office work at the kitchen table. Felix, the high schooler, had to take online classes in his room. Five-year-old Sean, who normally went to kindergarten, was sneaking around in the house playing home policeman. (a) **The kindergartener wanted to know what his family members were up to, and was checking up on everyone.**

(B)

"All right. I'm sure you're doing your work." Mom replied, and then sharply added a question. "Sean, what are you doing?" Sean's face immediately became blank, and he said, "Nothing." "Come here, Honey, and you can help me." Sean ran to the kitchen right away. "What can I do for you, Mom?" His voice was high, and Felix could sense that his brother was excited. Felix was pleased to get rid of (b) <u>the policeman</u>, and now he could concentrate on the lesson, at least till Sean came back.

(C)

While checking on his family, Sean interfered in their business as if it was his own. This time, (c) <u>the playful and curious boy</u> was interested in his brother Felix, who committed himself to studying no matter where he was. Sean secretly looked inside his brother's room from the door, and shouted toward the kitchen where Mom was working, "Mom, Felix isn't studying. He's just watching a funny video." Sean was naughtily smiling at his brother.

(D)

Felix was mad because (d) <u>his little brother</u> was bothering him. Felix was studying science using a video posted on the school web site. He made an angry face at the naughty boy. Right then, Mom asked loudly from the kitchen, "What are you doing, Felix?" Felix's room was located next to the kitchen, and he could hear Mom clearly. "I'm watching a lecture video for my science class." Felix argued against Sean's accusation and mischievously stuck (e) <u>his</u> tongue out at his little brother.

1. 주어진 글 (A)에 이어질 내용을 순서에 맞게 배열한 것으로 가장 적절한 것은?

① (B) – (D) – (C) 　　　　　② (C) – (B) – (D)
③ (C) – (D) – (B) 　　　　　④ (D) – (B) – (C)
⑤ (D) – (C) – (B)

2. 밑줄 친 (a)~(e) 중에서 가리키는 대상이 나머지 넷과 다른 것은?

① (a)　　　　② (b)　　　　③ (c)　　　　④ (d)　　　　⑤ (e)

3. 윗글에 관한 내용으로 적절하지 <u>않은</u> 것은?

① 엄마는 폭설로 인해 집에서 업무를 보고 있었다.
② Sean은 엄마가 불러서 주방으로 달려갔다.
③ Sean은 몰래 형의 방을 들여다보았다.
④ Felix는 자신의 방에서 게임을 하고 있었다.
⑤ Felix의 방은 주방 옆에 있었다.

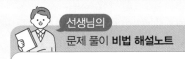

(A)

In this area, heavy snow in winter was not uncommon. Sometimes it poured down for hours and hours and piled up very high. Then, no one could go out. Today too, because of the heavy snow, Mom was doing her office work at the kitchen table. Felix, the high schooler, had to take online classes in his room. Five-year-old Sean, who normally went to kindergarten, was sneaking around in the house playing home policeman. (a) The kindergartener wanted to know what his family members were up to, and was checking up on everyone.

(B)

"All right. I'm sure you're doing your work." Mom replied, and then sharply added a question. "Sean, what are you doing?" Sean's face immediately became blank, and he said, "Nothing." "Come here, Honey, and you can help me." Sean ran to the kitchen right away. "What can I do for you, Mom?" His voice was high, and Felix could sense that his brother was excited. Felix was pleased to get rid of (b) the policeman, and now he could concentrate on the lesson, at least till Sean came back.

(C)

While checking on his family, Sean interfered in their business as if it was his own. This time, (c) the playful and curious boy was interested in his brother Felix, who committed himself to studying no matter where he was. Sean secretly looked inside his brother's room from the door, and shouted toward the kitchen where Mom was working, "Mom, Felix isn't studying. He's just watching a funny video." Sean was naughtily smiling at his brother.

(D)

Felix was mad because (d) his little brother was bothering him. Felix was studying science using a video posted on the school web site. He made an angry face at the naughty boy. Right then, Mom asked loudly from the kitchen, "What are you doing, Felix?" Felix's room was located next to the kitchen, and he could hear Mom clearly. "I'm watching a lecture video for my science class." Felix argued against Sean's accusation and mischievously stuck (e) his tongue out at his little brother.

핵심 문장인 이유

"The kindergartener wanted to know what his family members were up to, and was checking up on everyone." 이 문장은 꼬마가 가족들이 무엇을 하는지 확인하는 모습을 언급하고 있다. 글의 전개를 암시하기 때문에 핵심 문장에 해당한다.

본문 해설

1. (A)에 마지막 문장에 꼬마가 가족들이 무엇을 하는지 확인하려고 집을 돌아다니는 내용이 등장한다. 이에 이어질 내용으로 (C)에 첫 문장 'While checking on his family,'가 오는 것이 자연스럽다. (C)에 마지막 문장은 Sean이 엄마에게 Felix가 비디오를 본다고 고자질한다. 이어지는 (D)에서 Felix가 보고 있는 비디오가 과학 수업에 관련된 것이라고 언급하므로 자연스럽게 연결된다. Felix가 사실을 엄마에게 얘기하고, 이어서 (B)에 엄마가 대답하는 문장이 이어져야 한다.
2. 'stick ~ out(~을 내밀다)'는 표현을 참고하면 어린 동생에게 Felix가 혀를 내미는 행동임을 알 수 있다. 따라서 (a)~(d)는 모두 동생 'Sean'을 가리키고 (e)는 'Felix'를 가리킨다.
3. Felix는 게임을 하고 있는 것이 아니라, 과학 수업과 관련된 비디오를 보고 있었다. 따라서 ④는 글의 내용과 일치하지 않는다.

문제 풀이 전략

장문 독해 지문은 시간적인 여유가 없는 상태에서 집중도가 흐트러질 수 있다. 주의해야 할 점은 각 문항마다 지문을 다시 보는 것이 아니라 문항의 키워드를 정확히 확인하고 이를 상기시키며 지문을 읽어나가야 한다.

정답 1 ③　2 ⑤　3 ④

In this area, heavy snow in winter was not uncommon. Sometimes it poured down for hours and hours and piled up very high. Then, no one could go out. Today too, because of the heavy snow, Mom was doing her office work at the kitchen table. Felix, the high schooler, had to take online classes in his room. Five-year-old Sean, who normally went to kindergarten, ① was sneaking around in the house playing home policeman. The kindergartener wanted to know ② what his family members (a) were up to, and was checking up on everyone.

While checking on his family, Sean interfered in their business (b) as if it was his own. This time, the playful and curious boy was interested in his brother Felix, who committed ③ himself to studying (c) no matter where he was. Sean secretly looked inside his brother's room from the door, and shouted toward the kitchen where Mom was working, "Mom, Felix isn't studying. He's just watching a funny video." Sean was naughtily smiling at his brother.

Felix was mad because his little brother was bothering him. Felix was studying science using a video posted on the school web site. He made an angry face at the naughty boy. Right then, Mom asked loudly from the kitchen, "What are you doing, Felix?" Felix's room was located next to the kitchen, and he could hear Mom clearly. "I'm watching a lecture video for my science class." Felix argued against Sean's accusation and mischievously ④ stuck his tongue out at his little brother.

"All right. I'm sure you're doing your work." Mom replied, and then sharply added a question. "Sean, what are *you* doing?" Sean's face immediately became blank, and he said, "Nothing." "Come here, Honey, and you can help me." Sean ran to the kitchen right away. "What can I do for you, Mom?" His voice was high, and Felix could sense that his brother was excited. Felix was pleased to (d) get rid of the policeman, and now he could (e) concentrate on the lesson, at least till Sean ⑤ would come back.

수능형

윗글의 밑줄 친 부분 중, 어법상 틀린 것은?

내신형

윗글의 밑줄 친 (a)~(e) 중 바꿔 쓸 수 있는 표현으로 잘못 짝지어진 것은?

① (a): were doing   ② (b): as though

③ (c): wherever   ④ (d): get along with

⑤ (e): focus on

till(until)은 시간의 부사절을 이끄는 접속사이다. 따라서 미래시제를 사용할 수 없다.

① 문장의 주어는 'Five-year-old Sean'이기 때문에 'was'는 적절하다.
② 'be up to(~를 하다)'에서 전치사 to의 목적어가 없는 불완전한 문장이다. 따라서 'what(무엇을)'은 적절하다.
③ 문장의 주어 'Felix'가 공부에 몰두하고 있기 때문에 동사 'committed'의 목적어와 일치한다. 따라서 재귀대명사 'himself'가 적절하다.
④ 등위접속사 'and'로 동사 'argued'와 'stuck'은 병렬구조이다.

아래의 프롬프트를 챗GPT에 입력해 보세요.
"'be up to'의 의미를 모두 알려줘."

정답 ⑤

'get rid of(제거하다)'는 'get along with(~와 잘 지내다)'로 바꿀 수 없다.

아래의 프롬프트를 챗GPT에 입력해 보세요.
"'get rid of'의 유의어를 알려줘."

정답 ④

장문 독해(심화편)

 CASE 04

난이도 ★★☆☆☆

(A)

When Sally came back home from her photography class, she could hear Katie moving around, chopping things on a wooden cutting board. Wondering what her roommate was doing, (a) she ran to the kitchen. Sally watched Katie cooking something that looked delicious. But Katie didn't notice her because she was too focused on preparing for her cooking test the next day. **She was trying to remember what her professor had said in class that day**.

(B)

Katie, surprised by her roommate's words, turned her head to Sally and sighed, "I don't know. This is really hard." Stirring her sauce for pasta, Katie continued, "Professor Brown said that visual aspects make up a key part of a meal. My recipe seems good, but I can't think of any ways to alter the feeling of the final dish." Visibly frustrated, (b) she was just about to throw away all of her hard work and start again, when Sally suddenly stopped her.

(C)

"Wait! You don't have to start over. You just need to add some color to the plate." Being curious, Katie asked, "How can (c) I do that?" Sally took out a container of vegetables from the refrigerator and replied, "How about making colored pasta to go with (d) your sauce?" Smiling, she added, "It's not that hard, and all you need are brightly colored vegetables to make your pasta green, orange, or even purple." Katie smiled, knowing that now she could make her pasta with beautiful colors like a photographer.

(D)

In that class, Professor Brown said, "You have to present your food properly, considering every stage of the dining experience. Imagine you are a photographer." Recalling what the professor had mentioned, Katie said to herself, "We need to see our ingredients as colors that make up a picture." Sally could clearly see that Katie was having a hard time preparing for her cooking test. Trying to make (e) her feel better, Sally kindly asked, "Is there anything I can do to help?"

1. 주어진 글 (A)에 이어질 내용을 순서에 맞게 배열한 것으로 가장 적절한 것은?

① (B)−(D)−(C)   ② (C)−(B)−(D)

③ (C)−(D)−(B)   ④ (D)−(B)−(C)

⑤ (D)−(C)−(B)

2. 밑줄 친 (a)~(e) 중에서 가리키는 대상이 나머지 넷과 다른 것은?

① (a)   ② (b)   ③ (c)   ④ (d)   ⑤ (e)

3. 윗글에 관한 내용으로 적절하지 않은 것은?

① Sally는 사진 수업 후 집으로 돌아왔다.

② Brown 교수님은 음식에서 시각적인 면이 중요하다고 말했다.

③ Sally는 냉장고에서 채소가 든 그릇을 꺼냈다.

④ Sally는 색깔 있는 파스타를 만드는 것이 어렵다고 말했다.

⑤ Katie는 요리 시험 준비에 어려움을 겪고 있었다.

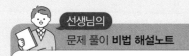
(A)

When Sally came back home from her photography class, she could hear Katie moving around, chopping things on a wooden cutting board. Wondering [what her roommate was doing,] (a) she ran to the kitchen. Sally watched Katie cooking something (that looked delicious.) But Katie didn't notice her because she was too focused on preparing for her cooking test the next day. She was trying to remember what her professor had said in class that day.

(B)

Katie, surprised by her roommate's words, turned her head to Sally and sighed, "I don't know. This is really hard." Stirring her sauce for pasta, Katie continued, "Professor Brown said that visual aspects make up a key part of a meal. My recipe seems good, but I can't think of any ways (to alter the feeling of the final dish.") Visibly frustrated, (b) she was just about to throw away all of her hard work and start again, when Sally suddenly stopped her.

(C)

"Wait! You don't have to start over. You just need to add some color to the plate." Being curious, Katie asked, "How can (c) I do that?" Sally took out a container of vegetables from the refrigerator and replied, "How about making colored pasta to go with (d) your sauce?" Smiling, she added, "It's not that hard, and all (you need) are brightly colored vegetables to make your pasta green, orange, or even purple." Katie smiled, knowing that now she could make her pasta with beautiful colors like a photographer.

(D)

In that class, Professor Brown said, "You have to present your food properly, considering every stage of the dining experience. Imagine you are a photographer." Recalling what the professor had mentioned, Katie said to herself, "We need to see our ingredients as colors (that make up a picture.") Sally could clearly see that Katie was having a hard time preparing for her cooking test. Trying to make (e) her feel better, Sally kindly asked, "Is there anything (I can do to help?")

핵심 문장인 이유

"She was trying to remember what her professor had said in class that day." 이 문장은 Katie가 요리 테스트가 얼마 남지 않은 시점에서, 배운 내용을 떠올리려 애쓰는 내용이다. 전반적인 글 전개에 영향을 줌으로써 핵심 문장에 해당한다.

본문 해설

1. (A)에 마지막 문장은 Katie가 수업 때 배운 내용을 기억하려 애쓰는 내용이다. 따라서 (D)에서 언급된 'In that class'가 이어지는 것이 자연스럽다. (D)에 마지막 문장은 Sally가 Katie에게 도와줄 게 없냐는 질문을 하므로 그에 대한 대답으로 (B)에 'I don't know. This is really hard.'가 자연스럽게 이어져야 한다. (B)에 마지막 문장에서 Sally가 Katie를 갑자기 멈추게 하는 내용이 언급되는데, 이는 (C)에서 등장하는 문장 'Wait! You don't have to start over.'에서 이유를 알 수 있다.

2. 주방으로 달려가는 사람은 Sally이다. (b)~(e)는 Katie를 가리킨다.

3. Sally는 다채로운 채소로 파스타를 만들면 색깔 있는 파스타도 어렵지 않다고 했다.

문제 풀이 전략

장문 독해 지문은 시간적인 여유가 없는 상태에서 집중도가 흐트러질 수 있다. 주의해야 할 점은 각 문항마다 지문을 다시 보는 것이 아니라 문항의 키워드를 정확히 확인하고 이를 상기시키며 지문을 읽어나가야 한다.

정답 1 ④ 2 ① 3 ④

When Sally came back home from her photography class, she could hear Katie moving around, chopping things on a wooden cutting board. Wondering ① <u>what</u> her roommate was doing, she ran to the kitchen. Sally watched Katie ② <u>cooking</u> something that looked delicious. But Katie didn't notice her because she was too focused on preparing for her cooking test the next day. She was trying to remember ③ <u>what</u> her professor had said in class that day.

In that class, Professor Brown said, "You have to present your food properly, considering every stage of the dining experience. Imagine you are a photographer." Recalling ④ <u>what</u> the professor had mentioned, Katie said to herself, "We need to see our ingredients as colors that make up a picture." Sally could clearly see that Katie was having a hard time ⑤ <u>to prepare</u> for her cooking test. Trying to make her feel better, Sally kindly asked, "Is there anything I can do to help?"

Katie, surprised by her roommate's words, turned her head to Sally and sighed, "I don't know. This is really hard." Stirring her sauce for pasta, Katie continued, "Professor Brown said that visual aspects make up a key part of a meal. My recipe seems good, but I can't think of any ways to alter the feeling of the final dish." Visibly frustrated, she was just about to throw away all of her hard work and start again, when Sally suddenly stopped her.

"Wait! You don't have to start over. You just need to add some color to the plate." Being curious, Katie asked, "How can I do that?" Sally took out a container of vegetables from the refrigerator and replied, "How about making colored pasta to go with your sauce?" Smiling, she added, "It's not Ⓐ <u>that</u> hard, and all you need are brightly colored vegetables to make your pasta green, orange, or even purple." Katie smiled, knowing that now she could make her pasta with beautiful colors like a photographer.

수능형

윗글의 밑줄 친 부분 중, 어법상 틀린 것은?

내신형

다음 보기 중, 밑줄 친 Ⓐ의 쓰임과 성격이 <u>같은</u> 것은?

① I don't think I can run <u>that</u> fast.
② Who is <u>that</u> boy?
③ The person <u>that</u> we met yesterday is my uncle.
④ She said <u>that</u> she would be late.
⑤ It is the window <u>that</u> Mike broke.

'have(spend)+시간+~ing'으로 동명사의 관용적 표현이다. 따라서 'to prepare' → 'preparing'이다.

① 간접의문문으로 '의문사+주어+동사' 어순을 가진다. 따라서 'what'은 적절하다.

② 5형식 문장에서 지각동사(watch)인 경우, 목적어와 보어가 능동관계이면 원형부정사/현재분사로 나타낸다. Katie가 요리를 하는 능동의 주체이므로 'cooking'은 적절하다.

③ 의문대명사, 관계대명사 'what'이 이끄는 문장은 불완전하다. 'had said'의 목적어가 없으므로 불완전하다. 따라서 'what'은 적절하다.

④ 의문대명사, 관계대명사 'what'이 이끄는 문장은 불완전하다. 'had mentioned'의 목적어가 없으므로 불완전하다. 따라서 'what'은 적절하다.

> 🐧 아래의 프롬프트를 챗GPT에 입력해 보세요.
> "동명사 –ing가 사용된 관용 표현들이 있어. 예를 들어 'busy –ing' 같은 거야. 그 밖에 동명사가 사용된 관용 표현들을 알려줘."

정답 ⑤

Ⓐ의 'that'은 형용사 'hard'를 수식하는 지시부사로 사용되었다. 의미는 '그렇게'이다.

② 명사 'boy'를 수식하는 지시형용사이다. 의미는 '그~'이다.

③ 선행사 'The person'을 수식하는 목적격 관계대명사 'that'이다.

④ 동사 'said'의 목적어절(명사절)을 이끄는 접속사 'that'이다.

⑤ 강조구문에서 사용하는 'that'이다.

> 🐧 아래의 프롬프트를 챗GPT에 입력해 보세요.
> "that의 종류를 예문을 가지고 설명해줘."

정답 ①

PART
06

어휘 및 어법

어휘 적절성 파악하기

CASE 01

난이도 ★★★☆☆

Everywhere we turn we hear about almighty "cyberspace"! The hype promises that we will leave our boring lives, put on goggles and body suits, and enter some metallic, three-dimensional, multimedia otherworld. When the Industrial Revolution arrived with its great innovation, the motor, we didn't leave our world to go to some ① remote motorspace! On the contrary, we brought the motors into our lives, as automobiles, refrigerators, drill presses, and pencil sharpeners. This ② absorption has been so complete that we refer to all these tools with names that declare their usage, not their "motorness." These innovations led to a major socioeconomic movement precisely because they entered and ③ affected profoundly our everyday lives. People have not changed fundamentally in thousands of years. Technology changes constantly. **It's the one that must ④ adapt to us**. That's exactly what will happen with information technology and its devices under human-centric computing. The longer we continue to believe that computers will take us to a magical new world, the longer we will ⑤ maintain their natural fusion with our lives, the hallmark of every major movement that aspires to be called a socioeconomic revolution.

윗글의 밑줄 친 부분 중, 문맥상 낱말의 쓰임이 적절하지 <u>않은</u> 것은?

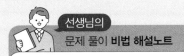
Everywhere we turn/we hear about almighty "cyberspace"! The hype promises that we will leave our boring lives, put on goggles and body suits, and enter some metallic, three-dimensional, multimedia otherworld. When the Industrial Revolution arrived with its great innovation, the motor, we didn't leave our world to go to some ① remote motorspace! On the contrary, we brought the motors into our lives, as automobiles, refrigerators, drill presses, and pencil sharpeners. This ② absorption has been so complete that we refer to all these tools with names that declare their usage, not their "motorness." These innovations led to a major socioeconomic movement precisely because they entered and ③ affected profoundly our everyday lives. People have not changed fundamentally in thousands of years. Technology changes constantly. It's the one that must ④ adapt to us. That's exactly what will happen with information technology and its devices under human-centric computing. The longer we continue to believe that computers will take us to a magical new world, the longer we will ⑤ maintain their natural fusion with our lives, (the hallmark of every major movement that aspires to be called a socioeconomic revolution.)

강조

핵심 문장인 이유

"It's the one that must adapt to us." 이 문장은 기술이 우리의 삶에 들어와 영향을 미치기 때문에 기술이 우리에 적응해야 한다는 내용이다. 우리가 기술에 의존하지 않고, 기술은 우리 삶의 용도로 사용되어야 한다는 주제를 담고 있으므로 핵심 문장에 해당한다.

본문 해설

'the natural fusion with our lives'는 기술이 우리 삶에 자연스럽게 융합하는 것을 의미한다. 따라서 기술에 대한 의존을 주장하는 것이 아니다. 컴퓨터가 마법 같은 세상으로 이끌어줄 거라고 더 오래 믿을수록 기술과의 자연스러운 융합은 '유지될(→지연될)' 것이다.

문제 풀이 전략

지문에 나오는 소재나 문제에 대해 긍정적인지 부정적인지를 우선적으로 파악해야 한다. 이를 바탕으로 글의 흐름을 놓치지 않고, 해당 문장이 부정문이라면 주의해서 읽어야 한다.

정답 ⑤

Everywhere we turn we hear about almighty "cyberspace"! The hype promises that we will leave our boring lives, put on goggles and body suits, and enter some metallic, three-dimensional, multimedia otherworld. When the Industrial Revolution arrived with its great innovation, the motor, we didn't leave our world to go to some remote motorspace! On the contrary, we brought the motors into our lives, as automobiles, refrigerators, drill presses, and pencil sharpeners. This absorption has been so complete that we refer to all these tools with names that declare their usage, not their "motorness." These innovations led to a major socioeconomic movement precisely because they entered and affected profoundly our everyday lives. People have not changed fundamentally in thousands of years. Technology changes constantly. It's the one that must adapt to us. That's exactly what will happen with information technology and its devices under human-centric computing. The longer we continue to believe that computers will take us to a magical new world, the longer we will delay their natural fusion with our lives, the hallmark of every major movement that aspires to be called a socioeconomic revolution.

윗글의 제목으로 가장 적절한 것은?

① Digital Dreams: Separating Fact from Fiction
② Human-Centric Computing: Adjusting to Real World
③ Sailing the Cyber Sea: A Reality Check
④ When Virtual Becomes Reality
⑤ Rethinking the Impact of Technology

Everywhere we turn we hear about almighty "cyberspace"! The hype promises that we will leave our boring lives, put on goggles and body suits, and ① enter some metallic, three-dimensional, multimedia otherworld. When the Industrial Revolution arrived with its great innovation, the motor, we didn't leave our world to go to some remote motorspace! On the contrary, we brought the motors into our lives, as automobiles, refrigerators, drill presses, and pencil sharpeners. This absorption has been so ② complete that we refer to all these tools with names that declare their usage, not their "motorness." These innovations led to a major socioeconomic movement precisely because they entered and affected ③ profoundly our everyday lives. People have not changed fundamentally in thousands of years. Technology changes constantly. It's the one that must adapt to us. That's exactly ④ what will happen with information technology and its devices under human-centric computing. The longer we continue to believe that computers will take us to a magical new world, the longer we will delay their natural fusion with our lives, the hallmark of every major movement that aspires to ⑤ call a socioeconomic revolution.

윗글의 밑줄 친 부분 중, 어법상 틀린 것은?

인간이 기술에 적응하는 것이 아니라 기술이 인간에게 적응해야 한다는 주장을 포함하고 있다. 따라서 기술이 인간의 삶에 맞춰 개발되고 적용되는 것에 관한 적절한 제목은 '② Human-Centric Computing: Adjusting to Real World'이다.

아래의 프롬프트를 챗GPT에 입력해 보세요.

"지문을 이해하는데 필요한 핵심 단어들을 모두 알려줘."

정답 ②

'to call'의 의미상 주어는 'the hallmark of every major movement'이다. 의미상 주어와 'a socioeconomic revolution'을 부르는 능동의 주체가 아닌 수동의 주체이기 때문에 'to be called'가 적절하다.

① 'live', 'put on'과 병렬관계이다.
② 'has been' 뒤에는 보어 자리이므로 형용사 'complete'는 적절하다.
③ 'affected'를 수식하는 부사 'profoundly'는 적절하다.
④ 선행사가 없고 'what'이 이끄는 절이 불완전하므로 적절하다.

아래의 프롬프트를 챗GPT에 입력해 보세요.

"to 부정사의 '태(Voice)'에 대해 자세히 알려줘."

정답 ⑤

어휘 적절성 파악하기

난이도 ★★★☆☆

It has been suggested that "organic" methods, defined as those in which only natural products can be used as inputs, would be less damaging to the biosphere. **Large-scale adoption of "organic" farming methods, however, would ① reduce yields and increase production costs for many major crops**. Inorganic nitrogen supplies are ② essential for maintaining moderate to high levels of productivity for many of the non-leguminous crop species, because organic supplies of nitrogenous materials often are either limited or more expensive than inorganic nitrogen fertilizers. In addition, there are ③ benefits to the extensive use of either manure or legumes as "green manure" crops. In many cases, weed control can be very difficult or require much hand labor if chemicals cannot be used, and ④ fewer people are willing to do this work as societies become wealthier. Some methods used in "organic" farming, however, such as the sensible use of crop rotations and specific combinations of cropping and livestock enterprises, can make important ⑤ contributions to the sustainability of rural ecosystem.

윗글의 밑줄 친 부분 중, 문맥상 낱말의 쓰임이 적절하지 <u>않은</u> 것은?

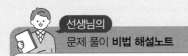
It has been suggested that "organic" methods, (defined as those in which only natural products can be used as inputs,)would be less damaging to the biosphere. Large-scale adoption of "organic" farming methods, however, would ① reduce yields and increase production costs for many major crops. Inorganic nitrogen supplies are ② essential for maintaining moderate to high levels of productivity for many of the non-leguminous crop species, because organic supplies of nitrogenous materials often are either limited or more expensive than inorganic nitrogen fertilizers. In addition, there are ③ benefits to the extensive use of either manure or legumes as "green manure" crops. In many cases, weed control can be very difficult or require much hand labor(if chemicals cannot be used,)and ④ fewer people are willing to do this work(as societies become wealthier.)Some methods used in "organic" farming, however, such as the sensible use of crop rotations and specific combinations of cropping and livestock enterprises, can make important ⑤ contributions to the sustainability of rural ecosystem.

핵심 문장인 이유

"Large-scale adoption of "organic" farming methods, however, would reduce yields and increase production costs for many major crops." 이 문장은 유기농법의 단점을 간결하게 요약하고 있다. 따라서 핵심 문장에 해당한다.

본문 해설

앞서 등장하는 문장에는 질소의 유기적 공급이 제한되거나 비싸다는 내용이다. 이어지는 'In addition(게다가)'를 사용해 앞의 내용에 부연 설명을 덧붙이고 있다. 하지만 이어지는 내용은 유기질에 대한 단점을 언급하고 있다. 따라서 '이익(→ 단점)'이다.

문제 풀이 전략

지문에 나오는 소재나 문제에 대해 긍정적인지 부정적인지를 우선적으로 파악해야 한다. 이를 바탕으로 글의 흐름을 놓치지 않고, 해당 문장이 부정문이라면 주의해서 읽어야 한다. 'In addition(게다가)'는 앞에서 말한 내용과 같은 맥락으로 추가적인 정보를 언급해야 한다.

정답 ③

It has been suggested that "organic" methods, defined as those in which only natural products can be used as inputs, would be less damaging to the biosphere. (①) Large-scale adoption of "organic" farming methods, however, would reduce yields and increase production costs for many major crops. (②) Inorganic nitrogen supplies are essential for maintaining moderate to high levels of productivity for many of the non-leguminous crop species, because organic supplies of nitrogenous materials often are either limited or more expensive than inorganic nitrogen fertilizers. (③) In addition, there are drawback to the extensive use of either manure or legumes as "green manure" crops. (④) Some methods used in "organic" farming, however, such as the sensible use of crop rotations and specific combinations of cropping and livestock enterprises, can make important contributions to the sustainability of rural ecosystem. (⑤)

글의 흐름으로 보아, 주어진 문장이 들어가기에 가장 적절한 곳을 고르시오.

In many cases, weed control can be very difficult or require much hand labor if chemicals cannot be used, and fewer people are willing to do this work as societies become wealthier.

실전! 내신대비! 　2022년 수능 30번 변형 문제　 난이도 ★★★★☆

It has been suggested that "organic" methods, defined as those in which only natural products can be used as inputs, would be ① <u>less</u> damaging to the biosphere. Large-scale adoption of "organic" farming methods, however, would reduce yields and ② <u>increase</u> production costs for many major crops. Inorganic nitrogen supplies are essential for maintaining moderate to high levels of productivity for many of the non-leguminous crop species, because organic supplies of nitrogenous materials often are either limited or ③ <u>more expensive</u> than inorganic nitrogen fertilizers. In addition, there are benefits to the extensive use of either manure or legumes as "green manure" crops. In many cases, weed control can be very difficult or require much hand labor if chemicals cannot be used, and fewer people ④ <u>are reluctant to</u> do this work as societies become wealthier. Some methods used in "organic" farming, however, such as the ⑤ <u>sensible</u> use of crop rotations and specific combinations of cropping and livestock enterprises, can make important contributions to the sustainability of rural ecosystem.

윗글의 밑줄 친 부분 중, 문맥상 낱말의 쓰임이 적절하지 <u>않은</u> 것은?

주어진 문장은 화학물질을 사용할 수 없다면, 잡초 제거가 어려워 수작업을 필요로 하게 된다는 내용이다. 화학물질을 사용하지 않은 작물은 녹비작물로 볼 수 있다. 이 내용이 이어지기 위해서는 녹비작물로서 거름과 콩과류를 광범위하게 사용하는 것에 대한 단점이 먼저 언급되어야 한다. 따라서 (④) 적절한 위치이다.

정답 ④

사회가 더 부유해지면서 잡초 제거를 'be reluctant to~(~하기를 꺼리다)' 사람들의 수가 더 줄어드는 것이 아니라 잡초 제거를 하려는 사람들의 수가 더 줄어드는 것이기 때문에 ④ ~하기를 꺼리다(→ ~하려 하다)이다.

> 아래의 프롬프트를 챗GPT에 입력해 보세요.
> "위에 소개한 지문의 핵심 단어들을 모두 고르고 뜻도 알려줘."

정답 ④

어휘 적절성 파악하기

난이도 ★★★☆☆

In economic systems what takes place in one sector has impacts on another; demand for a good or service in one sector is derived from another. For instance, a consumer buying a good in a store will likely trigger the replacement of this product, which will generate ① demands for activities such as manufacturing, resource extraction and, of course, transport. **What is different about transport is that it cannot exist alone and a movement cannot be ② stored**. An unsold product can remain on the shelf of a store until bought (often with discount incentives), but an unsold seat on a flight or unused cargo capacity in the same flight remains unsold and cannot be brought back as additional capacity ③ later. In this case an opportunity has been ④ seized, since the amount of transport being offered has exceeded the demand for it. The derived demand of transportation is often very difficult to reconcile with an equivalent supply, and actually transport companies would prefer to have some additional capacity to accommodate ⑤ unforseen demand (often at much higher prices).

윗글의 밑줄 친 부분 중, 문맥상 낱말의 쓰임이 적절하지 <u>않은</u> 것은?

 In economic systems/what takes place in one sector has impacts on another; demand for a good
           S
or service in one sector is derived from another. For instance, a consumer buying a good in a store
will likely trigger the replacement of this product, (which will generate ① demands for activities
such as manufacturing, resource extraction and, of course, transport.) What is different about
                           S
transport is that it cannot exist alone and a movement cannot be ② stored. An unsold product can
remain on the shelf of a store until bought (often with discount incentives), but an unsold seat on a
flight or unused cargo capacity in the same flight remains unsold and cannot be brought back as
additional capacity ③ later. In this case/an opportunity has been ④ seized,/since the amount of
transport (being offered) has exceeded the demand for it. The derived demand of transportation is
often very difficult to reconcile with an equivalent supply, and actually transport companies would
prefer to have some additional capacity (to accommodate ⑤ unforseen demand (often at much
higher prices).)

핵심 문장인 이유

"What is different about transport is that it cannot exist alone and a movement cannot be stored." 이 문장은 운송과 상품의
다른 점을 보여준다. 교통 수요와 공급의 균형을 맞추는 것이 어려운 이유를 명확히 보여 줌으로써 핵심 문장에 해당한다.

본문 해설

상품은 구매될 때까지 매장 진열대에 남아 있을 수 있지만, 운송량은 수요를 초과할 경우 그것을 이후에 사용할 기회가 ④ 포착된다(→ 상
실된다)이다.

문제 풀이 전략

지문에 나오는 소재나 문제에 대해 긍정적인지 부정적인지를 우선적으로 파악해야 한다. 이를 바탕으로 글의 흐름을 놓치지 않고, 해당 문
장이 부정문이라면 주의해서 읽어야 한다. 'since(때문에)'가 이끄는 내용은 원인을 나타냄으로써 발생하는 결과와 같은 맥락으로 서술되
어야 한다.

정답 ④

In economic systems what takes place in one sector has impacts on another; demand for a good or service in one sector is derived from another. For instance, a consumer buying a good in a store will likely trigger the replacement of this product, which will generate demands for activities such as manufacturing, resource extraction and, of course, transport. What is different about transport is that it cannot exist alone and a movement cannot be stored. An unsold product can remain on the shelf of a store until bought (often with discount incentives), but an unsold seat on a flight or unused cargo capacity in the same flight remains unsold and cannot be brought back as additional capacity later. In this case an opportunity has been missed, since the amount of transport being offered has exceeded the demand for it. The derived demand of transportation is often very difficult to _____ with an equivalent supply, and actually transport companies would prefer to have some additional capacity to accommodate unforseen demand (often at much higher prices).

윗글의 빈칸에 들어갈 말로 가장 적절한 것을 고르시오.

① interfere ② coordinate

③ associate ④ replace

⑤ connect

In economic systems what takes place in one sector ① has impacts on another; demand for a good or service in one sector is derived from another. For instance, a consumer buying a good in a store will likely trigger the replacement of this product, ② which will generate demands for activities such as manufacturing, resource extraction and, of course, transport. What is different about transport is ③ that it cannot exist alone and a movement cannot be stored. An unsold product can remain on the shelf of a store until bought (often with discount incentives), but an unsold seat on a flight or unused cargo capacity in the same flight remains unsold and cannot be brought back as additional capacity later. In this case an opportunity ④ has missed, since the amount of transport ⑤ being offered has exceeded the demand for it. The derived demand of transportation is often very difficult to reconcile with an equivalent supply, and actually transport companies would prefer to have some additional capacity to accommodate unforseen demand (often at much higher prices).

윗글의 밑줄 친 부분 중, 어법상 틀린 것은?

운송 수요는 상품 수요와 달리 상응하는 공급과 조정하거나 일치시키기가 쉽지 않다는 것을 의미한다. 교통회사들이 일반적으로 예측하지 못한 추가 수요를 여분의 용량을 가지고 있기를 선호한다는 내용을 통해 수요와 공급(용량)을 일치하기 어렵다는 것을 추론할 수 있다.

> 🔊 **아래의 프롬프트를 챗GPT에 입력해 보세요.**
> "'reconcile 조화를 이루다' 와 같은 유의어들을 알려줘."

정답 ②

'an opportunity'와의 수식 관계가 수동이다. 따라서 'has been missed'가 적절하다.

① 관계절의 동사를 보고 관계대명사 what이 포함한 선행사가 단수명사라는 것을 알 수 있다. 따라서 'has'는 적절하다.
② 계속적 용법의 주격 관계대명사 'which'이다.
③ 보어 자리에 절을 이끄는 접속사 'that'이다.
⑤ 'the amount of transport'를 수동관계로 수식하는 분사구 'being offered'는 적절하다.

> 🔊 **아래의 프롬프트를 챗GPT에 입력해 보세요.**
> "that 뒤가 불완전/완전 문장인지에 따라 that의 쓰임이 달라지는 경우를 설명해줘."

정답 ④

어휘 적절성 파악하기

CASE 04

난이도 ★★★☆☆

If I say to you, "Don't think of a white bear', you will find it difficult not to think of a white bear. In this way, 'thought suppression can actually increase the thoughts one wishes to suppress instead of calming them'. One common example of this is that people on a diet who try not to think about food often begin to think much ① more about food. This process is therefore also known as the *rebound effect*. **The ② ironic effects seems to be caused by the interplay of two related cognitive processes**. This dual-process system involves, first, an intentional operating process, which consciously attempts to locate thoughts ③ unrelated to the suppressed ones, Second, and simultaneously, an unconscious monitoring process tests whether the operating system is functioning effectively. If the monitoring system encounters thoughts inconsistent with the intended ones, it prompts the intentional operating process to ensure that these are replaced by ④ inappropriate thoughts. However, it is argued, the intentional operating system can fail due to increased cognitive load caused by fatigue, stress and emotional factors, and so the monitoring process filters the inappropriate thoughts into consciousness, making them highly ⑤ accessible.

윗글의 밑줄 친 부분 중, 문맥상 낱말의 쓰임이 적절하지 <u>않은</u> 것은?

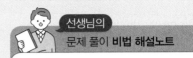
If I say to you, "Don't think of a white bear', you will find it difficult not to think of a white bear. In this way, 'thought suppression can actually increase the thoughts one wishes to suppress instead of calming them'. One common example of this is that people (on a diet)(who try not to think about food) often begin to think much ① more about food. This process is therefore also known as the *rebound effect*. The ② ironic effects seems to be caused by the interplay of two related cognitive processes. This dual-process system involves, first, an intentional operating process, (which consciously attempts to locate thoughts ③ unrelated to the suppressed ones,) Second, and simultaneously, an unconscious monitoring process tests whether the operating system is functioning effectively. If the monitoring system encounters thoughts (inconsistent with the intended ones,) it prompts the intentional operating process to ensure that these are replaced by ④ inappropriate thoughts. However, it is argued, the intentional operating system can fail due to increased cognitive load (caused by fatigue, stress and emotional factors,) and so the monitoring process filters the inappropriate thoughts into consciousness, making them highly ⑤ accessible.

핵심 문장인 이유

"The ironic effects seems to be caused by the interplay of two related cognitive processes." 이 문장은 억제하려는 생각이 오히려 증폭되는 원인을 인지과정의 상호작용을 통해 설명한다. 이후에 이어지는 모니터링 과정에 대한 상세한 내용들을 이해하는데 중요한 역할을 하므로 핵심 문장에 해당한다.

본문 해설

Monitoring system과 Intentional operating process가 잘 작동하는지 확인하는 시스템이다. Intentional operating process 관련 없는 생각을 의식적으로 억압한다. 만약 의도된 생각과 일치하지 않는 생각을 만난다면 ④ 적절하지 않은(→ 적절한) 생각으로 대체된다.

문제 풀이 전략

지문에 나오는 소재나 문제에 대해 긍정적인지 부정적인지를 우선적으로 파악해야 한다. 이를 바탕으로 글의 흐름을 놓치지 않고, 해당 문장이 부정문이라면 주의해서 읽어야 한다. 'However(그러나)' 뒤에 Intentional operating process가 실패하는 내용을 담고 있으므로, 앞에 내용은 반대되는 내용이 나와야 한다. 따라서 거꾸로 올라가 '적절한' 생각으로 대체되어야 하는 것으로 확인할 수 있다.

정답 ④

If I say to you, "Don't think of a white bear', you will find it ① difficult not to think of a white bear. In this way, 'thought suppression can actually increase the thoughts one wishes to suppress instead of calming them'. One common example of this is that people on a diet ② who try not to think about food often ③ beginning to think much more about food. This process is therefore also known as the *rebound effect*. The ironic effects seems to be caused by the interplay of two related cognitive processes. This dual–process system involves, first, an intentional operating process, which consciously attempts to locate thoughts unrelated to the suppressed ones, Second, and simultaneously, an unconscious monitoring process tests whether the operating system is functioning effectively. If the monitoring system encounters thoughts inconsistent with the intended ④ ones, it prompts the intentional operating process to ensure that these are replaced by appropriate thoughts. However, it is argued, the intentional operating system can fail due to increased cognitive load ⑤ caused by fatigue, stress and emotional factors, and so the monitoring process filters the inappropriate thoughts into consciousness, making them highly accessible.

윗글의 밑줄 친 부분 중, 어법상 틀린 것은?

If I say to you, "Don't think of a white bear', you will find it difficult not to think of a white bear. In this way, 'thought suppression can actually increase the thoughts one wishes to suppress instead of calming them'. One common example of this is that people on a diet who try not to think about food often begin to think much more about food. This process is therefore also known as the *rebound effect*. The ironic effects seems to be caused by the interplay of two related cognitive processes. This dual–process system involves, first, an intentional operating process, which consciously attempts to locate thoughts unrelated to the suppressed ones, Second, and simultaneously, an unconscious monitoring process tests whether the operating system is functioning effectively. If the monitoring system encounters thoughts inconsistent with the intended ones, it prompts the intentional operating process to ensure that these are replaced by appropriate thoughts. However, it is argued, the intentional operating system can fail due to increased cognitive load caused by fatigue, stress and emotional factors, and so the monitoring process filters the inappropriate thoughts into consciousness, making them highly accessible.

윗글에 관한 내용과 일치하지 <u>않는</u> 것은?
① 생각을 억제하려는 시도는 억제하는 데 도움이 되지 않는다.
② 의도적 과정은 무관한 생각을 억제한다.
③ 무의식적 모니터링 과정은 의도적 과정을 감시한다.
④ 모니터링 과정은 적절하지 않은 생각을 적절한 생각으로 대체한다.
⑤ 증가된 인지부화는 적절하지 않은 생각을 접근하기 쉽게 만든다.

접속사 that이 이끄는 보어절에서 동사가 없으므로 'beginning → begin'이다.

① 가목적어, 진목적어는 5형식 문장에서 나타난다. 따라서 목적격보어 'difficult'는 적절하다.
② 선행사 people을 수식하는 주격 관계대명사 'who'는 적절하다.
④ 복수명사 thoughts를 대신하는 대명사 'ones'이다.
⑤ increased cognitive load를 수식하는 'caused'는 수동관계이므로 적절하다.

아래의 프롬프트를 챗GPT에 입력해 보세요.
"'You will find it difficult not to think of a white bear.'와 같은 문장 구조를 가진 예문을 5개 알려줘."

정답 ③

모니터링 과정은 적절하지 않은 생각을 '의도적 과정'이 적절한 생각으로 대체하도록 촉구하는 역할을 수행한다.

아래의 프롬프트를 챗GPT에 입력해 보세요.
"글의 전개를 간략하게 나누어서 설명해줘."

정답 ④

유형

18

어법 정확성 파악하기

CASE 01

기출문제
정복하기

2024년 6월
평가원
29번 문제

난이도 ★★★☆☆

Consider The Wizard of Oz as a psychological study of motivation. Dorothy and her three friends work hard to get to the Emerald City, overcoming barriers, persisting against all adversaries. They do so because they expect the Wizard to give ① them what they are missing. **Instead, the wonderful (and wise) Wizard makes them aware that they, not he, always had the power ② to fulfill their wishes.** For Dorothy, home is not a place but a feeling of security, of comfort with people she loves; it is wherever her heart is. The courage the Lion wants, the intelligence the Scarecrow longs for, and the emotions the Tin Man dreams of ③ being attributes they already possess. They need to think about these attributes not as internal conditions but as positive ways ④ in which they are already relating to others. After all, didn't they demonstrate those qualities on the journey to Oz, a journey ⑤ motivated by little more than an expectation, an idea about the future likelihood of getting something they wanted?

윗글의 밑줄 친 부분 중, 어법상 틀린 것은?

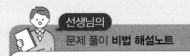
Consider The Wizard of Oz as a psychological study of motivation. Dorothy and her three friends work hard to get to the Emerald City, overcoming barriers, persisting against all adversaries. They do so because they expect the Wizard to give ① them what they are missing. Instead, the wonderful (and wise) Wizard makes them aware that they, not he, always had the power ② to fulfill their wishes. For Dorothy, *home* is not a place but a feeling of security, of comfort with people she loves; it is wherever her heart is. // The courage (the Lion wants), the intelligence (the Scarecrow longs for), and the emotions (the Tin Man dreams of) ③ being attributes (they already possess.) // They need to think about these attributes / not as internal conditions but as positive ways ④ in which they are already relating to others.) After all, didn't they demonstrate those qualities on the journey to Oz, a journey ⑤ motivated by little more than an *expectation,* an idea about the future likelihood of getting something they wanted?

핵심 문장인 이유

해당 문장은 전체 내용의 주된 메시지, 즉 스스로를 믿는 힘과 자립성을 가장 잘 요약한다. 동기에 대한 심리학적 연구로서의 이야기를 전체적으로 해석하는데 결정적인 역할을 하기 때문에 가장 중요한 핵심 문장에 해당한다.

본문 해설

③ 문장의 주어는 The courage ~ and the emotions이고, 밑줄 친 부분은 문장의 술어 동사가 와야 할 자리이므로, being을 수와 시제가 표시된 동사 are이 적절하다.

① to give의 의미상 주어는 the Wizard이므로, give의 목적어 역할을 하는 대명사 them은 어법상 적절하다.
② the power를 수식하는 형용사적 용법의 to부정사 to fulfill은 어법상 적절하다.
④ positive ways를 수식하는 관계절을 이끄는데, 뒤에 완전한 절(they are ~ to others)이 이어지고 있으므로, '전치사+관계사'의 구조인 in which는 어법상 적절하다.
⑤ a journey와 이를 수식하는 분사구가 수동 관계에 있으므로 과거분사 motivated는 어법상 적절하다.

문제 풀이 전략

다양한 어법과 문장 구조 관련 전략을 활용하여 주어진 텍스트의 정확성을 파악하고 적절한 답을 선택한다.
※ 어법 체크리스트 참고 (p.312)

정답 ③

> They need to think about these attributes not as internal conditions but as positive ways in which they are already relating to others.

Consider The Wizard of Oz as a psychological study of motivation. (①) Dorothy and her three friends work hard to get to the Emerald City, overcoming barriers, persisting against all adversaries. (②) They do so because they expect the Wizard to give them what they are missing. (③) Instead, the wonderful (and wise) Wizard makes them aware that they, not he, always had the power to fulfill their wishes. (④) For Dorothy, home is not a place but a feeling of security, of comfort with people she loves; it is wherever her heart is. The courage the Lion wants, the intelligence the Scarecrow longs for, and the emotions the Tin Man dreams of are attributes they already possess. (⑤) After all, didn't they demonstrate those qualities on the journey to Oz, a journey motivated by little more than an expectation, an idea about the future likelihood of getting something they wanted?

글의 흐름으로 보아, 주어진 문장이 들어가기에 가장 적절한 곳을 고르시오.

Consider The Wizard of Oz as a psychological study of motivation. Dorothy and her three friends work hard to get to the Emerald City, overcoming barriers, persisting against all adversaries. They do so because they expect the Wizard to give them what they are missing. Instead, the wonderful (and wise) Wizard makes them aware that they, not he, always had the power to fulfill their wishes. For Dorothy, home is not a place but a feeling of security, of comfort with people she loves; it is wherever her heart is. The courage the Lion wants, the intelligence the Scarecrow longs for, and the emotions the Tin Man dreams of are attributes they already possess. They need to think about these attributes not as internal conditions but as positive ways in which they are already relating to others. After all, didn't they demonstrate those qualities on the journey to Oz, a journey motivated by little more than an expectation, an idea about the future likelihood of getting something they wanted?

윗글의 주제로 가장 적절한 것은?

① The Value of Technological Progress in Oz
② The Role of Magic in Personal Transformation
③ The Importance of Self—Realization and Motivation
④ The Effects of Industrialization on Personal Identity
⑤ The Difference between an expectation and a reality

주어진 문장은 그들은 이러한 속성을 내적인 조건이 아니라 이미 자신들이 다른 이들과 관계를 맺는 긍정적인 방식으로 생각할 필요가 있다는 내용을 담고 있다.

여기서 'these attributes'란 앞문장에서 구체적으로 언급되었던 예시인 사자의 용기, 허수아비의 지성, 양철 인간의 감정을 통칭하고 있다. 또한, 다음 문장에서 그들이 'those qualities'를 오즈로 가는 여행에서 보여주지 않았는가? 라고 하며 결국 그들은 자신들이 원하는 무언가를 얻을 수 있을 거라는 미래의 가능성에 관한 생각을 나타낸다.

따라서 주어진 문장이 들어가기에 가장 적절한 곳은 ⑤번이다.

정답 ⑤

이 지문은 도로시와 그녀의 친구들이 갖고 싶은 것을 얻기 위해 어떻게 노력하는지, 그 과정에서 그들이 이미 원하는 속성을 가지고 있음을 발견하는 과정을 보여준다. 또한, 그들의 욕망이 미래의 성취를 위한 중요한 동기부여 역할을 하는 것을 강조하는 내용의 글이므로, 글의 주제로 가장 적절한 것은 ③ '자아실현과 동기부여의 중요성'이다.

① 오즈에서 기술 발전의 중요성
② 개인적 변화에서 마법의 역할
④ 산업화가 개인 정체성에 미치는 영향
⑤ 이상과 현실 사이의 차이

🐾 아래의 프롬프트를 챗GPT에 입력해 보세요.
"위에 소개한 지문의 핵심 단어들을 모두 고르고 뜻도 알려줘."
"위에 소개한 지문의 주제를 영어 한 문장으로 요약해줘."

정답 ③

어법 정확성 파악하기

CASE 02

난이도 ★★★☆☆

Trends constantly suggest new opportunities for individuals to restage themselves, representing occasions for change. To understand how trends can ultimately give individuals power and freedom, one must first discuss fashion's importance as a basis for change. The most common explanation offered by my informants as to why fashion is so appealing is ① that it constitutes a kind of theatrical costumery. Clothes are part of how people present ② them to the world, and fashion locates them in the present, relative to what is happening in society and to fashion's own history. **As a form of expression, fashion contains a host of ambiguities, enabling individuals to recreate the meanings ③ associated with specific pieces of clothing.** Fashion is among the simplest and cheapest methods of self-expression: clothes can be ④ inexpensively purchased while making it easy to convey notions of wealth, intellectual stature, relaxation or environmental consciousness, even if none of these is true. Fashion can also strengthen agency in various ways, ⑤ opening up space for action.

윗글의 밑줄 친 부분 중, 어법상 틀린 것은?

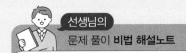
　　Trends constantly suggest/new opportunities for individuals to restage themselves, representing occasions for change. To understand/how trends can ultimately give individuals power and freedom,/ one must first discuss/fashion's importance as a basis for change.//The most common explanation offered by my informants as to why fashion is so appealing) is ① that it constitutes a kind of theatrical costumery.//Clothes are part of/how people present/② them to the world,/ and fashion locates them in the present,/ relative to what is happening/in society and to fashion's own history./As a form of expression,/ fashion contains a host of ambiguities, enabling individuals to recreate the meanings/③ associated with specific pieces of clothing./Fashion is among the simplest and cheapest methods of self-expression:/clothes can be ④ inexpensively purchased while making it easy to convey notions of wealth, intellectual stature, relaxation or environmental consciousness,/ even if none of these is true.//Fashion can also strengthen/agency in various ways,⑤ opening up space for action.

핵심 문장인 이유

해당 문장은 전체 내용의 주된 메시지, 즉 스스로를 믿는 힘과 자립성을 가장 잘 요약한다. 동기에 대한 심리학적 연구로서의 이야기를 전체적으로 해석하는데 결정적인 역할을 하기 때문에 가장 중요한 핵심 문장에 해당한다.

본문 해설

② 주어인 people이 자신들을 세상에 보여주는 것이므로 them은 재귀대명사인 themselves가 적절하다.

① 문장의 보어 역할을 하는 명사절을 이끄는 접속사 that은 어법상 적절하다.
③ the meanings를 수식하는 과거분사구를 이끄는 associated는 어법상 적절하다.
④ 동사인 purchased를 수식하므로 부사 inexpensively는 어법상 적절하다.
⑤ 앞 절 내용의 결과를 보여주는 분사구문을 이끄는 opening은 어법상 적절하다.

문제 풀이 전략

다양한 어법과 문장 구조 관련 전략을 활용하여 주어진 텍스트의 정확성을 파악하고 적절한 답을 선택한다.
※ 어법 체크리스트 참고 (p.312)

정답 ②

Trends constantly suggest new opportunities for individuals to restage themselves, representing occasions for change. To understand how trends can ultimately give individuals power and freedom, one must first discuss fashion's importance as a basis for change. The most common explanation offered by my informants as to why fashion is so appealing is that it constitutes a kind of theatrical costumery. Clothes are part of how people present themselves to the world, and fashion locates them in the present, relative to what is happening in society and to fashion's own history. As a form of expression, fashion contains a host of ambiguities, enabling individuals to recreate the meanings associated with specific pieces of clothing. Fashion is among the simplest and cheapest methods of self-expression: clothes can be inexpensively purchased while making it easy to convey notions of wealth, intellectual stature, relaxation or environmental consciousness, even if none of these is true. Fashion can also _____, opening up space for action.

수능형

윗글의 제목으로 가장 적절한 것은?

① The Economic Implications of Fashion
② The History and Evolution of Clothing
③ The Environmental Impact of Fast Fashion
④ Famous Fashion Designers and Their Influence
⑤ Fashion: A Medium of Expression and Empowerment

내신형

윗글의 빈칸에 들어갈 말로 가장 적절한 것을 고르시오.

① strengthen agency in various ways
② restrict the range of action for individuals
③ weaken individuals' interest in societal events
④ limit individuals' perspectives on current trends
⑤ reduce the importance of individual style preferences

지문에서 패션을 개인들이 자신을 세상에 어떻게 제시하는지의 일부분으로서의 역할을 강조하며, 이것을 '표현의 수단(Medium of Expression)'으로 보는 것을 강조한다. 또한, 패션은 개인들이 특정 의복과 연관된 의미를 재창조하고 다양한 개념을 전달하는 능력을 부여함으로써, 그들의 '권력과 자유(Empowerment)'를 강화한다고 이야기한다.

따라서 글의 제목으로 가장 적절한 것은 ⑤ '패션: 표현과 자기 주도력의 매체'이다.

① 패션의 경제적 영향
② 의류의 역사와 진화
③ 패스트 패션의 환경적 영향
④ 유명한 패션 디자이너와 그들의 영향력

🔁 아래의 프롬프트를 챗GPT에 입력해 보세요.
"명사를 수식하는 현재분사와 과거분사 표현 예시를 3개씩 알려줘."
"분사구문의 쓰임과 예시를 알려줘."

정답 ⑤

여기서 "agency"는 개인이나 그룹이 스스로의 의지로 행동하고, 자신들의 상황을 바꾸는 능력을 의미하므로 즉, 패션을 통해 개인이 자신의 아이덴티티를 표현하고, 사회적 위치를 설정하고, 의미를 재창조하고, 새로운 행동의 여지를 열 수 있게 되는 등 개인의 행동 능력을 강화하는 것으로 볼 수 있다.

따라서 빈칸에 들어갈 말로 가장 적절한 것은 ① '다양한 방식으로 개인의 능력을 강화하다'이다.

② 개인들의 행동 범위를 제한하다
③ 개인들의 사회적 사건에 대한 관심을 약화시키다
④ 개인들의 현재 트렌드에 대한 시각을 제한하다
⑤ 개인적인 스타일 선호도의 중요성을 감소시키다

정답 ①

어법 정확성 파악하기

CASE 03

난이도 ★★★☆☆

Recognizing ethical issues is the most important step in understanding business ethics. **An ethical issue is an identifiable problem, situation, or opportunity that requires a person to choose from among several actions that may ① be evaluated as right or wrong, ethical or unethical.** ② <u>Learn</u> how to choose from alternatives and make a decision requires not only good personal values, but also knowledge competence in the business area of concern. Employees also need to know when to rely on their organizations' policies and codes of ethics or ③ <u>have</u> discussions with co-workers or managers on appropriate conduct. Ethical decision making is not always easy because there are always gray areas ④ <u>that</u> create dilemmas, no matter how decisions are made. For instance, should an employee report on a co-worker engaging in time theft? Should a salesperson leave out facts about a product's poor safety record in his presentation to a customer? Such questions require the decision maker to evaluate the ethics of his or her choice and decide ⑤ <u>whether</u> to ask for guidance.

윗글의 밑줄 친 부분 중, 어법상 틀린 것은?

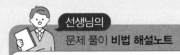
Recognizing ethical issues is the most important step in understanding business ethics.//An ethical issue is an identifiable problem, situation, or opportunity that requires a person to choose from among several actions (that may ① be evaluated as right or wrong, ethical or unethical.))②
Learn[how to choose from alternatives and make a decision]requires/not only good personal values, but also knowledge competence/in the business area of concern.//Employees also need to know/ when to rely on [their organizations' policies and codes of ethics] or ③ have [discussions with co-workers or managers on appropriate conduct.]Ethical decision making is not always easy/because there are always gray areas ④ that create dilemmas/ no matter how decisions are made.) For instance/ should an employee report on/a co-worker engaging in time theft? Should a salesperson leave out/facts about a product's poor safety record in his presentation to a customer? Such questions require/the decision maker to evaluate/the ethics of his or her choice and decide ⑤ whether to ask for guidance.//

핵심 문장인 이유

해당 문장은 "ethical issue"라는 핵심 키워드를 명확히 정의하며, 이를 통해 비즈니스 윤리에 대한 깊은 이해를 가능하게 한다.

또한, 이 문장은 여러 행동을 평가하고 선택하는 과정이 윤리적 판단의 중심임을 강조하며, 이러한 판단이 비즈니스 환경에서 어떻게 이루어져야 하는지에 대한 나머지 토론의 기본적인 틀을 제공하므로 가장 중요한 핵심 문장이라고 할 수 있다.

본문 해설

② Learn은 동사 requires의 주어 역할을 할 수 없으므로 주어 역할을 할 수 있는 동명사 Learning 이나 To learn이 적절하다.

① 조동사 may 뒤에 위치하며 "as right or ～"로서 평가받으므로 수동태 표현은 적절하다.
③ 등위접속사 or에 의해 앞서 "when to rely on"의 to부정사와 병렬관계이므로 to가 생략된 동사원형 형태는 적절하다.
④ 앞의 선행사 "gray areas"를 수식하는 주격 관계대명사 that은 적절하다.
⑤ "to ask for guidance"를 할 것인지, 하지 않을 것인지 선택 사항을 나타내는 복합관계대명사 whether은 적절하다.

문제 풀이 전략

다양한 어법과 문장 구조 관련 전략을 활용하여 주어진 텍스트의 정확성을 파악하고 적절한 답을 선택한다.
※ 어법 체크리스트 참고 (p.312)

정답 ②

Recognizing ethical issues is the most important step in understanding business ethics. An ethical issue is an identifiable problem, situation, or opportunity that requires a person to ① choose from among several actions that may be evaluated as right or wrong, ethical or unethical. Learning how to choose from alternatives and make a decision requires not only good ② personal values, but also knowledge competence in the business area of concern. Employees also need to know when to ③ rely on their organizations' policies and codes of ethics or have discussions with co-workers or managers on appropriate conduct. Ethical decision making is not always ④ challenging because there are always gray areas that create dilemmas, no matter how decisions are made. For instance, should an employee report on a co-worker engaging in time theft? Should a salesperson leave out facts about a product's poor safety record in his presentation to a customer? Such questions require the decision maker to ⑤ evaluate the ethics of his or her choice and decide whether to ask for guidance.

윗글의 밑줄 친 부분 중, 문맥상 낱말의 쓰임이 적절하지 <u>않은</u> 것은?

Recognizing ethical issues is the most important step in understanding business ethics. An ethical issue is an identifiable problem, situation, or opportunity that requires a person to choose from among several actions that may be evaluated as right or wrong, ethical or unethical. Learning how to choose from alternatives and make a decision requires not only good personal values, but also knowledge competence in the business area of concern. Employees also need to know when to rely on their organizations' policies and codes of ethics or have discussions with co-workers or managers on appropriate conduct. Ethical decision making is not always easy because there are always gray areas that create dilemmas, no matter how decisions are made. For instance, should an employee report on a co-worker engaging in time theft? Should a salesperson leave out facts about a product's poor safety record in his presentation to a customer? Such questions require the decision maker to evaluate the ethics of his or her choice and decide whether to ask for guidance.

윗글의 내용을 한 문장으로 요약하고자 한다. 빈칸 (A), (B)에 들어갈 말로 가장 적절한 것은?

Recognizing ethical issues and making informed decisions based on values, knowledge, and _____(A)_____ policies are essential for understanding business ethics and navigating ethical _____(B)_____.

	(A)		(B)		(A)		(B)
①	organizational	……	dilemmas	②	personal	……	thoughts
③	governmental	……	guidances	④	governmental	……	situations
⑤	organizational	……	capabilities				

challenging 바로 뒷문장에서 because there are always gray areas that create dilemmas, no matter how decisions are made. 결정이 어떻게 내려지든 딜레마를 만드는 회색 영역이 늘 있기 때문이라는 내용이 나오므로 윤리적 의사결정이 항상 '쉬운 것은 아니다'는 내용이 자연스럽다.

따라서 ④의 challenging을 easy와 같은 낱말로 바꾸어 '항상 딜레마가 따르기 때문에 윤리적 의사결정이 쉽지 않다'고 하는 것이 적절하다.

정답 ④

지문에 따르면 비즈니스 윤리를 이해하고 윤리적인 딜레마를 해결하기 위해서는 윤리적 문제를 인식하고 가치관, 지식, 조직 정책을 기반으로 한 정보를 바탕으로 결정을 내려야 한다.

이는 상황을 평가하고 올바른 행동과 잘못된 행동 사이에서 선택을 하는 것을 포함하며, 윤리적인 딜레마에 직면했을 때는 조언을 구하는 것이 필요하다는 내용의 글이므로, 빈칸 (A), (B)에 들어갈 말로 가장 적절한 것은 ① '조직의 – 딜레마'이다.

② 개인의 – 생각
③ 정부의 – 보조
④ 정부의 – 상황
⑤ 조직의 – 능력

> 🔖 **아래의 프롬프트를 챗GPT에 입력해 보세요.**
> "위에 소개한 지문의 핵심 단어들을 모두 고르고 뜻도 알려줘."
> "위에 소개한 지문의 주제를 영어 한 문장으로 요약해줘."

정답 ①

어법 정확성 파악하기

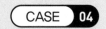

CASE 04

난이도 ★★★☆☆

Like whole individuals, cells have a life span. During their life cycle (cell cycle), cell size, shape, and metabolic activities can change dramatically. A cell is "born" as a twin when its mother cell divides, ① producing two daughter cells. Each daughter cell is smaller than the mother cell, and except for unusual cases, each grows until it becomes as large as the mother cell ② was. During this time, the cell absorbs water, sugars, amino acids, and other nutrients and assembles them into new, living protoplasm. After the cell has grown to the proper size, its metabolism shifts as it either prepares to divide or matures and ③ differentiates into a specialized cell. **Both growth and development require a complex and dynamic set of interactions involving all cell parts.** ④ What cell metabolism and structure should be complex would not be surprising, but actually, they are rather simple and logical. Even the most complex cell has only a small number of parts, each ⑤ responsible for a distinct, well-defined aspect of cell life.

윗글의 밑줄 친 부분 중, 어법상 틀린 것은?

Like whole individuals, cells have a life span.//During their life cycle (cell cycle), [cell size, shape, and metabolic activities] can change dramatically. A cell is "born"/as a twin/when its mother cell divides, ① producing two daughter cells.//Each daughter cell is smaller than the mother cell, and except for unusual cases, each grows until it becomes/as large as the mother cell ② was.//During this time,/the cell absorbs [water, sugars, amino acids, and other nutrients] and assembles [them]/into new, living protoplasm.//After the cell has grown to the proper size, its metabolism shifts/as it either prepares to divide or matures and ③ differentiates into a specialized cell. Both growth and development require/a complex and dynamic set of interactions (involving all cell parts.) ④ What [cell metabolism and structure should be complex] would not be surprising, but actually, they are rather simple and logical.//Even the most complex cell has only a small number of parts,/each ⑤ responsible for a distinct, well-defined aspect of cell life.

(annotations: S, V markings; =daughter cell; V①, V②; A, B; That over What; being under responsible)

핵심 문장인 이유

해당 문장은 세포의 '성장'과 '발달'이 모든 세포 부분을 포함한 복잡하고 동적인 상호작용의 집합을 필요로 한다는 것을 강조하며 세포의 '구조', '기능', 그리고 '생명 과정'에 관련된 핵심 키워드들을 포함하고 있다.

이러한 키워드들은 세포의 성장과 발달에 대한 이해를 중요하게 하는 요소들로서, 세포 생물학과 관련된 핵심 개념들을 나타내기 때문에 핵심 문장에 해당한다.

본문 해설

④ 문장의 술부 would not be surprising 앞에 위치하여 절을 이끌면서 주어 역할을 하는 That이 적절하다.

① 주절의 주어를 의미상의 주어로 하는 분사구문 producing~을 쓴 것은 어법상 적절하다.

② as the mother cell was large에서 large가 생략된 것으로 어법상 적절하다.

③ 상관접속사 either A or B 구조에서 A와 B에 오는 말은 병렬구조를 이루어야 하므로 prepares와 마찬가지로 matures and differentiates~를 쓴 것은 어법상 적절하다.

⑤ each being responsible~의 분사구문에서 being이 생략된 것으로 어법상 적절하다.

문제 풀이 전략

다양한 어법과 문장 구조 관련 전략을 활용하여 주어진 텍스트의 정확성을 파악하고 적절한 답을 선택한다.
※ 어법 체크리스트 참고 (p.312)

정답 ④

During this time, the cell absorbs water, sugars, amino acids, and other nutrients and assembles them into new, living protoplasm.

Like whole individuals, cells have a life span. During their life cycle (cell cycle), cell size, shape, and metabolic activities can change dramatically. (①) A cell is "born" as a twin when its mother cell divides, producing two daughter cells. (②) Each daughter cell is smaller than the mother cell, and except for unusual cases, each grows until it becomes as large as the mother cell was. (③) After the cell has grown to the proper size, its metabolism shifts as it either prepares to divide or matures and differentiates into a specialized cell. (④) Both growth and development require a complex and dynamic set of interactions involving all cell parts. (⑤) That cell metabolism and structure should be complex would not be surprising, but actually, they are rather simple and logical. Even the most complex cell has only a small number of parts, each responsible for a distinct, well−defined aspect of cell life.

글의 흐름으로 보아, 주어진 문장이 들어가기에 가장 적절한 곳을 고르시오.

Like whole individuals, cells have a life span. During their life cycle (cell cycle), cell size, shape, and metabolic activities can change dramatically. A cell is "born" as a twin when its mother cell divides, producing two daughter cells. Each daughter cell is smaller than the mother cell, and except for unusual cases, each grows until it becomes as large as the mother cell was. During this time, the cell absorbs water, sugars, amino acids, and other nutrients and assembles them into new, living protoplasm. After the cell has grown to the proper size, its metabolism shifts as it either prepares to divide or matures and differentiates into a specialized cell. Both growth and development require a complex and dynamic set of interactions involving all cell parts. That cell metabolism and structure should be complex would not be surprising, but actually, they are rather simple and logical. Even the most complex cell has only a small number of parts, each responsible for a distinct, well−defined aspect of cell life.

윗글의 제목으로 가장 적절한 것은?

① Mother Cells: The Origin of Life
② The Role of Water in Cellular Life
③ Amino Acids: The Building Blocks of Cells
④ The Simple Components of Complex Organisms
⑤ The Intricate Journey of Cell Growth and Development

주어진 문장은 이 기간 동안 세포가 다른 영양소들을 흡수하여 새로운 살아있는 원형질로 조합한다는 내용이다.

③번을 기준으로 앞 문장에 나온 각 딸세포가 각각 모세포의 크기만큼 커질 때까지 자란다는 내용이 나오는데 주어진 문장의 'during this time'이 바로 모세포만큼 커지는 기간을 의미한다.

바로 뒷 문장에서는 세포가 적절한 크기로 성장한 후, 물질대사가 변화한다는 내용이 나오므로 주어진 문장은 ③번에 들어가는 것이 적절하다.

> 🔁 아래의 프롬프트를 챗GPT에 입력해 보세요.
> "분사구문의 주어가 주절의 주어와 다른 경우 예시를 3개 알려줘."
> "상관접속사 either A or B 구조말고 비슷한 다른 종류 알려줘."

정답 ③

세포는 수명이 있는데, 세포 주기 동안 크기와 모양이 변화하며 새로운 생명 프로토플라즘을 조립하여 성장 및 발달을 거쳐 모체세포가 분열한다. 이 모체세포가 두 개의 작은 딸세포로 태어난 후, 각 딸세포는 모체세포와 같은 크기가 될 때까지 자란다. 발달 과정에서 세포가 생명 주기 동안 크기와 형태를 변화시키며 영양분을 흡수하고 분열하거나 전문화하는 과정을 설명하는 글이다.

따라서 글의 제목으로 가장 적절한 것은 ⑤ '세포 성장과 발달의 복잡한 여정'이다.

① 모체세포: 생명의 기원
② 물의 역할: 세포 생명에 있어서
③ 아미노산: 세포의 구성 요소
④ 복잡한 생물체의 단순한 성분들

> 🔁 아래의 프롬프트를 챗GPT에 입력해 보세요.
> "위에 소개한 지문의 핵심 단어들을 모두 고르고 뜻도 알려줘."

정답 ⑤

어법 체크리스트

	어법 정확성 체크 항목	O	X
1	주어–동사 수, 시제가 일치하는가?	☑	☑
2	관계사와 접속사(상관접속사 등)가 적절하게 사용되었나?	☑	☑
3	완전한 문장인가? (동사, 목적어가 빠지진 않았는가?)	☑	☑
4	형용사와 부사의 위치와 용법이 올바른가?	☑	☑
5	동사의 변화나 형태가 문맥에 맞게 사용되었나?	☑	☑
6	대명사가 명확하게 지칭하는 대상을 가르키나?	☑	☑
7	관용구와 숙어가 올바르게 사용되나?	☑	☑
8	문장 내에서 병렬 구조가 일관되나?	☑	☑
9	불필요한 단어나 구절이 반복되진 않나?	☑	☑
10	인용문이나 구두점의 사용은 올바른가?	☑	☑
11	시간적이나 공간적 관계를 나타내는 표현이 적절한가?	☑	☑
12	전치사가 올바르게 사용되었나?	☑	☑
13	명사를 수식하는 분사(능동 – 현재분사, 수동 – 과거분사)가 적절한가?	☑	☑
14	to부정사의 용법은 적절한가? (명사적, 형용사적, 부사적 용법)	☑	☑
15	관계부사가 올바르게 사용되었나? (시간, 장소, 방법 등)	☑	☑
16	강조구문이 적절하게 사용되었나?	☑	☑
17	분사구문이 적절하게 사용되었나?	☑	☑
18	수동태 표현이 적절하게 사용되었나? (수, 시제 일치 등)	☑	☑